Property Finance

D0474885

By the same author

The Valuation of Property Investments (with N. Enever)

Property Companies: Share Price and Net Asset Value (with N. Woodroffe)

Property Investment

Property Development

Property Valuation Principles

Property Valuation Techniques (with T. Steeley)

Urban Economics: A Global Perspective (with P. N. Balchin and J. Chen)

Property Finance

Second Edition

David Isaac
Professor of Real Estate Management
Director of Research
University of Greenwich

First edition 1994
Reprinted five times
Second edition 2003

Published by
PALGRAVE MACMILLAN
Houndmills, Basingstoke, Hampshire RG21 6XS and
175 Fifth Avenue, New York, N.Y. 10010
Companies and representatives throughout the world

PALGRAVE MACMILLAN is the global academic imprint of the Palgrave
Macmillan division of St. Martin's Press, LLC and of Palgrave Macmillan Ltd.
Macmillan® is a registered trademark in the United States, United Kingdom
and other countries. Palgrave is a registered trademark in the European
Union and other countries.

ISBN 0–333–98714–4

This book is printed on paper suitable for recycling and made from fully
managed and sustained forest sources.

A catalogue record for this book is available from the British Library.

10   9   8   7   6   5   4   3   2   1
12   11   10   09   08   07   06   05   04   03

Printed and bound in Great Britain by
Creative Print & Design (Wales), Ebbw Vale

To Simon and Katie

Contents

List of Figures

List of Tables

List of Boxes

Preface to the First Edition

This book is an introduction to property finance, bringing together the professional disciplines related to finance and to property investment and development. The book intends to do three things: establish the basic concepts of finance, examine the applications of these concepts in practice and, finally, give an overview of the market – its history and present position as of 1993. As you will appreciate, this is a wide field and I have tried to be as selective as possible in the text.

I believe the book will be useful for a number of different groups, including students in property-related areas, practitioners who are not specialist in the area or who have limited experience of it and those professionals involved in developing, investing in and administering property assets. For the student, it provides a text at second- or third-year undergraduate level and is also useful as an introductory text at postgraduate level for those without previous knowledge in the area. Finance is an essential, and arguably the paramount element in the process of land and construction management. Estate and land managers, surveyors, construction and project managers, architects and engineers need an understanding in this area and, at the same time, those involved in finance, commerce and business require an insight into finance as applied to the property asset. The book provides an overview for progressing to more advanced and specialised texts. For those concerned with property and construction, I hope the book will provide a view into the area of applied economics in the same way that, for those with a business background, the text will help to explain some of the peculiarities of dealing with land, property and construction.

I have endeavoured to structure the book by initially establishing the basic concepts and then looking in some detail at the main characteristics of finance, the instruments involved and the players. Where possible, I have introduced recent research and make no apologies for using and referencing this work to bring the reader up to date in a rapidly changing sector. Where possible, simple case studies have been added to assist in the understanding. I would have liked to have incorporated more extensive applications but this was beyond the scope and scale of this text.

I believe the book comes at an important time in the development of the property market; hopefully, we are now seeing the signals of partial recovery in both the residential and commercial sectors, and with recovery it is hoped that the practitioners and financiers involved in the market will be older and wiser, and that both the lessons of the slump of 1973–4 and the false hopes of the booming late 1980s will be understood and taken on board. In fact, it will be expected of professionals in the market to be older and wiser. In a previous book entitled *Property Valuation Techniques* (written with Terry Steley, Macmillan Press, 1991), we wrote about the need to clarify valuation techniques to make them more accessible and applicable; the intention here is to provide an insight into property finance that will also seek to clarify this process.

Chapter 2 is about the theory of finance; and some readers may wish to bypass this in the first instance if they find it difficult or wish to move on. Hopefully they will come back to it at a later time when the overall picture becomes clear and they feel more suited to the material. I have endeavoured to keep the chapters self-contained and apologise for any duplication of material; the intention is to reduce cross-referencing and provide easier reading.

Finally, I would like to thank those who have assisted me in writing this book, Professor Ivor Seeley, the series editor, who has stimulated me to write what will hopefully be a number of texts for the series, and Malcolm Stewart, my publisher. I would also like to thank Mike Riley and his staff at Chesterton Financial, who over the years have provided me with valuable insights into the practice of financial services. Many colleagues and external organisations have provided me with information and assistance and these are listed in the acknowledgements below. I would also like to thank Terry Steley and Maxine Davies of the University of Greenwich and Neil Woodroffe of South Bank University for their help. Finally, I am reliant on the continued support of Professor David Wills, Lewis Anderson and the staff of the School of Land and Construction Management at the University of Greenwich to develop my research and studies and I am grateful for their help.

University of Greenwich, 1994   DAVID ISAAC

Preface to the Second Edition

In this second edition, I have updated the material and data and introduced new concepts that have arisen with the passage of time. I have also taken the opportunity to go through the text and revise sections that I hope will increase the readability of the material. Certain chapters, especially those relating to new innovations in the market, have been revised and brought up to date. Chapter 1 (Introduction) and Chapter 4 (Property Lenders) have been substantially revised, as have the Chapters 12 (on Securitisation) and 13 (on Financial Accounts). That said, there have been additions and corrections to all other chapters and additional research and references have been included in the text.

The book, hopefully, will continue to be a useful text and reference for practitioners and students of many disciplines involved in the study and applications of property finance. For this second edition I would also like to thank my publisher, Becky Mashayekh, for her support, guidance, patience and understanding.

University of Greenwich, 2003   DAVID ISAAC

Acknowledgements

The author and publishers wish to thank the following for the use of copyright material:

> Butterworths: for the use of extracts from *Real Estate Finance; Estates Gazette;* the Journals of MCB University Press.
> S. G. Warburg Securities, UBS Philips & Drew and Paribas Capital Markets.
> Chesterton, Savills Research, DTZ Research, Richard Ellis.

Every effort has been made to trace all the copyright-holders, but if any have been inadvertently overlooked the publishers will be pleased to make the necessary arrangement at the first opportunity.

Disclaimer
This book is intended as an academic text and should not be used without additional professional advice for investment/finance/development purposes.

List of Abbreviations

ACT	advance corporation tax
APT	Arbitrage Pricing Theory
APUTs	Authorised Property Unit Trusts
ASB	Accounting Standards Board
CAPM	Capital Asset Pricing Model
CMI	commercial mortgage indemnity
CML	Capital Market Line
CSO	Central Statistical Office
EBIT	earnings before interest and taxes
FHBR	Finance Houses base rate
FIMBRA	Financial Intermediaries, Managers and Brokers Regulatory Association
FRA	forward rate agreements
FRNs	floating rate notes
FRS	Financial Reporting Standard
GDMR	Gross Domestic Mortgage Rate
IPD	Investment Property Databank
JVC	joint venture company
LIBOR	London Interbank Offered Rate
LIFFE	London International Financial Futures and Options Exchange
LLP	Limited Liability Partnership
LTV	loan to value
MBOs	management buy-outs
MBS	mortgage backed security
MOF	multi-option facility
NAV	net asset value
NPV	net present value
NRV	net realisable value
PFI	Private Finance Initiative
PINCs	Property Income Certificates
PPP	Public–Private Partnership
PUTs	Property Unit Trusts
REITs	Real Estate Investment Trusts
RICS	Royal Institute of Chartered Surveyors
SAPCOs	Single Asset Property Companies
SIB	Securities and Investment Board
SPOTs	Single Property Ownership Trusts
SPUTs	Securitised Property Unit Trusts
SPV	special purpose vehicle

SROs	self-regulating organisations
SSAP	Statements of Standard Accounting Practice
UPS	Underwriting Property Service
USM	Unlisted Securities Market

1
Introduction

1.1 Introduction

A property or building can be owner-occupied or rented; that is, an investment property. The property may of course be vacant, resulting from being surplus to the owner's requirements or a poor investment! From the beginning it should be noted that a large proportion of property is owner-occupied but most of the texts and theories are applied to an investment market. The commercial property industry is a relatively young one in terms of the realisation that profit can be earned by producing and renting space.

Property finance is money raised on the back of existing properties or raised for the purpose of expenditure on properties. Whether the property is owner-occupied or an investment property may alter the criteria for the raising and application of the funds, but the fundamental concepts may well be the same. For instance, funds could be raised internally or externally by an organisation but the criteria for the internal loan or transfer of funds may well need to match those in the market. In this text, the presentation is mainly about the application of funds to property in the investment market and funds are considered to be private rather than public sector monies. This is to make the analysis simpler but, as has already been said, the principles and concepts could well be similar.

The investment market for property cannot be seen in isolation from other investment markets. The application of funds to property has to reflect competition from other forms of investment. The decision to invest in a particular area will be a comparison of risk and return, for instance; thus, knowledge of alternative investments and, more interestingly from a property financing point of view, knowledge of the application of finance to other investments could be very important. This can clearly be seen in the securitisation and unitisation of property, which are discussed later. Another important point to be made is in respect of the nature of the lender and the property to which finance is applied. At its simplest, it is an individual purchasing a single property with a single loan. This is rarely the case. Much finance is raised by corporate entities such as property companies, lending on the back of existing property and other assets for the purchase of a portfolio of assets which may include property assets, but not exclusively so.

Finally, it is important to realise the significance of property and its finance to the economy. The importance can be shown in three different ways: as a factor of production, as a corporate asset and as an investment. As a factor of production, property is the space in which economic activity will take place; the efficiency and costs of such space will affect the cost of goods and services produced. As a corporate asset, it forms the major asset value in the balance sheet and the majority of corporate debt is secured against it. As an investment, it is one of the major types of investment held by the financial institutions on which pensions and assurance benefits depend (Fraser 1993).

The London Business School estimated in the mid-1990s that the total value of commercial property in the UK – including private investment, owner-occupation and overseas investment – is greater than £250 billion; this had probably increased to £300 billion by 2000. In addition, the value of all residential property exceeds £1,000 billion (Freeman Publishing 2000).

1.2   The structure of the investment market

There are three major areas of traditional investment opportunity (ignoring gold, commodities and works of art): fixed interest securities, company stocks and shares, and real property. The Stock Exchange provides a market for listed shares and certain fixed interest securities such as those issued by the government, local authorities and public bodies. The market in real property contrasts with that of company shares and other securities. The property market is fragmented and dispersed whilst that of shares and other securities is highly centralised. The London Stock Market is an example of this centralisation. The centralisation of markets assists the transferability of investments, as does the fact that stocks and shares can be traded in small units thereby assisting transferability. Compared with other traditional investment opportunities, real property investment has the distinguishing features of being heterogeneous, indivisible and having inherent problems of management. The problems of management may include collecting rents, dealing with repairs and lease renewal and thus, together with the other problems noted, may lead to real property being an unattractive proposition for the small investor. A decentralised market will tend to have high costs of transfer of investments and also there will be an imperfect knowledge of transactions.

Thus, the nature of the real property market makes property difficult to value. There is no centralised market price to rely on, as the price may be too difficult to ascertain unless a transaction has recently taken place. Many of the problems of valuation relate to difficulties of trying to relate comparable transactions to properties being valued or even trying to assess what transactions could be considered comparable. Because of the nature of the real property market, individual investors have tended to withdraw from the market. This is also due to the channelling of savings into collective organisations, such as pension funds and insurance companies, rather than individuals using their savings for direct investment.

The structure of control of UK commercial property has changed over the last 25 years. Two distinct trends have emerged. First, traditional owners such as the landed estates (including the Grosvenor Estates, the Crown Estates, those owned by Oxford and Cambridge colleges, the public utilities and the public sector estates of local and central government) have diminished in influence. In the last 20 years, foreign ownership of property has increased dramatically, especially in the major centres. The second trend relates to the shift in control away from the financial institutions, the pension funds and insurance companies towards separate fund managers and property companies. In the 1990s, the effects of privatisations and outsourcing have extended to the institutions and it is considered that the power base is now in specialist fund management operations (Freeman Publishing 2000).

Property company shares

Property company shares provide a medium for indirect investment in property that deals with some of the disadvantages of direct investment outlined above. Equities are available in smaller units and can be easily traded. Property shares, specifically, have been viewed as an effective protection against inflation because of the durability of property. Shares of a property investment company where most of the revenue to the company is derived from rental income also provide the investor with a high degree of income security. Thus, property shares traditionally were seen to provide both an element of protection against the effects of inflation and greater security to the investor.

Two types of property company are discernible. An investment company normally holds property for long periods and takes its revenue from rental income. A trading company will develop and sell property, earning revenues on disposal of the property rather than through income. Because of different tax positions, the functions should be kept separate but the most extensive developers will also often be investment companies which may or may not retain a completed development within the portfolio of the investment company.

Despite the fact that the value of all land and buildings in the UK is greater than the value of all the quoted shares and government securities added together, property shares only make up a small fraction of the value of the Stock Exchange. The UK property industry appears insignificant to an equities fund manager (Freeman Publishing 2000). Only one property company, Land Securities, qualifies for inclusion in the FTSE 100, the top 100 companies on the Stock Market as measured by market capitalisation (the value of all the shares). In 2000, the total market capitalisation of all 110 quoted property companies was only £30 billion, which represents less than 2 per cent of the market capitalisation of the London Stock Exchange. On the other hand, institutional investors hold nearly £100 billion in commercial property.

1.3   Financial structures

Property finance is important in the property investment market. The costs and availability of finance will affect the cost of the provision of new investment property and therefore its supply. It is through finance that the structure of the investment in property may be created, so finance has an effect on the form of the property interest created. Whilst the costs and availability of funding are obvious in the case of the funding of development property, it is important to realise that it is critical to the investment market also. The value of an investment may be driven by the opportunities or lack of opportunities to fund it and, of course, this was the main impetus of the move into the securitisation of property; a repackaging of the property asset into appropriate financial packages which add value. Securitisation is covered in Chapter 12.

Shown below are some basic principles that define the financial structure and which have been identified by Fraser (1993) among others:

1 A company must maintain a balance between equity and debt capital. Traditionally property companies are highly geared, which means that these companies carry a high level of debt capital relative to equity or total capital. The issues of gearing are covered in Chapter 2. The security of property and the growth in rental values and capital value have provided an appropriate environment for increasing debt capital. Apart from the balance of equity and debt, the nature and composition of equity and debt in themselves are important.

2 There should be a balance of maturity dates of the debt with the majority being long term. Redemptions (the paying-off of debt) should be spread evenly to avoid the risk of a major refinancing operation occurring at a time of adverse financial conditions. The needs of a major refinancing could have an adverse effect on the market, making available monies scarce and putting up the costs. A proportion of the money should be flexible so that it can be repaid without cost or penalty at any time during the duration of the term.

3 A company should match short-term assets with short-term liabilities and long-term assets with long-term liabilities; this is asset matching. If long-term property investment is funded through short-term borrowing (for instance, overdraft or short-term debt) then there could be major problems for refinancing as an appropriate stock of new capital may not be available at the crucial time of refinancing. This may mean that the property asset would have to be disposed of at an inappropriate time leading to a collapse in its value.

4 Companies should maintain a balance between fixed interest money and variable interest money. Fixed interest rates protect the company in a period of rising interest rates but obviously are expensive if rates fall, so they provide a hedge against future risk. A hedge is a means of avoiding financial risks, associated in this case with changes in interest rates; this aspect is covered in Chapter 4. Variable rate monies need to be available if interest rates fall so that the benefits of the reduced cost of money can be obtained. Excessive high fixed interest money could have a disastrous effect on a property company in a period of low inflation.

5 Debt should be structured so that interest repayments are spread over the year so as to even out the cash flow for the company or to coincide with income received.

6 To avoid foreign currency risk, companies with operations overseas should reduce their exposure to this risk by matching overseas assets and debts in the same currency.

7 The financial structure should aim to maximise the tax shield: that is, the avoidance of tax payment to maximise the after-tax cash flow. Thus, where appropriate, the interest repayments should have tax relief and be available to offset against income.

8 Apart from interest rates, the arranging costs should be minimised. The price of capital is related to not just the interest rates, but also commitment and arrangement fees, penalties for early repayment, frequency of repayment and how interest is calculated on the outstanding amount.

The finance function

Management and finance theory tells us that in a well-organised business, each section of the business should arrange its activities to contribute to the attainment of corporate goals. Central to this function in a corporate entity is the maximisation of shareholders' wealth. This is basically done by the generation and management of cash, which is the fundamental concern of finance. Pike and Neale (1993) suggest the simple cash flow diagram shown in Figure 1.1.

The questions which may be key in our understanding of what finance is all about in a generalised corporate context are listed below:

1 What long-term investment strategy should a company take on?
2 How can cash be raised for the required investments?
3 How much short-term cash flow does a company need to pay its bills?

These are strategic decisions that will determine the strategy for generating cash and at the same time ensure that the company is liquid (has cash available to pay its bills).

One way that companies raise cash to finance their investment activities is by selling or issuing securities. These securities are also called financial instruments or claims, as they are claims on the cash and assets of the company. These securities may be roughly classified as equity or debt and are loosely called respectively stock or bonds in the USA and shares and loan stock in the UK. The differences in terminology do make this a problem when dealing with finance literature from the USA. Sometimes the basic concepts behind a security or its operation may differ in the two countries, as in the operation of financial options that are discussed later.

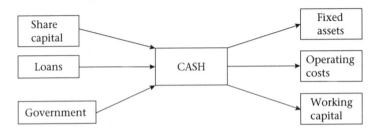

Figure 1.1 The importance of cash
Source: Adapted from Pike and Neale (1993), p. 8.

The difference between equity and debt is a basic distinction of the modern theory of finance and this book uses the distinction to classify the instruments available. To summarise, all the securities of a firm are claims that depend on (or are contingent on) the value of the firm. Maximising shareholders' wealth is the primary goal of the company and thus financial decisions are made to increase value for shareholders. A company raises cash by issuing securities to the financial markets. There are two basic types of financial markets, the money markets and the capital markets. Money markets deal with debt securities that pay off in the short term, usually less than one year. Capital markets are the markets for long-term debt and equity shares.

The balance sheet model of the firm

The concept of the finance function as a corporate activity can be seen easily in the use of a balance sheet model of the firm shown in Figure 1.2 (Ross, Westerfield and Jaffe 1993). The balance sheet is a yearly snapshot of the assets and liabilities of the firm.

The assets of the firm are shown on the left side of the balance sheet, and these are current or fixed assets. Fixed assets are those that last a long time and are durable, such as buildings and plant. Some fixed assets are tangible, such as machinery and equipment; others intangible, such as patents, goodwill and trade-marks. The other category of assets is current assets which have short lives and are intended to be turned to cash. For a property company, the distinction between fixed and current assets may be between properties held for investment and those which it intends to trade in the short term.

In order to invest in these assets, the company must raise the cash to pay for the assets and this is shown on the right side of the balance sheet. The firm will sell claims to its assets in the form of debt (loan agreements) or equity shares. Just as

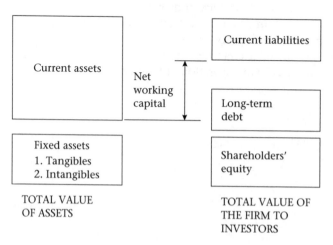

Figure 1.2   Balance sheet model of the firm

Source: Ross, Westerfield and Jaffe (1993), p. 5.

assets are classified as long or short term, so are liabilities. Short-term debt is a current liability and consists of loans and other obligations that must be repaid in one year. Long-term debt is thus that debt whose repayment date is more than one year from issue. Shareholders' equity is the difference in value between the assets and debt of the firm and is thus a residual claim.

The balance sheet model highlights the questions that have already been mentioned and provides an appropriate response:

1 In what long-term assets should the company invest? This is a question about the left side of the balance sheet. The type and proportions of the assets invested in will depend on the nature of the business. Making and managing expenditure on long-term assets is called *capital budgeting*.
2 How can a firm raise cash for the required capital expenditures? This question concerns the right hand side of the balance sheet and the answer involves the firm's *capital structure* that represents the proportion of the firm's finance coming from current and long-term debt and equity.
3 How should the short-term operating cash flow be managed? There is a mismatch between the timing of cash inflows and outflows during operating activities; financial managers must manage these gaps in cash flow by managing the firm's net working capital (current assets less current liabilities). This is the subject of *short-term finance.*

From a property perspective we may see these activities as, respectively, the areas of property investment, finance and operational financial management. This book is essentially about finance, but examined in the context of property investment and financial management.

1.4   The financing of property since the Second World War

The history of the postwar UK property market can be divided into a number of periods. These are the postwar development boom, the financial boom of 1967–73, the investment boom of the late 1970s and the finance-led development boom of the late 1980s with the subsequent collapse into the 1990s (Brett 1997). Differences between the periods reflect the different finance sources and methods available during each period.

The postwar boom period

In the period immediately after the Second World War there was an acute shortage of space. This was especially true of the office sector where the shortage of office accommodation had been fuelled by the destruction of approximately 750,000 square metres of office space by aerial bombing during the war. The economy was beginning to grow at a reasonable rate against a background of low interest rates and low inflation. Because property had been destroyed during the war and space was scarce, this led to a growth in rental values. At the beginning of the 1950s, the Conservative government of the time recognised the need for economic growth and encouraged a period of rapid economic expansion. Because interest rates were low at this time, the yields on property investments were higher than long-term borrowing rates. Fixed interest loans were available from financial institutions and were readily used by the property companies. Financial partnerships between institutions and property companies were also frequently established. The financing of property investments could thus be carried out using long-term mortgage funds at low rates that were fixed; typically these funds would be provided by an insurance company. Short-term finance for the construction of the buildings usually came from bank sources or else from the building contractor. There was an overall attempt by developers to raise the total funds necessary for the property development from lending sources, to avoid committing any of their own money. Property developments were thus intended to be 100 per cent debt financed with no equity involvement. Developers subsequently held on to their completed developments rather than selling them; this was partly a response to the tax system, as tax was payable on the trading profit but there was no tax on the capital surplus created by the developer until the property was sold. Developers such as Land Securities and Hammerson became established at this time. Some new funding was achieved by the floating of property companies on the Stock Exchange in the late 1950s and early 1960s. These flotations achieved cash for new developments without the developers having to sell their existing properties. Developers at this time let their buildings on leases without rent review and were not concerned with the effects of inflation on their income stream but instead concentrated on income from development profits. Fixed interest financing by financial institutions became standard practice by the 1960s and was linked to shareholdings, options and conversion rights taken up in development companies by the institutions. Inflation then began to rise in the early 1960s and institutions, providing finance as mortgages or debentures, started to take a share of equity initially by conversion rights (converting their debt arrangements in the companies to equity) and then eventually by establishing joint companies with the developers. The insurance companies were especially active at this time. Developers who wanted to retain their properties had to give away some equity to ensure finance at lower rates. Sale and leaseback, where the developer offered to sell the proposed building subject to the investor leasing the building back, became the dominant form of funding arrangement. This approach had many advantages including avoiding falling under the government's credit control measures of the time (Savills 1989).

By the early 1960s, recession affected demand and credit squeezes made short-term financing difficult. The office development boom in London was eventually brought to an end by the Labour Government in 1964 with the Control of Office and Industrial Development Act 1965. This so-called 'Brown Ban', named after George Brown, the politician who initiated the legislation, in fact artificially restricted the supply and sowed the seed of the next boom in the 1970s (Fraser 1993).

The financial boom 1967–73

A renewed stock market boom commenced in 1967 and lasted until the crash in 1974. Institutional finance was being provided to the property companies in the form of leasebacks. Pension funds in this period joined the insurance companies in buying out completed developments and they dominated the investment market (Cadman and Catalano 1983). New forms of indirect investment, such as property bonds and property unit trusts, were established. The market was characterised by a series of takeovers in the late 1960s and this activity continued on in the early 1970s. By March 1972, property shares had risen over five times from the low point of 1967 (Brett 1983b). The assets of existing property companies were becoming more and more valuable because of the effect of the shortage of investment properties. The value of property companies was thus increasing because of the scarcity of space rather than because of accumulated development profits. Due to inflation in this period rent reviews were introduced, initially on a 14-yearly basis; these were reduced to 7-yearly reviews and then to 5-yearly reviews. By 1975, some leases had 3-yearly reviews. Between 1964 and 1974 there was a reduction of 40 per cent in the number of quoted companies due to amalgamation and liquidation (Ratcliffe 1978).

To summarise, in the postwar era in the 1950s and 1960s the modern property developer had emerged and property companies had established themselves. The stimulation to development was based on the shortage of property in a period of low inflation. This meant that the rental levels of developments increased dramatically during the period whilst building costs were static. The other major stimulants to the developers were the fixed interest rates and the lack of equity input. The growth of the property developers was on the basis of refinancing the development on a fixed interest mortgage for 20 to 30 years. The institutions were providing finance for the developments and there was some link-up between developers and institutions. Over this period the institutions, generally insurance companies, insisted on having a greater share in the equity returns available. They purchased shares in the property companies and then made mortgage debenture loans convertible to shares so that an increased equity stake could be obtained if the scheme were a success. However, the taxation structure in the late 1960s affected this arrangement; gross funds (financial institutions not paying tax) suffered from the taxation of income and dividends and new structures of finance emerged. In the late 1960s and early 1970s developers began using sale and leaseback; the property was financed in the development stage using bank finance and was sold on completion. As time wore on, a shortage of schemes became apparent and the institutions (the insurance companies and later, the pension funds) purchased development sites directly with agreements for building and leaseback with the developer. Developers borrowed short term for their developments or to finance acquisitions, because they thought rising asset values would counterbalance the deficit finance. They ignored their cash flow and borrowed against the increased value of their properties to meet the income shortfall between rental and interest payments.

The crash of 1974/75 showed how the economic indications had changed since the 1950s and 1960s. High interest rates, lessened demand and inflation of costs meant that profit levels were not achieved because of increased capital costs and income voids during which interest arrears fluctuated. The highly-geared property companies had been fuelled by debt finance provided under fairly lax lending criteria.

In the aftermath of the oil crisis of 1973, interest rates were raised to a penal level; secondary banks were heavily committed to property and began to collapse.

Accounting conventions of the time had disguised the sharply negative cash flow of most property companies with large development programmes. It thus became impossible to sell a property and it was not possible to borrow on it. Property shares collapsed, as did the direct market in property (Brett 1997).

The investment boom (late 1970s)

In the late 1970s, the institutions were keen buyers of property and values rose sharply during this period. Large institutions were undertaking direct development or using developers as project managers. Insurance companies became very active developers during this period. Larger property companies were borrowing on the hope that the cash flow (rent less interest paid) would be positive at the first rent review.

The rental boom (late 1980s)

In the 1980s and 1990s, the usual approach to funding was that the funder was invited to purchase the site and provide finance for the building contract. Interest would be rolled up during the development period and added to the development costs. On completion and letting of the building, the profit on the development would be paid over to the developer by the funder. On this basis, developers built up a large turnover; they were basically matching their site funding and project management skills with the institutional investors' financial resources. Such approaches greatly reduced the risk exposure of the developer to the project. Forward funding meant that the project was financed, in terms of the development, by the end purchaser at a keep rate (an interest rate based on the long-term investment rate rather than short-term money market rates) but generally the project was valued for purchase at the end of the project at a higher yield (a cheaper capital value).

In the early 1980s, the recession and rising unemployment had affected the demand for property and rental increases fell while yields increased. Property lagged behind the rest of the economy in its recovery. There was not another boom until 1986/87. The institutions were now less important as providers of funds for property and their net purchases dropped as they re-weighted their portfolios towards equities and gilts, disappointed with the performance of their property assets. In 1980, around 20 per cent of insurance companies' and 10 per cent of pension funds' portfolios was invested in property; by the mid-1980s this had been reduced to 7 per cent and 5 per cent respectively. A development boom, funded by the banks, had begun. The banks were prepared to lend on an individual development and roll up the interest until the property was disposed of; thus developers were traders rather than investment companies. 'Big Bang', the era of the deregularisation of the Stock Exchange and the globalisation of financial activities in the City of London, produced huge levels of liquidity provided by the banks and by the end of the 1980s bank lending had reached an all-time record. By the beginning of the 1990s, rental growth had tailed off and the market was collapsing. There were no buyers for the completed developments. Speculative developments, especially office and shopping centres, were empty and the properties were sold at a great discount. The banks had to extend their development loans beyond the development period because there were no institutional funders in the market to buy the completed developments. Development loans were thus converted to investment loans, committing banks to staying in the market. Innovative financial techniques, in the absence of traditional institutional finance, were the key developments of the 1980s.

Recession and stability (the 1990s on)

At the beginning of 1990, there were 140 banks lending to property companies and developers in the UK, and 40 per cent of these were overseas banks. In terms of bank loans, £30 billion was outstanding to property lending which equates to 7.5 per cent of all bank lending. Lending had increased 20 per cent per annum from 1981 to 1990 and the Bank of England had become concerned. The lending banks' response was to reduce loan to value ratios (see section 1.5 for an explanation) from between 75 per cent and 80 per cent to between 66 per cent and 70 per cent, but they were still lending as they had to make profits.

Some comparison has been made between the lending crisis of the 1990s and the property crash in 1974 but they were very different. In the 1974 crash, banks were unable to deal with unpaid loans and had a weaker capital base. There was also weaker tenant demand at the time. The strong investor demand in 1974 was pushing yields down and thus trading profits were based on investor reaction rather than rental growth. The developers had poor covenants (financial strength). There was also poor market research being undertaken by banks and property companies. From the 1990s on, there have been better financial controls and banks are taking more security for loans (not withstanding non-recourse deals). The property sector in the 1990s was driven more by tenant demand rather than investment markets so yields moved but not significantly.

Between the summers of 1990 and 1994, around 15 quoted property companies including Olympia & York, Mountleigh, Rosehaugh and Speyhawk became insolvent, putting major schemes such as Canary Wharf and the Broadgate development in the City of London into the hands of their bankers. By 1992, a London office building might have been worth some 50 per cent of its value at the 1989 peak (Freeman Publishing 2000).

The financial market up to the present is considered later in the chapter.

Present lenders in the market

The present players in the lending market include:

Clearing banks Merchant banks (also providing an advisory role)	} Banks
Insurance companies Pension funds	} Institutions
Private individuals Overseas investors	} Investors

1.5   Vocabulary of finance

At this stage, the introduction of a few basic concepts could be useful. Some of the simpler terms are set out below.

Base rate

The lowest rate at which banks can borrow from the Bank of England. Changes in this minimum lending rate are likely to trigger corresponding changes in the base rate of commercial banks.

Debt

Someone else's money: for instance, an overdraft, a term loan or debenture (loan secured on an asset).

Equity

Your money. Money put into a project. Company equity is ordinary share capital.

Security

When money is lent for the purchase of an asset, the lender will usually have the right to sell the asset in the case of any default. This is achieved by way of a legal charge. Security could be just related to a single project and lenders therefore have no recourse back to the parent company or other assets. This is known as a non-recourse deal. When there is some partial recourse back to the parent company (for instance, rental guarantees), this is known as a limited recourse transaction.

Loan to value ratio

The ratio of the amount a lender will lend to the total value of the asset used as a security. Usually expressed as a percentage. A 75 per cent loan to value ratio will mean that a £100,000 asset will raise £75,000 of loans.

Risk

Banks are not in the business of taking risks, only making money. They generally consider any loan in excess of 70 per cent of value to be riskier and would expect to be compensated by a greater return.

LIBOR

The London Interbank Offered Rate. The average interest rate that the banks will lend to one another. It is the credit quality of banks. Interest rates are linked to this rate and are expressed as a margin over LIBOR: for example, 50 basis points over LIBOR (1 basis point is 0.01 per cent).

Interest rate margin

Sometimes the interest rate will be sub-LIBOR (depending on the strength of the lender in the case of a major multinational company, say). Generally, however, a margin is added to the LIBOR rate. This could be between 0.1 per cent and 1 per cent for a good covenant, 1–2 per cent for a medium covenant and more than 2 per cent for other property transactions.

Gilt rate

Gilts are government bonds issued with a fixed (or index-linked) coupon or interest rate, usually with a fixed redemption rate. For instance, Treasury 5 per cent 2002 means that the bond has been issued by the Treasury at an initial coupon based on the par (issue value) of 9 per cent which will be repaid in 2002. As the price of the gilt changes in the market, so does the initial yield and the redemption yield (respectively the current income yield, and the yield which takes into account the repayment of the principal at the expiry date). Some longer-term loans are priced off the gilt rate (the average rate for government bonds of a specific duration).

Drop-lock

Drop-lock is a mechanism within a long-term floating rate facility which, when triggered, allows the borrower to fix the interest rate over the remaining period of the facility. The trigger is the reduction of long-term interest rates to a predetermined level.

Deep-discounted bonds

Deep-discounted bonds are a means of raising long-term finance with a low initial interest rate. Attractions include:

(a) interest payments can be stepped to rise every 5 years to equate to a property yield;
(b) tax relief can be claimed on the implied annual interest expense over the life of the bond.

These bonds can only really be issued by leading companies whose credit worthiness ensures marketability in the bond market.

1.6 Overview of the finance market

Over the last decade or so, the lending market has been difficult, and Berkley (1991) blamed the poor position of property lending on four factors.

1 Relatively new lenders in the market, such as building societies and foreign banks who had money to finance property but little expertise of adjusting the terms of the loans to the risks being taken.
2 The use of commercial indemnity insurance (CMI, covered later in this book) to increase the debt proportion of value from 70 per cent to 85 per cent, say. CMIs were abused, especially on development loans, and insurers have had to face considerable claims. Insurers failed to differentiate between the risks involved in indemnifying comparatively secure investment loans and the top slice position in a development or trading opportunity. (The top slice is the slice of income that has the least priority of charge.)

3   There was pressure on lenders to evolve innovative schemes that dealt with high interest rates. These underestimated how high interest rates would go during the period. Even clearing banks allowed overdrafts to increase to reflect the higher interest rates and, as more overdrafts reached their limits, so there were directives to call in the loans. This, in turn, put more pressure on the secondary bank market to lend.

4   In a good market, it is easier to obtain a report to confirm the borrower's bullish projections, whereas since the early 1990s valuers have become more cautious. A satisfactory offer of finance will not be forthcoming from a lender without a suitable valuation to support it.

The activity in the financial markets has developed, especially in the areas of debt finance, joint ventures and mezzanine finance. The main criteria in these areas are outlined below to give an indication of the nature of the financial products and structures in the market. This is really a selective introduction to the more extensive overview of debt and equity that is outlined later in the book.

Debt finance

Clearing banks and, to a lesser extent, merchant banks have been prepared to provide loans for property development. Generally these loans are secured on collateral beyond the property to be developed. Interest is charged on a fixed or variable basis. Non-recourse finance is now more popular; it can be defined as loans on property unsupported by outside collateral. Finance is available from banks for up to 70 per cent loan to value ratio without outside security being provided. Banks take first charge over the site and advance monies during the development phase. Interest rates are between 1 per cent and 2 per cent over LIBOR but this is reduced with pre-let or pre-sale.

Loans generally have limited recourse with developers undertaking to:

- pay cost overruns;
- inject equity stakes either up-front or side-by-side;
- pay interest from completion of the deal;
- complete within certain time limits; and
- complete within certain costs.

Banks will normally allow interest to be capitalised during the construction period and developers generally include this as a construction cost, thus not affecting profits during the development process. The main types of debt finance available are as follows.

Commercial mortgages

These are straightforward loans where the interest rate is either paid currently or capitalised. The principal is either amortised over the term of the loan or repaid by a single payment at the end. The interest rate can be fixed or variable and other capital market instruments can be used including caps (preventing interest rises over a certain rate), floors (preventing interest rate rises over a certain level) and collars (restricting the movement of interest rates between a floor and a cap rate). These instruments are used to minimise interest fluctuations, thereby reducing risk and obtaining finer pricing. The length of loan will vary but the maximum for many banks is five years, although insurance companies and building societies may lend up to 25 years.

Equity participation or convertible mortgages

This structure allows the lender to share in the uplift of the value of the property for a reduction in the interest rate payable.

Mortgage debenture issues

This is a traditional method of raising corporate finance. It involves a loan raised on a debenture issue that is secured against the property or other assets and yields either a fixed or index-linked return.

Multi-option facilities

In this structure a group of banks agree to provide cash advances at a pre-determined margin for a certain period.

Deep-discounted bonds

Deep-discounted bonds are a method of raising long-term finance with a low initial interest rate. Interest payments can be stepped to accord with rent review and there are also tax advantages. Bonds can be placed with institutional investors and can be very finely priced. It is anticipated that bond issues will become increasingly used to finance major projects to overcome the need to refinance on completion of the development.

Joint ventures

There are a number of different types of joint venture; the concept involves the coming together of two or more parties to undertake a transaction. Joint ventures are a useful means of bringing parties together with different interests in order to complete deals. The reasons for increased use of joint ventures include: pressure from the Bank of England to reduce the level of bank debt in the property sector; increased risk in property development; lack of equity in the property market and thus property companies being unable to raise new funds in the stock market, and demand from overseas investors who have a preference for joint venture arrangements.

Forms of joint venture structures are:

- limited liability companies
- partnership (one party must have unlimited liability)
- profit participation.

The decision on how to create the joint venture will depend on the purposes of the joint venture. This is turn will depend on whether this is being organised for a single property project or for a number of schemes, on the tax situation of the parties and the venture, and finally, whether there are stamp duty (transaction tax) considerations which will affect the costs of transfer and which accordingly should be minimised under the structure agreed.

On negotiation of a joint venture agreement important points to consider are:

- the level of funding to be provided
- the development period/time
- who will control the decision-making process
- how the profit is going to be distributed
- what the provisions are for dissolution in the event of failure
- how disputes are to be settled.

Joint ventures are considered in detail in Chapter 11.

Mezzanine finance

There are often gaps between the costs of development and limited recourse loans and this is filled by a mezzanine loan. The amount of mezzanine finance varies but can take debt up to 95 per cent of cost. Mezzanine funders can require rates of return between 30 and 40 per cent, secured on a subordinated loan (i.e., charged after the main loan) with a share of profit, normally side-by-side with a cap at an agreed level. Should the project run into problems, the priority return that the mezzanine financier seeks can quickly diminish any profit. Interest payable on the mezzanine finance can be capitalised, producing cash flow benefits.

The finance market

Bank of England property lending figures at the beginning of the 1990s showed that there was too much debt and too little equity in the market. Banks had continued to lend on the basis that the financial institutions or foreign investors would be around to refinance the property projects. 'Big Bang' (the deregulation of the Stock Exchange in October 1986) and the deregulation of the financial services market sparked an increase in property lending by the foreign banks; £35 billion of bank debt was outstanding to the property sector in 1993. Had restrictions on loans been introduced, the sector could have been in serious trouble. Despite the subsequent slowdown in the economy, property transactions were still being financed and some international banks, especially the Japanese, regarded the situation as an opportunity to increase their market share. American banks, however, reduced their exposure at this time. Clearing banks started to take a cautious view in the 1990s as initially, with property values falling, they had to be very careful not to cause a collapse through unwarranted liquidations. The problems arising from the Rush & Tompkins (a major building contractor) collapse in the early 1990s, and the domino effect triggered by the collapse, demonstrated this.

Building societies became increasingly active in the market but the demise of one or two of their major investments in the early 1990s caused them to reappraise the situation. During the early 1990s, few banks lent on speculative development schemes and even pre-let schemes could only be financed where an exit route for the financier was clearly demonstrated. Borrowers were expected to provide guarantees for any cost overruns and interest was payable during the development period. Equity injections were required from the developer and the banks demanded a substantial level of recourse. The amount of equity initially required increased as most banks were not prepared to lend above 70 per cent of cost and this equity was demanded up-front. At this time, by comparison, banks were still keen to lend on good quality investment property although they would not capitalise interest over long periods. This created difficulties with reversionary properties. Loans above the normal loan to value of 70 per cent were available if mortgage indemnity policies were used or the bank received a share of profits.

During the early 1990s, there was clearly a need for further liquidity in the property sector through increased equity injections. More funds did enter the market through Authorised Property Unit Trusts but, despite the tax transparency (the avoidance of excessive taxation, covered later in the book) of these trusts, their impact was limited in the short term because of falling property values during the period. The London Future and Option Exchange was established to introduce a property futures contract which would provide further liquidity; however, this was abandoned soon after. Using the exchange, investors could increase their exposure to the property market by purchasing contracts that could be used to hedge the risk of a trading or investment portfolio.

In the market of the early 1990s any loan structure which capitalised interest was very sought after because of the need to provide funds to refinance development loan facilities. This was one reason why deep-discounted bond issues increased in popularity. Convertible mortgages offered another alternative whereby the borrower provided the lender or investor with equity in the scheme in return for a higher loan advance and reduced obligations to pay interest. Both discounted bonds and convertible mortgages, though, suffered to a degree because of higher interest rates in international markets at this time. The situation by the mid-1990s was that, until new investments or investment products could bolster the amount of equity in the market, property loans on new transactions remained difficult to secure.

In terms of prospects for equity finance in the 1990s, there was some encouragement in the sector with, for instance, increases in property share prices. In the early 1990s, many property shares were showing a premium to net asset value as opposed to the usual discount. Savills' survey on financing property (Savills 1993a) suggested that 1992 had been dominated by the events in September of that year that led to the devaluation of the pound and the withdrawal of the UK from the Exchange Rate Mechanism. After that event, a yield gap developed between average property yields and borrowing rates, and also between property yields and those on gilts and equities. Property yields generally remained higher over this period. The FTA Property Index fell to an historic low in September 1992 but afterwards recovered. The rise in property share values resulted in the narrowing of discounts on share price to net asset value (see Chapter 10 for a definition and discussion of this measure of performance). The long-term average discount of 30 per cent fell to 13 per cent at the beginning of 1993, was reduced to 7 per cent in April 1993 and reached a 4 per cent premium in June 1993 (Savills 1993a). The trend was further upwards with a 21 per cent premium by the end of 1993.

Table 1.1   Movement of prime yields by sector
1992–3 (%)

	1992	1993
Retail	5.25	4.75
Office	8.75	7.50
Retail warehouse	9.25	7.50
Industrial	9.00	7.50

Source: Savills (1993b).

The period around 1992–3 was a critical juncture as financiers and investors in the property markets were endeavouring to ascertain whether the sector was lifting out of the slump following the boom of the late 1980s. The speculation and institutional interest in property shares in the market at this time meant that share prices rose as indicated above, and this enabled the property companies on their re-rating (their increased valuation on the stock market) to raise new capital. This capital was used to improve balance sheets and enable them to buy into the weak property market. Thus, the direct property market started to show a slow but positive progress due to the weight of institutional and overseas money, which led to a downward pressure on yields, as shown in Table 1.1, and also a general expectation of recovery in the sector.

Reports from DTZ Debenham Thorpe (*Money into Property*, 1993, and other research), confirms that the demand for property assets had strengthened at this time and that, led by the major property companies, the potential demand in 1993 was the highest for 5 years. Thus, there was in prospect a better balance between the demands of institutions and property companies and between the demands for debt and equity. This balance helped to avoid the same destabilising effect that happened with the influx of bank property lending in the late 1980s (DTZ Debenham Thorpe 1993). The institutions thus found themselves underweight with property in their portfolios and this, combined with the cash-raising activities of the property companies, led to a number of rights issues. Banks continued to reduce their exposure at the same time and the figures for loans at March 1993 were down to £36.8 billion, down 85 per cent from 1991 (Evans 1993). It was suggested that these indications meant that the severe lack of liquidity experienced in the market since 1989 had at last begun to ease.

Figure 1.3 shows the flow of new money into property around the period of the boom and slump of the 1980s and early 1990s. The figures for 1993 are for the first quarter only.

The recovery that took place in 1993 was clearly shown in published surveys of confidence at the time; for instance, the Chesterton Financial/*CSW* Confidence Barometer showed a substantial change of attitude in the market. The Confidence Barometer is an overall measure of confidence amongst commercial property lenders and is based on whether the respondents are pessimistic or optimistic in the future across a number of criteria. The measure of net confidence is the percentage surplus or deficit of optimists over pessimists and the survey noted a dramatic change in attitudes from January to July 1993 (Chesterton Financial/*CSW* 1993). For the first time since the confidence barometer was first launched, all measures of net confidence were positive by July 1993 (see Tables 1.2 and 1.3).

Respondents to the Confidence Barometer survey had expected an improvement in the overall state of their property lending, lower bad debt provisions, fewer borrowers in breach of loan covenants and a lower rate of receivership amongst borrowers as indicated by their responses. This confidence carried on through the following years as the investment position of property consolidated.

By the late 1990s, a substantial rise in the support for commercial property was evident amongst the financial institutions, the insurance companies and pension funds. The recovery by the end of the decade was such that research carried out

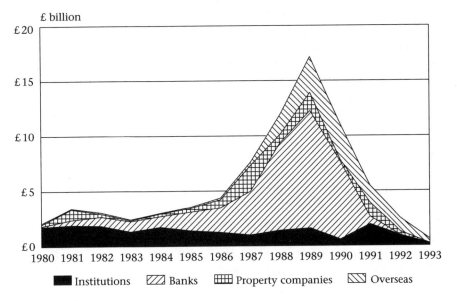

Figure 1.3 New money into property
Source: DTZ Research (2001).

Table 1.2 Chesterton/*CSW* Confidence Barometer: next 6 months (%)

The measures of overall net confidence for the 6-month period following the survey were:

	July '91	Jan. '92	July '92	Jan. '93	July '93
Optimistic	8	8	9	16	43
Pessimistic	−48	−49	−48	−39	−13
No change	44	43	44	45	44
Net confidence	−40.3	−40.8	−39.2	−22.6	29.7

Note: Figures are rounded except for net confidence.
Source: Chesterton Financial/*CSW* (1993).

Table 1.3   Chesterton/*CSW* Confidence Barometer: next 12 months (%)

The measures of overall net confidence for the 12-month period following the survey were:					
	July '91	Jan. '92	July '92	Jan. '93	July '93
Optimistic	31	27	22	36	62
Pessimistic	−31	−35	−26	−27	−8
No change	38	39	52	36	30
Net confidence	0.5	−8.3	−3.5	9.2	53.6

Note: Figures are rounded except for net confidence.
Source: Chesterton Financial/*CSW* (1993).

estimated that net capital inflows to the UK commercial property market amounted to £29.7 billion by 2000. This represented an increase of two-thirds over 1999 and was the largest annual total recorded, even after allowing for capital value inflation. The increase was driven by record levels of net investment from institutional and overseas investors and particularly high levels of finance committed by providers of loan finance. Predictions by DTZ Research (2001) suggested lower capital inflows in 2001, perhaps around £20 billion. In 2000, net investment by financial institutions increased £6.1 billion over the previous year; this increase was dominated by the pension funds who provided £3.7 billion. Overseas investment registered its highest increase in 2000. In terms of capital issues, with the re-rating of property shares, they out-performed the wider equities market and the average discount to net asset value (NAV) narrowed from 36 per cent in February 2000 to 16 per cent at the end of the first quarter of 2001. Debt finance contributed £81 billion in 2000, up 24 per cent from 1999. After accounting for capital value inflation, the level of debt was up 20 per cent from that outstanding at the top of the last lending cycle (DTZ Research 2001). However, the rate of property lending was slowing in 2001. Bank lending over the previous year to June 2001 was £15 billion to make a total of £63.7 billion outstanding. Although this is the largest annual increase recorded to date, higher even than the £10.6 billion increase in lending in 1989, the percentage increase over the year was 31 per cent, half the increases of 50–60 per cent measured in the boom years of the late 1980s. However, with respect to these figures, there is an expectation that many property lenders will securitise their loan books (see Chapter 12 for a discussion of securitisation). This securitisation will reduce the loan amount covered by the Bank of England property lending survey further which, even at this time, accounted for only two-thirds of total commercial lending (Keers 2001).

Towards the end of the 1990s, the suggestion was that the fundamentals for commercial property investment remained sound, but a yield gap had opened up between long-dated gilt rates in the money markets and the higher yielding average property yields. Development activity in the sector was also being sustained. Key developments in the market related to:

• the increased debt outstanding to the sector, with worries about the debt problems of the late 1980s and early 1990s

- the diversity of investment products available for funding matched by the diversity of finance sources available, especially from overseas
- the growth of indirect vehicles for investment, especially those based on limited partnerships (DTZ Debenham Thorpe 1999).

The central question that arose following the property market recession of the early 1990s was whether property could ever fully regain the growth status that it had enjoyed for most of the postwar period. In what appears to be a more relaxed market, it is unlikely that a shortage of good-quality property that has fuelled rental growth previously will recur. Also, if inflation remains at a permanently lower level, as has been the case recently, then property values are unlikely to increase from this source either (Brett 1997).

By 1999, debt secured on property assets in the UK was around £42.4 billion (around 6 per cent of UK lending). The actual total lending figure to property companies is higher than that quoted by the Bank of England as the Bank's figures exclude loans from building societies, insurance companies, unauthorised banks and securitised debt. Including these categories, it is likely the figure was more than £60 billion. At this time, over a 100 banks were prepared to lend on UK property. The German banks were the most competitive for the larger prime deals, with the UK clearing banks and building societies tending to dominate the smaller market with deals of less than £10 million and also the secondary market (Freeman Publishing 2000). The top 10 per cent of banks at this time accounted for 73 per cent of all property lending, and the emergence of the large German lenders has added to this trend towards concentration. The German banks at this time were responsible for 12 per cent of UK property lending. The types of finance provided included investments in the traditional sectors of office, retail and industrial, but there has also been increased attention in the leisure and hotel sector. The preferred securities for lending are modern properties on leases with more than 10 years unexpired, let to good covenants. Lending on portfolios of properties and multi-lets is becoming more popular amongst lenders because of location and tenant diversification respectively. Development finance is reserved for pre-let schemes let to good covenants that are easily funded; only prime speculative schemes would be funded. Mezzanine finance is provided by a number of lenders, mainly investment and merchant banks and specialist finance houses. Bank debt by nationality of lending in 1999 was concentrated in the hands of UK (67 per cent) and other EU banks (23 per cent).

Debt outstanding to property companies increased by 24 per cent in 2000 to £81 billion. This was 28 per cent higher (after accounting for capital inflation) than that outstanding at the top of the last lending cycle. The expansion of loan finance has led to the relaxation of some lending criteria. The securitisation of loan books is a new growth area: 80 per cent of lenders appear intent on expanding their loan books. DTZ Research (2001) suggest that there is no evidence presently in the market that the expansion in lending is fuelling speculative development but the principal risk would be an economic slowdown leading to tenant defaults and loan delinquencies.

1.7   The globalisation of finance

Financial, capital and money markets have moved from national to international dominance. These markets are globalised, deregulated and freer in which to operate. Thus, stateless finance, outside the jurisdiction of any one country and its regulatory institutions, can manipulate the market. Innovations in the finance of property have been a product of this globalisation. The traditional funding of development projects by short-term bank funding and long-term institutional finance has been replaced. Innovations in finance have also had to deal with the inherent illiquidity and lumpiness of property. Investor interest in liquidity, flexibility, the management of risk, yield analysis and portfolio management have been met by new advances of financing property (Pugh 1991).

The context of property financing in the 1980s and 1990s was the globalisation of the investment markets of different asset classes; this began after the abolition of exchange controls for investment funds in the UK in the late 1980s. Banks became interested in the globalisation because they were following the needs of business occupiers as well as property investors. Property investment globalisation accelerated with the presence of Scandinavians, Japanese and other foreign investment which was having an influence in the European markets in the late 1980s (Sieracki 1993). Until 'Big Bang' (the deregularisation of the Stock Exchange in the mid-1980s) the City of London was nearly all UK owned, only 3 per cent being foreign owned; by 2000, this proportion has risen to 25 per cent (Freeman Publishing 2000).

DTZ Research (2001) found that the fastest growing source of lending was that by foreign banks entitled to establish branches in the UK and lending institutions entitled to provide service on a cross-border basis. This group is dominated by German mortgage banks that specialise in long-term real estate lending as well as infrastructure-related loans to the public sector at fixed interest rates. From 1991, German mortgage banks were allowed to engage in cross-border lending and, since then, this activity has increased dramatically, such that the debt outstanding to UK commercial property (on the basis of figures published by the German Mortgage Bank Association) was almost £6 billion by 2000. At the same time, US investment has been falling; much of the US investment is from Real Estate Investment Trusts (REITs) and deals often involve participation in joint ventures. For instance, in 1999 BL Universal (the joint venture between British Land and Great Universal Stores) linked up with the American pension fund, Teachers Annuity, to acquire the freehold interest in Microsoft's UK headquarters for around £100 million (DTZ Debenham Thorpe 1999).

1.8   Summary

The late 1970s were a critical period for property investment; its returns were outperforming inflation. By the early 1980s, average rental growth was underperforming inflation and returns from the capital markets were falling in certain sectors. According to the Richard Ellis Monthly Indices, only since 1986 has property begun to show significant real returns. In the early 1990s, wider performance measures, matched by increasingly sophisticated market research and analysis as property returns fell, produced a much keener understanding of the components of property investment of yield, rent and valuations methods and by the mid-1980s, property was being measured relatively as well as absolutely. In the late 1970s, capital growth was driven by falling yields; in 1987–88, capital growth was generated by rental growth. In 1988, Richard Ellis tested the hypothesis that the property market moves counter-cyclically to equities and gilts and is thus a good prospect for the diversification of a portfolio. This study found:

- *very limited similarity* between property returns and equities (0.10 correlation coefficient)
- *no similarity* between property returns and gilts (0.03 correlation coefficient)
- gilts and equity returns were *more in line* (0.44 correlation) (Barter 1988).

If one takes away the sentiment of land and building, then a property investment is basically a flow of income arising from the property asset which can be distributed in many different ways to offer investors differing degrees of risk and thus differing yields and capital values. This is the basis of property securitisation and the innovative forms of property finance which have been developed; these new financial techniques attempt to overcome property's inherent illiquidity and inflexibility. Jones Lang LaSalle have provided the longest available run of consistent annual data describing the performance of a diversified portfolio of real properties. The data show the following:

- property returns have been lower than the returns of equities and similar to the returns on gilts
- property volatility has been less than the volatility of both equities and gilts
- property has been much less well correlated with equities and gilts than equities and gilts have been correlated with one another
- property smoothes the overall performance of a portfolio with the three asset classes, and thus property offers risk reductions to holders of gilts and equities (Freeman Publishing 2000).

The key concerns about property as an investment medium, as noted by Barter (1988), still remain as follows.

1 *Illiquidity* Properties take three months to buy and sell. There is no certainty of price and terms until contracts are exchanged. This problem is acute for properties with capital values above £20 million because of the relatively small supply of potential single purchasers in the market, especially when there are no international purchasers. There are problems in appraising and financing the more substantial developments.

2 *Inflexibility* There is a high unit cost with property purchases and little flexibility in the purchase; one needs to buy the whole. There are problems in portfolio diversification and management here. Property shares and property units offer some opportunity to diversify, but property companies are taxed in the same way as other companies and unauthorised property unit trusts are only available

to pension funds and certain types of charities and cannot be listed. Now there are authorised trusts for the general public but these may remain unlisted and have a corporation tax liability on the income. Some of the problems of illiquidity and inflexibility have been addressed by 'swapping' properties in matched deals. This avoids the exposure and bad publicity of putting properties up for sale in a poor market. An example in the UK was a swap valued at £35.35 million in the UK in which the Provident Mutual sold a mixed portfolio of six office, retail and industrial properties to Allied London in exchange for eight retail warehouses, valued at £21.6 million, together with £12.75 million in cash (*Estates Times* 1993).

3   *Growth of debt finance*   There has been a substantial increase in bank lending to the property sector in recent years and this has replaced new equity investment by institutions. This may pose a threat to the property market and is discussed later in the book; although the inflow of money into property from banks decreased in the early 1990s, it is now increasing again. After 1997, a yield gap developed as all property yields remained high, around 8 per cent, whilst the rate on 15-year gilts fell from around 8 per cent towards 4 per cent; this gap made the debt financing of property more profitable. In the last 25 years, the available data has disguised the returns that have been available to property investors who finance their purchases partly with equity and partly with borrowed money. In periods of rising values and low interest rates, investors can use debt finance to increase returns on their equity (Freeman Publishing 2000).

4   *Valuation methodology and precision*   Conventional valuation methods are inflexible. The all-risk yield approach of traditional valuation methods is difficult to apply to more illiquid properties such as major shopping centres and substantial office buildings. Cases such as the Queens Moat Houses valuations carried out in the UK in the early 1990s, where there were critical variations in the valuation of a portfolio of hotels, confirm this. Conventional valuations also have difficulty in the valuation of over-rented property where rents are expected to fall on review. As markets have improved in the 1990s, although the particular problem of over-renting has become less important, the general problems related to valuation methodology have not lessened. Research findings from the property profession themselves seem to bear this out: Harvard (2001) suggests that the normal behaviour of valuers and the procedures followed by valuation firms lead to a higher risk of an unsupportable valuation where valuers are working in relatively unfamiliar areas. Research in psychology and decision making has shown that humans adopt heuristic strategies when making judgements in complex task environments. Heuristics, of which several types have been identified, are short cuts that simplify tasks. They are essential strategies, often characterising expert behaviour, enabling humans, who have limited processing capacity, to reduce the amount of information to be dealt with. The downside of this approach is that it can, however, lead to biased or sub-optimal decisions being made.

5   *The future role of the property profession*   The liberalisation of the financial markets and the increased importance of debt in property funding require new competencies for chartered surveyors. New competition has come from fund managers who can access large sums of capital for business development or co-invest

in large blocks of properties alongside clients, which surveyors cannot (Freeman Publishing 2000). The demands of the UK Financial Services Act (1986) for those providing information on finance and funding will require different and greater competence in the financial area. The Act poses problems of conflicts of interest amongst surveying firms who act in transaction business as well as in investment management. In these areas and others, the property profession is reorienting itself to the market.

Short-termism

Property is a long-term investment and cannot compete on similar terms with investments that pay off on a much shorter time horizon. Recent attitudes of funders and managers of companies in the UK indicate a short-term approach to investment and performance that may be a reflection of the difficult times in which these companies have had to operate. Companies have sometimes opted for very short-term investment appraisals and rapid payback. The pressure to perform has not only led fund managers to increase their management activity but also to short-term perspectives of investment strategy. This strategy focuses on the short-term performance of companies in arriving at the valuation of a company's worth with emphasis on current profit performance and dividend payments. This perspective has many consequences across the spectrum of companies including:

- the neglect of the long-term by corporate management leading to a failure to undertake important long-term investments in resources and research and development
- the volatility of short-term corporate results becoming exaggerated in securities markets, producing unacceptable fluctuations in share prices.

Because of its long-term production cycle, these consequences are likely to be very damaging to property and construction. A survey carried out by the UK Department of Industry's Innovation Advisory Board in 1990 concluded that the City of London's (representing the financial centre) influence on corporate activity led to companies prioritising short-term profits and dividends at the expense of research and development. This practice was also at the expense of other innovative investment. The report found that the practices of key financial institutions sustained these priorities. Researchers in the USA have concluded that the increasing shareholder power of institutional investors has had a damaging effect on research and development expenditure amongst US firms. The City of London rejects this criticism by saying that much of the responsibility for the lack of long-term innovation investment is attributable to corporate managers, to their preference for growth by acquisition, their poor record of commercial development and their reward systems based on short-term targets (Pike and Neale 1998).

The implications for property in this respect are very clear; property development and the development of its associated transport, social and services infrastructure are long-term projects. Development and refurbishment underpin the property investment market. Projects on difficult town-centre sites or involving major infrastructure works encounter problems of risk and uncertainty as they extend into the future. There are also problems of high transfer cost and illiquidity in property; for instance, to force a sale of a development or investment property at an inappropriate time (say, halfway through a building contract) could cause a collapse in the price of the asset. This effect is accentuated because of the location attributes of property, as markets are localised and imperfect. Short-termism is inappropriate to property finance where long-term strategy and long-term returns are the key to success.

These short-term aspects have, in the past been reflected in the way finance has been provided. Maguire and Axcell (1994), in their comparison between the term structure of loans in the UK and those of France and Germany, found that debt finance provision in the UK is predominantly short term compared to those countries. They conclude, for instance, that the widespread use of long-term financial instruments to fund owner-occupied property may have had a stabilising effect on supply and demand in property markets in both France and Germany. Another point to be made here relates to liability matching; many investors (for instance, pension funds) have future liabilities based on future wage levels and thus may need to achieve real growth in their investments. These liabilities are longer term and, because of this, property investment may be a more attractive proposition because of the long-term returns of property even if, in the short term, property investment's annual performance may appear poor.

References and further reading

Balchin, P. N., Isaac, D. and Chen, J. (2000) *Urban Economics: A Global Perspective*, Palgrave, Basingstoke/New York.

Barter, S. L. (1988) 'Introduction', in S. L. Barter (ed.), *Real Estate Finance*, Butterworths, London.

Berkley, R. (1991) 'Raising Commercial Property Finance in a Difficult Market', *Journal of Property Finance*, 1(4), 523–9.

Brett, M. (1983b) 'Indirect Investment in Property', in C. Darlow (ed.), *Valuation and Investment Appraisal*, Estates Gazette, London.

Brett, M. (1990b) *Property and Money*, Estates Gazette, London.

Brett, M. (1997) *Property and Money*, Estates Gazette, London.

Cadman, D. and Catalano, A. (1983) *Property Development in the UK – Evolution and Change*, College of Estate Management, Reading.

Chesterton Financial/CSW (1993) *Property Confidence Barometer*, Chesterton Financial, London, July.

Debenham, Tewson & Chinnocks (1984) *Property Investment in Britain*, Debenham, Tewson & Chinnocks, London.

DTZ Debenham Thorpe (1993) *Money into Property*, DTZ Debenham Thorpe, London, August.

DTZ Debenham Thorpe (1999) *Money into Property*, DTZ Debenham Thorpe, London, May.

DTZ Research (2001) *Money into Property*, DTZ Research, London, edition 26, June.

Dubben, N. and Sayce, S. (1991) *Property Portfolio Management*, Routledge, London.

Estates Times (1993) 'Swaps not cash', *Estates Times*, 19 November, 24.

Evans, P. H. (1993) 'Statistical Review', *Journal of Property Finance*, 4(2), 75–82.

Fraser, W. D. (1993) *Principles of Property Investment and Pricing*, Macmillan, London.

Freeman Publishing (2000) *Guide to the Property Industry*, Freeman Publishing, London, June.

Harvard, T. (2001) *Valuation Behaviour and Valuer Reliability*, Royal Institute of Chartered Surveyors Foundation, London (web address: http://www.rics-foundation.org).

Keers, H. (2001) 'Property lending cools despite £15 bn increase', *Property Week*, 10 August, 68.

Maguire, D. and Axcell, A. (1994) 'Real Estate Finance: France, Germany and the UK', *Journal of Property Finance*, 5(1), 29–40.

Pike, R. and Neale, B. (1993) *Corporate Finance and Investment*, Prentice-Hall, London.

Pike, R. and Neale, B. (1999) *Corporate Finance and Investment: Decisions and Strategies*, Prentice-Hall, London.

Pugh, C. (1991) 'The Globalisation of Finance Capital and the Changing Relationships between Property and Finance', *Journal of Property Finance*, 2(2) and (3).

Ratcliffe, J. (1978) *An Introduction to Urban Land Administration*, Estates Gazette, London.

Riley, M. and Isaac, D. (1993b) 'Commercial Property Lending: Confidence Survey', *Journal of Property Finance*, 4(3/4), 45–51.

Ross, S. A., Westerfield, R. W. and Jaffe, J. F. (1993) *Corporate Finance*, Irwin, Boston, MA.

Savills (1989) *Financing Property 1989*, Savills, London.

Savills (1993a) *Financing Property 1993*, Savills, London.

Savills (1993b) *Investment and Economic Outlook*, Savills, London, Issue 3, October.

Sharpe, W. F., Alexander, G. J. and Bailey, J. V. (1995) *Investments*, Prentice-Hall, Englewood Cliffs, NJ.

Sieracki, K. (1993) 'U.K. Institutional Requirements for European Property', *Estates Gazette*, 17 July, 116.

2
Theories of Finance

2.1 Introduction

In the last 30 years, a branch of applied microeconomics has been developed and this has specialised in modern finance theory. It is important to understand some of the developments in this theory and how they underpin the principles for raising and pricing property finance. It is not within the range of this text to provide details of the theory or any extensive discussion and you are referred to one of the specialist texts as shown in the bibliography to this chapter. The beginning of the separate development of modern finance theory was with Markowitz's work around 1958 when he was developing portfolio theory, which is now applied in the selection of investment portfolios. In addition, Modigliani and Miller were working on capital structure and gearing at this time. Modern finance theory emphasises the analytical and quantitative skills of management rather than a descriptive approach to the understanding of finance; however, you should appreciate that, in a text of this nature, a descriptive approach is used as well as the application of theory.

2.2 Financial theory

Copeland and Weston (1988) suggest that there are seminal and internally consistent theories on which modern finance theory is founded. These are listed below, together with brief explanations. All these theories attempt to answer the common problem related to economics: 'How do individuals and society allocate scarce resources through a price system based on the valuation of risky assets?'

1 *Utility theory*: the basis of rational decision-making in the face of risky alternatives; how do people make choices?
2 *State preference theory*
3 *Mean variance theory and the capital asset pricing model*
4 *Arbitrage pricing theory*
5 *Option pricing theory*
6 *Modigliani–Miller theorems*
7 *Market efficiency*

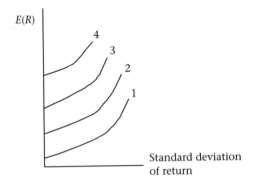

Figure 2.1   Utility theory

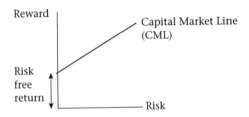

Figure 2.2   The relationship between risk and reward

Utility theory shows how people make choices. State preference theory, mean variance theory, arbitrage and option pricing theory describe the objects of choice. Combining the theory of choice with the objects of choice shows how risky alternatives are valued. If correctly assigned, asset prices should provide the appropriate indicators for resource allocation. Modigliani–Miller theory asks, 'Does the method of financing have any effect on the value of assets, particularly the firm?'

Utility theory

In Figure 2.1, utility theory suggests that investors will maximise expected utility as their preferred outcome. This can be done by selecting the best combination of risk and return. The indifference curves for a number of assets (1–4) for a risk-averse investor are shown as functions of risk and return. $E(R)$ represents mean return. The standard deviation of return (often represented as σR) shows how expected return can vary and represents risk (see Figure 2.2).

State preference theory

Prices of investments represent the aggregate risk preference of individuals and firms. The development of state preference theory provides a means to determine the optimal portfolio decisions for individuals and the optimal investment rules for firms in a world of uncertainty. In a perfect capital market a set of prices for market securities can be derived. These prices are determined by:

(a) individual time preference for consumption and the investment opportunities of firms;
(b) probability beliefs concerning pay-offs that are dependent on the assumptions of the scenarios possible at the time of the pay-off (state contingents);
(c) individual preferences towards risk and the level of non-diversifiable risk in the economy.

Mean variance theory

Mean variance theory combines the theory of investor choice (utility theory) with the objects of investor choice (the portfolio opportunity set) to show how risk-averse investors wishing to maximise expected utility will choose their optimal portfolios. Measures of risk and return can be combined with probability to show the risk and return for a portfolio of risky assets, called portfolio theory.

From this theory two theoretical models can be derived that enable us to price risky assets in equilibrium; these are the Capital Asset Pricing Model (CAPM) and the Arbitrage Pricing Theory (APT). In the CAPM the appropriate measure of risk is the covariance of returns between the risky asset in question and the market portfolio of all assets. The CAPM is a useful conceptual framework for capital budgeting and the cost of capital. Although the model is not perfectly validated by empirical tests its main implications appear correct:

- systematic (market) risk β (beta) is a valid measure of risk
- the model is linear
- the trade-off between return and risk is positive.

The CAPM is shown graphically in Figure 2.3, where:

R_F = risk-free return
$E(R)$ = mean return
beta or β = risk

The CAPM says that the required rate of return on any asset is equal to the risk-free rate of return plus a risk premium. The risk premium is the price of risk

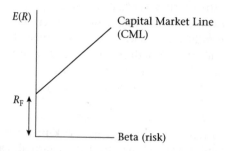

Figure 2.3   The Capital Market Line

multiplied by the quantity of risk. In the terminology of the CAPM, the price of risk is determined by the slope of the line, the difference between the expected rate of return on the market portfolio and the risk-free rate of return. The quantity of risk is called beta (β).

Arbitrage pricing theory

APT is more general than the CAPM discussed above. It suggests that many factors, not just the market portfolio, may explain asset returns. For each factor, the appropriate measure of risk is the sensitivity of asset returns to changes in the factor. For normally distributed returns the sensitivity is analogous to the beta or systematic risk of the CAPM. APT can be applied to cost of capital and capital budgeting problems.

Option pricing theory

The theory assumes that all financial assets are contingent claims. For example, ordinary shares are really a call option on the value of the assets of a firm. Similarly, other securities may also be thought of as options.

Option prices are functions of five parameters: the price of the underlying security, its instantaneous variance, the exercise price of the option, the time to maturity and the risk-free rate. All variables are observable except the instantaneous variance; this is the variation of the rate of return on the underlying asset. The holder of a call option will prefer more variance in the price of the stock as this will increase the probability that the price of the stock will exceed the exercise price and this will thus be of some value to the call holder. The option price does not, in this theory, depend on either individual risk preferences or the expected rate of return on the underlying asset. Options are discussed further in Chapter 6.

Modigliani–Miller theorems

The cost of capital is used as a basis for a rate of return. This rate needs to be defined so that a project's returns can be assessed against required criteria. For a firm, the main criterion is usually taken as whether the project improves the wealth position of the current shareholders of the firm. The original Modigliani–Miller theorems have been extended using the CAPM so that a risk-adjusted cost of capital may be obtained for each project. When the expected cash flows of the project are discounted at the correct risk-adjusted rate, the result is the net present value (NPV) of the project.

In a world without taxes, the value of the firm is independent of its capital structure. With the introduction of corporate and personal taxes, the firm is unaffected by the choice of financial gearing. However, although no completely satisfactory theory has yet been found to explain the existence of an optimal capital structure, casual empiricism suggests that firms behave as though it does exist. Thus, the estimated weighted average cost of capital can be calculated using a target capital structure. Empirical evidence suggests there is a gain from being geared.

Market efficiency

The hypothesis of capital market efficiency says that the prices of securities instantaneously and fully reflect all available relevant information. Capital market efficiency relies on the ability of arbitrageurs (dealers who capitalise on dealing in assets which are over- or undervalued on the market) to recognise that prices are out of line and to make a profit by driving them back to an equilibrium value consistent with available information. In an efficient market, securities will be traded at correct prices. This provides confidence to investors and the best allocation of funds.

For a stock market to be perfect, the following conditions need to apply:

1 The market needs to be frictionless without transaction costs and taxes. No constraining regulations limiting freedom of entry and exit for investors and companies seeking funds. All shares should be perfectly marketable.
2 All services in the market should be provided at the average minimum cost, with all participants being price takers.
3 All buyers and sellers should be rational and wish to maximise their expected utility maximisers.
4 There should be many buyers and sellers.
5 The market should be efficient from an informational point of view; information should be costless and received simultaneously by all individuals.

No market satisfies all these conditions. It is possible to relax some of the assumptions and still have an efficient market. The assumptions of costless information, a frictionless marketplace and many buyers and sellers are not necessary preconditions for the existence of an efficient capital market.

The capital market approach used in finance theory is important in respect of financial decisions made; the approach is only tenable if markets are efficient. If markets are efficient then the market prices will reflect the effects of decisions made in the market. The market price is the present value of future returns expected by the participants in the market discounted at a rate that reflects the risk-free rate and an appropriate risk premium. The stock market is essentially a secondary market: a place to buy and sell established securities. The influence of the market on sources of new capital is very high. The conditions necessary for efficiency in the capital markets are not as stringent as those defined by a perfect capital market.

The efficient market requires that:

- dealing costs be not too high
- the relevant information be available to a largish number of participants
- no individual dominates the market.

If people disagree on other individuals' judgements on future returns, this leads to transactions taking place. The sum of the transactions process will produce unbiased valuations in an efficient market. Such a market is a 'fair game' one. If it is a fair game, then *ex-post* gains or losses cannot be predicted *ex-ante*.

2.3 The theories developed

Capital market theory

Capital market theory relates both to the CAPM and to APT. The theory is about discounting risky cash flows, and has a number of important aspects that are covered below point by point:

How is risk measured?

The risk is related to an asset (we can use a company stock for ease of understanding). It relates to the variability of returns, measured by their variance or standard deviation. This is applicable to a single asset or security.

How is risk measured in a portfolio of securities?

Investors generally hold diversified portfolios, so we are interested in the contribution of a security to the risk of the entire portfolio. Because a security's variance is dispersed in a large diversified portfolio, the security's variance/standard deviation no longer represents the security's contribution to the risk of a large portfolio. In this case, the contribution is best measured by the security's covariance with the other securities in the portfolio.

For example, if a stock has high returns when the overall return of the portfolio is low and vice versa, the stock has a negative covariance with the portfolio. It acts as a hedge against risk, reducing the risk of the portfolio. If the stock has a high positive covariance, there is a high risk for the investor.

What is the measure of diversification?

β (beta) is the appropriate measure of the contribution of a security to the risk of a large portfolio.

What are the criteria for holding an investment?

Investors will only hold a risky investment if its expected return is high enough to compensate for its risk. There is a trade-off between risk and reward. The expected return on a security should be positively related to the security's beta.

$$\text{Expected return on a security} = \text{Risk-free rate} + [\text{beta} \times (\text{Expected return on market portfolio} - \text{Risk-free rate})]$$

(Ross, Westerfield and Jaffe 1993)

The term in brackets is positive so the equation relates the expected return on a security as a positive function of its beta. This equation is the basis of the Capital Asset Pricing Model. The Arbitrage Pricing Theory also derives a relationship between risk and return but not in this form. The APT draws basically the same conclusions but makes assumptions that the returns on securities are driven by a number of market factors.

Capital Asset Pricing Model

$$\bar{R} = R_F + \beta(\bar{R}_M - R_F)$$

where $\bar{R}_M$ is the expected return on the market, $\bar{R}$ is the expected return on the security, R_F is the risk-free rate and β is the measure of risk. Beta is a measure of the security's sensitivity to movements in an underlying factor, a measure of systematic risk. Systematic risk affects a large number of assets and is also called market, portfolio or common risk. Diversifiable risk is a risk that affects a single asset or small group of assets; this is also called unique or unsystematic risk.

The total risk for an individual security held in a portfolio can thus be broken down:

Total risk of individual security = portfolio risk + unsystematic or diversifiable risk

Thus, total risk is the risk borne if only one security is held. Portfolio risk is the risk still borne after achieving full diversification. Portfolio risk, as we have seen, is also called systematic or market risk. Diversifiable, unique or unsystematic risk is that risk which can be diversified away in a large portfolio.

Gearing and the cost of capital

The expected return on any asset depends on its beta. If a project has a beta risk similar to the firm, then it can be used in the CAPM. If a project's beta is different, then it should be used in assessing the return, or else the average beta of similar projects in the industry could be used. The beta of the company is determined by the revenue cycle, operating gearing and financial gearing (Ross, Westerfield and Jaffe 1993).

The cost of capital is the weighted average of the firm's cost of equity and debt. If the cost of equity is r_S and the cost of debt is r_B, the total cost of capital can be shown as:

$$\frac{S}{S+B} r_S + \frac{B}{S+B} r_B$$

where S is the percentage of equity to total capital and B is the percentage of debt to total capital.

Operating gearing is based on the differences between fixed and variable costs, but one cost alters with the quantity of output and the other does not. If there are higher fixed costs and lower variable costs, then there is a higher operating gearing defined as:

$$\frac{\text{Change in EBIT}}{\text{EBIT}} \times \frac{\text{Sales}}{\text{Change in sales}}$$

EBIT = earnings before interest and taxes. Operating gearing measures the percentage change in EBIT for a given percentage change in sales, and operating gearing increases as fixed costs rise and variable costs fall (see Chapter 13 for a further discussion on operating gearing).

Financial gearing is the extent to which a firm relies on debt. A highly geared firm has to make interest payments regardless of the firm's sale or income, so this is a fixed cost of finance. The risk (β) of an asset or of a company is reflected by its cost of capital and is determined by its capital structure, thus:

The firm's $\beta = \beta$ of ordinary shares if the firm is only financed with equity, otherwise:

$$\beta \text{ asset} = \frac{\text{debt}}{\text{debt} + \text{equity}} \times \beta \text{ debt} + \frac{\text{equity}}{\text{debt} + \text{equity}} \times \beta \text{ equity}$$

β debt is very low and in practice can be assumed to be 0. Thus, (Ross, Westerfield and Jaffe 1993):

$$\beta \text{ asset} = \frac{\text{equity}}{\text{debt} + \text{equity}} \times \beta \text{ equity} = \text{equity gearing} \times \text{risk of equity}$$

Because $\frac{\text{equity}}{\text{debt} + \text{equity}}$ must be < 1 for a geared firm, it follows that β asset $< \beta$ equity. β in an ungeared firm must be less than the β of equity in an otherwise identically geared firm.

Efficient markets

Efficient markets suggest that current market prices reflect available information. If valuations are a good proxy for prices, then valuations should reflect all known information (Brown 1991). There are several forms of market efficiency: weak, semi-strong and strong. If markets are efficient, they can process the information available and the information is thus incorporated into the price of the security. Thus, systems for playing the market cannot succeed, and abnormal returns cannot be expected. The definition of the types of market depends on the information the market uses to determine prices.

1 *Weak form* – incorporates the past history of prices and is efficient with respect to these prices, so stock selections based on patterns of past stock price movements are no better than random choice.
2 *Semi-strong form* – this market makes use of all publicly available information which is reflected in the price of stocks; thus, investors will not be able to outperform the market by using the same information.
3 *Strong form* – the market has all information and uses all the available information that anyone knows about the stocks, including inside information, to price the stocks.

Evidence from different financial markets supports the weak form and semi-strong efficiency but not the strong form. Thus, it is still not possible for the investor to use available information to beat the market and the share prices conform to a 'random walk'. Efficient markets enable us to say something about the way assets should be priced. If the market is a fair game, investors should be compensated for that part of the total risk that cannot be reduced by diversification. An efficient market implies valuers are doing a good job impounding information into valuations. Although there is a widespread belief that property markets are inefficient, the only real test of this in market efficiency is whether property investors are able to earn abnormal returns consistently over many periods. Evidence suggests this is not the case (Brown and Matysiak 2000).

Capital structure

In a no-tax world, Modigliani and Miller suggest that the value of the firm is unaffected by gearing, but with taxes the firm's value is an increasing function of gearing.

The expected rate of return is related to gearing and before taxes:

$$r_S = r_O + \frac{B}{S}(r_O - r_B)$$

where r_S is the cost of equity, r_O is the cost of equity in an ungeared firm, r_B is the cost of debt, S = percentage of equity, and B is percentage of debt to total capital.

Chaos theory

The efficient market hypothesis is based on the assumption that rational investors rapidly absorb new information about a company's prospects which then is built into the share price. Thus, the market has no memory; all price-sensitive events are random and independent of one another. The crash of 1987, possibly attributed to the market's realisation that shares were overvalued and triggered by the collapse of a relatively minor buy-out deal, has uncovered evidence that share price movements do not always conform to a 'random walk'.

A new branch of mathematics, chaos theory, has been used to explain these features. Chaos theory is based on the study of natural systems such as weather patterns and river systems. Observations of such systems give a chaotic impression of the elements lurching from one extreme to another. But chaos theorists suggest that these apparently unpredictable patterns are governed by sets of complex subsystems that react interdependently and can be modelled. Predictions of the behaviour of chaotic systems are very sensitive to the precise conditions specified at the start of the estimation period, so a small error in the specification can lead to major errors in the model. It has been suggested that stock markets are chaotic in this sense, and that markets do have memories, are prone to major swings and do not behave randomly. In the UK, some evidence has been found that today's price movement is influenced by changes in the past. If price moves were persistent (i.e., if previous moves in price had been upwards), then the subsequent price move was also found to be more likely to be up than down. Yet chaos theory also suggests that persistent trends are more likely to result in major reversals. Other observers of the market suggest that markets are essentially rational and efficient but succumb to chaos on occasions with bursts of chaotic frenzy being attributable to specific acts, which suggests some scope for informed insiders to out-perform the market during such periods. The true nature of the market is still in debate but it seems likely that corporate financial managers cannot necessarily regard today's market price as a fair assessment of company value. However, the market may well correctly value a company over a period of years (Pike and Neale 1993).

2.4 The application of theory to practice

Financial decisions

Financial management is concerned with answering three questions:

1 What specific assets should an enterprise acquire?
2 What total volume of funds should an enterprise commit?
3 How should the funds required be financed?

The study of finance is an extension to microeconomic theory. Financial decisions are made within certain parameters:

- expected returns
- risk
- capital markets
- the firm's cost of capital.

The firm's cost of capital is used in assessing the expected returns and capital market conditions affect the firm's cost of capital. The fundamental model is the relationship between risk and expected returns. Thus, financial decisions are a trade-off between risk and return.

Profit and wealth maximisation

The firm's operating objective is generally taken simply as the maximisation of profit. Wealth maximisation is more satisfactory or, more specifically, the maximisation of shareholders' wealth (for a corporate entity).

The objections to profit maximisation criteria are set out below:

1 The future is uncertain. It is not possible to express objective probabilistic distributions of the various returns possible. It is not possible to maximise the unknown.
2 Financial decision-making concerns the trade-off of risk and return. The concept of profit maximisation cannot embrace this view of decision-making.
3 The conditions of uncertainty are such that decisions of profit maximisation cannot be made. Companies tend to a level performance that satisfies rather than maximises objectives. The satisficing goal is consistent with the behavioural theory of the firm and is also consistent with wealth maximisation. The decision-maker will satisfice in situations where the costs of searching for a better solution are thought to be equal or greater than the benefits to be had from the possibly sub-maximal course adopted.
4 The view of profit maximisation is a narrow one. There are a number of external constraints to this approach. Wealth maximisation is unrealistic but maximisation could mean the maximum possible difference between the value of the input of resources into the firm and the value of the output of goods and services.

If a wider viewpoint is taken and the ultimate decision is a trade-off between risk and reward (and decision-maker attitudes towards these will vary), then utility maximisation is the goal of financial decision-making. Profit maximisation and wealth are subsumed under utility maximisation.

The cost of capital is important in these decisions. The firm will embark on projects that offer the prospect of a return greater than the firm's cost of capital. The firm's cost of capital will be determined by the finance markets. Market participants assess the performance of the firm and a collective judgement is made on the market. This assessment is a significant factor in pricing the firm's equity and rate of interest on debt.

Significance of capital markets

Finance uses the capital market approach as the basis for decision-making. Such an approach is only useful if the capital markets are efficient.

The point made by the theory discussed previously on efficient markets is that in efficient markets, investors cannot consistently achieve above-average returns other than by chance. In October 1987, on 'Black Monday', there was a sudden and dramatic fall in share prices on most of the world's stock markets with share prices falling by 30 per cent or more. Had this been triggered by a particular event, shareholders' reaction could have been explained as the efficient market reacting to new information. However, this collapse was not due to external events but rather to a recognition that the bull market had ended and the speculative share price bubble had burst. The equity returns in US markets were out of alignment compared to returns on government stocks and there was a sharp international adjustment starting with this realisation and accentuated by futures dealing and 'program trading' which triggered sales of stocks and shares automatically as prices fell. This crash brought into question the validity of the simple efficient markets hypothesis and a view developed that there may not be a single 'true' value for the level of shares but a range.

Pike and Neale (1993) suggest that there are a number of implications for managing finance, which arise from market efficiency:

1 Investors are not easily fooled by glossy financial reports or 'creative accounting' techniques which boost corporate reported earnings but not underlying cash flows.
2 Corporate management should endeavour to make decisions that maximise shareholders' wealth.
3 There is little point in bothering with the timing of new issues. Market prices are a 'fair' reflection of the information available and rationally evaluate the degree of risk in shares.
4 Where corporate managers possess information not yet released to the market (termed 'information asymmetry'), there is some opportunity for influencing prices. Release of this information can be carried out strategically, such as when an unwelcome takeover bid occurs (Pike and Neale 1993).

Capital structure and gearing

Money lent to the business by third parties is debt finance or loan capital. Most companies borrow money on a long-term basis by issuing stocks or debentures.

The supplier of the loan will specify the amount of loan, rate of interest, date of payment and method of repayment. The finance manager of a firm will monitor the long-term financial structure of the firm by examining the relationship between loan capital (where interest and loan repayments are contractually obligatory) and ordinary share capital (where dividend payment is at the discretion of the directors). This relationship between debt and equity is called gearing (known in the USA as leverage). Strictly, gearing is the proportion of debt capital to total capital in the firm (Pike and Neale 1993).

The capital structure of a property company is a key factor in how a company is viewed in terms of its attractiveness for an investor or lender. The property sector is characterised by a high level of gearing due to the availability of fixed interest finance during the first postwar boom from 1954 to 1964. This availability led to many property companies being highly geared.

High gearing is of benefit when property values are rising ahead of interest charges but can be dangerous if the real rate of interest is rising at a greater rate than property values. A simple example of gearing applied to house purchase is shown in Box 2.1.

With the exception of major institutional investors, other property investors will tend to gear up. In the 2000s, it is evident that even the major institutions, the life assurance companies especially, are joining this trend to share in the

Box 2.1 Example of the effect of gearing in house purchase

House is purchased for £100,000
The growth rate in house prices is 20 per cent
70 per cent is borrowed on mortgage
The interest rate on the mortgage is 10 per cent p.a.
The house is sold after 1 year

1 What is the equity return?
2 What is the return if you borrow 50 per cent?

1 Sale price   £120,000
   less mortgage   £70,000
   plus interest   £7,000
   Balance   £77,000
   Profit   £43,000

   Return on capital $= \dfrac{£43,000}{£30,000} \times 100\% = 143\%$

   $= 43\%$ profit

2 Sale price   £120,000
   less mortgage   £50,000
   plus interest   £5,000
   Balance   £55,000
   Profit   £65,000

   Return on capital $= \dfrac{£65,000}{£50,000} \times 100\% = 130\%$

   $= 30\%$ profit

increased returns available from gearing. Evidence suggests that property companies may gear up to around 30 per cent as an average but private investment portfolios may gear up to the extent of 80–90 per cent of cost (Freeman Publishing 2000).

2.5   The comparison of property returns with other investment media

The relationship of property yield movements to interest rate changes is an interesting one. Short-term interest rates (bank base rates) or yields on long-term stocks generally move in the opposite direction to property yields. This is so whether prime yields are considered or even average yields. Secondary property, where rental yields are higher and likely to provide a greater proportion of overall return than with prime property, may have yields that may be more related to interest rate movements. In 1978–79 average yields fell but interest rates rose sharply. In 1982 and 1983 property yields began moving up while interest rates were falling. In 1988, the average property yield fell as short- and long-term interest rates increased (Brett 1997). Logically one would expect yields to decrease as expectation of rental growth increases.

In theory, returns on different kinds of investment should have impact on others. If yields on government stocks are high, then one expects a higher return on shares. Interest rates and yields have three elements: a time-preference element, an inflation element and a risk element (Isaac and Steley 2000).

Time-preference element

This exists as a compensation to the investor who now cannot spend the investment monies immediately but will need to wait until the investment can be liquefied. The compensation stems from the premise that people prefer to have money now and not later; the money, after all may be put to use either in consumption or in alternative investment, and thus immediate satisfaction or alternative investment opportunities are obtained. The interest rate needs an element to entice people to part with their monies and delay consumption or to compete with alternative investment. From the analysis above, the rate on index-linked Treasury stock is a measure of this. Ignoring redemption, the interest rate has the elements of risk (none) and inflation covered; it thus represents an indication of the time-preference element. This rate varies with market conditions, but for ease of calculation we have assumed a 3 per cent allowance in the following calculations.

Inflation

It is important that this element used in interest rates is a reflection of investors' anticipation of the inflation rate, which may differ from the expectations of the rate used by the government, first because various financial advisers may be using different economic models to advise the government, and second because the investors' index of inflation may differ from the one used by the government. Our calculation of a possible inflation allowance can be assessed for the investors' view of the difference between index-linked gilts and ordinary undated Treasury stock. The calculation uses the relationship between market rates of interest, which are inclusive of inflation, and real rates of interest, which exclude inflation:

$$i = \frac{(1 + e)}{(1 + g)} - 1$$

Here, let us use i as the inflation-proof yield rate (index-linked, say, 3 per cent) and e as the inflation-prone rate of undated ordinary government stock (say 10 per cent). Thus, to find g (the rate of inflation):

$$0.03 = \frac{(1 + 0.1)}{(1 + g)} - 1$$

$$(1 + g) = \frac{1.1}{1.04} = 1.0577, \text{ so } g = \text{say, } 5.8\%$$

The returns on index-linked government stock are shown in financial newspapers, as is the rate for undated stock; the latter is listed as consols, being an abbreviation of consolidated loan stock (the government national debt).

Risk premium

Much work has been done in the property and other investment sectors on this question of risk premium. This is the addition to the risk-free interest rate to take into account the risk of the investment. This risk may relate to the inability to predict the level of return and perhaps the likelihood of payment.

The relationship between risk and return is direct: for instance, the monetary rewards of university lecturers may be low to reflect the security of their position (this is probably an historic analysis), while a market-maker in the City of London may obtain colossal earnings if successful in trading but runs the risk of being made redundant if earnings fall. A person investing in a building society will not expect very high rates of interest as the investor believes the investment to be secure; on the other hand, couriers running drugs into Singapore may request large returns to cover the risk of a potential early end to their careers.

This relationship between risk and reward is called the Capital Market Line, being the price on the market for raising capital given different risk rates. This line can be represented diagrammatically as shown in Figure 2.2 earlier in this chapter, but note that the relationship between the two may not be a simple linear one (i.e., not a straight line function: Isaac 1998).

Conclusion

Yields on different kinds of investment may influence those on others, but rental growth in property is more likely to be determined by supply and demand and the general economic situation. Inflation and risk attitudes may differ between investors in the different asset classes. Property yields do react to rental growth but with delay and in a haphazard fashion; property cycles drive rental growth. Property values do not always rise as a result of inflation. In the long run, inflation has an effect on building costs and profit which lead to expectations of higher costs and rents but growth in rents and capital values has taken place in periods of relatively low inflation (1978–88) and the property crash of 1974–76 took place whilst inflation was at its highest level (Brett 1997).

References and further reading

Brett, M. (1997) *Property and Money*, Estates Gazette, London.

Brown, G. R. (1991) *Property Investment and the Capital Markets*, E. & F. Spon, London.

Brown, G. R. and Matysiak, G. A. (2000) *Real Estate Investment: A Capital Market Approach*, Pearson Education, Harlow.

Copeland, T. E. and Weston, J. F. (1988) *Financial Theory and Corporate Policy*, Addison-Wesley, Wokingham.

Enever, N. and Isaac, D. (2001) *The Valuation of Property Investments*, Estates Gazette, London.

Freeman Publishing (2000) *Guide to the Property Industry*, Freeman Publishing, London, June.

Isaac, D. (1998) *Property Investment*, Macmillan, London.

Isaac, D. and Steley, T. (2000) *Property Valuation Techniques*, Macmillan, London.

Lee, C. F. (1985) *Financial Analysis and Planning: Theory and Application*, Addison-Wesley, Wokingham.

Levy, H. and Sarnat, M. (1994) *Capital Investment and Financial Decisions*, Prentice-Hall, Englewood Cliffs, NJ.

Neave, E. H. (1998) *Capital Investment and Financial Decisions*, Prentice-Hall, Englewood Cliffs, NJ.

Pike, R. and Neale, B. (1993) *Corporate Finance and Investment*, Prentice-Hall, London.

Pike, R. and Neale, B. (1999) *Corporate Finance and Investment: Decisions and Strategies*, Prentice-Hall, London.

Ross, S. A., Westerfield, R. W. and Jaffe, J. F. (1993) *Corporate Finance*, Irwin, Boston, MA.

Ross, S. A., Westerfield, R. W. and Jaffe, J. F. (1999) *Corporate Finance*, McGraw-Hill, London.

Samuel, J. M., Wilkes, F. M. and Brayshaw, R. E. (1995) *Management of Company Finance*, Chapman Hall, London.

Van Horne, J. C. (1998) *Financial Management and Policy*, Prentice-Hall, London.

3
The Structure of Finance

3.1 Introduction

The cash flow approach to the firm and the balance sheet model were discussed in Chapter 1. These approaches, besides looking at the application of company funds for the purchase of assets, also differentiated between the sources of the funds, in particular the difference between long-term debt and shareholders' equity in the firm. An understanding of the difference between equity and debt is fundamental to an understanding of how finance works. The structure of finance can be analysed in two different ways: debt versus equity, or project versus corporate funding.

In the past, most interest in property concentrated on project finance but, with the size of schemes increasing and innovatory techniques of funding derived from the USA and other economic sectors, there is more interest in corporate finance. Generally, firms offer two basic types of securities to investors: debt securities are contractual obligations to repay corporate borrowing; while equity securities are shares of common stock and preferred stock that represent non-contractual claims on the residual cash flow of the firm. Issues of debt and equity that are publicly sold by the firm are then traded on the financial markets. These distinctions are clarified below.

Debt versus equity

Equity is money and resources provided by the developer, partners, investors and funds that participate in the risk and profit of the scheme. Debt finance basically consists of loans raised from banks and other sources against the project (project specific) and non-project specific loans raised in the market. This is not always a useful distinction as corporate funding, the raising of finance against the assets of a company, can be based on equity as well as debt.

Project versus corporate finance

Project finance is finance provided where the principle or only security for the finance is the property itself, although supporting guarantees and additional collateral may also be requested. Corporate finance is finance raised on the back of

Box 3.1   Funding matrix

	Corporate funding	**Project finance**
Equity finance	Share issues	Partnership funds Single asset unitisation
Debt finance	Loan stock Fixed interest debentures	Bank overdrafts Short-term funds for development

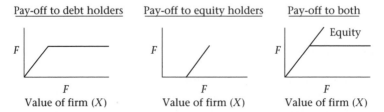

Figure 3.1   Pay-offs to debt and equity
Source: Ross, Westerfield and Jaffe (1993).

the corporate entity rather than the project. Traditionally, property and other companies provided funds for new projects from retained earnings, the issue of new shares and borrowings. In the postwar era, fixed interest mortgages and debentures were also used. Nowadays, there may be a complex corporate package of different types of funds. Using the parameters above, the funding matrix can distinguish amongst the financing methods available and this is shown in Box 3.1.

Capital structure

Financing arrangements determine how the value of a company is sliced up. The persons or institutions that buy debt from the firm are creditors. The holders of the equity shares are shareholders. The size of the company's balance sheet will determine how well the company has made its investment decisions. The size of the firm is its value in the financial markets:

$V = D + E$
Value of company = Value of debt + Value of equity
(Ross, Westerfield and Jaffe 1993)

Corporate securities issued are a contingent claim on the value of the company. The shareholders' claim on the value of the company is a residual after payment to the debt holder; they get nothing if the value of the company is equal to or less than the amount promised to the debt holders.

In Figure 3.1, F is the promised pay-off to debt holders. $X-F$ is the pay-off to equity shareholders if $X-F > 0$; if not, then pay-off = 0.

Financial markets

The financial markets are a means of bringing together buyers and sellers of financial securities composed of the money markets and the capital markets. Money markets are the markets for debt securities that pay-off in the short term (usually less than 1 year). Capital markets are the markets for long-term debt and equity shares. Primary markets are used when governments or companies initially sell securities. Companies offer their shares through public placings or public offerings (this is discussed in greater detail in Chapter 6 on corporate finance), and these are primary markets. Secondary markets come into operation for the resale of securities. The primary market itself can be sub-divided into seasoned and unseasoned new issues. A seasoned new issue refers to the offering of an additional amount of already existing security, whereas an unseasoned new issue involves the initial offering of a security to the public. Unseasoned new issues are often referred to as initial public offerings, or 'ipos'.

Debt and equity are traded in the security markets. There is a distinction between auction markets and dealer markets: equity securities tend to be sold in auction markets (a stock exchange), while debt securities are sold in dealer markets. Auction markets differ from dealer markets in two ways:

1 Trading in an auction exchange takes place at a single site on the floor of the exchange or with a centralised screen system. In October 1986, the Stock Exchange changed its system of trading post-'Big Bang' (the deregulation of the Stock Exchange) from trading on the floor of the exchange to an electronic marketplace. The Stock Exchange Automated Quotation System (SEAQ) moved the system of trading into dealing rooms equipped with computer screens.

2 The transaction prices of shares traded on the auction exchange are communicated almost immediately to the public by means of computers and other devices, whereas this is not the case in dealer markets (Ross, Westerfield and Jaffe 1993).

Direct investment versus property vehicles

The concept of project versus corporate finance can be looked at from a different perspective, that of direct investment in property as against investment through a property vehicle. Venmore-Rowland (1991) has considered the advantages and disadvantages of investment by these two approaches and these are shown in Box 3.2.

Two factors are working in opposite directions: correlation to other investments and liquidity. Correlation is important to obtain a diversified portfolio of investment and therefore spread risks. Direct property has a relatively low correlation to equities but is more illiquid. Property vehicles are liquid but are more highly correlated to equities (Venmore-Rowland 1991).

3.2 Categories of finance

Finance available for transactions can generally be divided into traditional debt and pure equity, but in between these mezzanine debt can also be available.

Box 3.2   Direct property and property vehicles

Direct property	
Advantages	**Disadvantages**
low risk relative to equities	illiquid
diversification benefits	management intensive
hedge against inflation	minimum portfolio size required
good for matching inflation-prone long-term liabilities	
Property vehicles	
Advantages	**Disadvantages**
liquidity	loss of control
divisibility	tax slippage
management expertise	short term, relatively poor performance
specialisation of vehicle	high correlation to stock market
gearing	
can shift weight/exposure	
income benefits from the discount to net asset value	

To distinguish this from traditional debt, mezzanine debt is often referred to as junior debt, as opposed to traditional debt which is called senior debt. Assuming a property is purchased for £1 million, then 70–80 per cent may be provided by senior debt (depending on the loan to value ratio agreed) and the remaining up to 90 per cent could be covered by mezzanine debt leaving 10 per cent of the purchase price to be provided from equity. The structure of this approach is very significant as, in terms of security, the senior debt will be the most secure, the mezzanine finance next and equity third. There is thus a ranking of security from senior debt to equity, and as we move between these ranks it can be seen that risks increase and thus, in accordance with the capital market line described in Chapter 2, the rate of return required by the funder also increases.

The following analysis of different categories of finance is based on a suggested classification by Brett (1997) and is summarised in Box 3.3.

Debt or equity

The distinction between debt and equity depends on whether the money is borrowed (debt), and here the lender has no direct involvement in the project, or whether the money has been invested on the basis of sharing both the risk and the returns of the project (equity). Borrowed money needs to be repaid and interest will be paid on the outstanding amount until the debt is repaid. The equity return for the person who puts up the money is determined by the success of the enterprise. The person shares the profits and, if there are none, then there is no return.

The most obvious form of equity is ordinary share capital. Equity shares can also exist in development situations where a financier is entitled to a share in profits of the scheme. There are also deferred forms of equity such as convertible loans,

Box 3.3   Summary of categories of finance

Categories of finance

Debt or equity
Project finance or corporate finance
Loan or traded security
Secured or unsecured
Fixed rate or variable rate
Long term or short term
Recourse, non-recourse or limited recourse loans
Domestic or euromarket loans

Main criteria

Debt or equity
Project or corporate finance

Finance matrix

	Debt	Equity
Project finance		
Corporate finance		

which start as debt instruments paying a fixed rate of interest, but later the loans may be converted into equity shares.

If we consider mezzanine finance in this analysis, we can see that equity is the investment in a project and thus has a return based on a profit share and no interest payments. Debt is purely a loan with no profit share but interest is received. In between, mezzanine finance may operate as debt but could be quasi-equity in the sense that, although it is more risky and would attract a higher interest rate, an alternative might be to convert all or part of the debt into equity. This conversion would thus include an option to take a profit share in place of all or part of the interest payments made. The profit share may replace or lessen the interest payments being made but, alternatively, if a profit share were not part of the deal, we would expect interest payments to be at a higher rate for the mezzanine finance to reflect the additional risk. Mezzanine finance is discussed further in Chapter 8.

Project finance or corporate finance

Project finance is the money borrowed for a project, usually a development project. The loan is based on the project itself and this becomes the main security. A larger company may be able to borrow on the strength of the assets of the company itself rather than its individual projects; this is asset-based or corporate finance. Interest will generally be lower for corporate loans than for project loans because there will be more collateral available for security rather than relying on the risk of a single project. Many companies are undertaking developments of such a size that they dwarf the company's own resources and the developer may then be concerned that, if anything went wrong with the project, the lenders may have recourse to other assets of the company, which may undermine the company's financial position. In this case, each development may need to be financed separately on a project basis and the developer may try to make the project 'off-balance sheet' if possible.

Loan or traded security

Borrowed money may simply be a simple loan or a bond in the form of an instrument (a negotiable piece of paper) which is transferable. This is a form of IOU note and is called a security rather than a straightforward loan, and this can be sold on to other investors. The purchasers receive interest each year and also have the right for the original cost to be repaid at the end of the agreed duration of the security. If the purchasers do not wish to wait for this repayment date, they can sell the rights to other investors, who then become entitled to receive the interest and the eventual repayment monies. Securities of this kind are bought and sold on the stock market.

Secured or unsecured

Lenders will normally require security for the money they provide; they want collateral (security) for the loans and thus will charge assets to cover the loan, either the specific assets of a business related to the project or the assets of a business as a whole. If the borrower fails to pay the interest or capital repayments as required, then the lender can put a receiver into the company and the receiver will repay the loans from the proceeds of the sale of the company's assets or other available revenues. A secured loan is safer than an unsecured loan but well-established companies may be able to raise unsecured loans because the safeguard for the lender is the company's established profit record, out of which the interest can be paid. Most borrowings in the euromarkets are unsecured, as are borrowings in the commercial paper market. The company's name and standing are the main guarantees.

Fixed rate or variable rate (floating rate) interest

Sometimes the rate of interest is agreed at the outset of the loan and remains unchanged over the life of the loan. With other loans, the interest rate will change according to movements in money market rates or other rates agreed. For large-scale floating rate borrowings, the most common yardstick of interest rates is the London Interbank Offered Rate, or LIBOR. This is the rate of interest at which the banks themselves are prepared to lend to each other. It is agreed at the outset, say, that the company will pay a margin over the LIBOR rate, perhaps 2.5 percentage points (or 250 basis points, which is the same thing as a basis point is 0.01 per cent) over LIBOR. You can choose a LIBOR floating rate and then fix it. Short-term borrowings are most likely to be at the floating rate of interest. Long-term borrowings such as mortgage debentures are more likely to be at a fixed rate. The borrower can buy a cap for floating-rate borrowing. This is a form of insurance policy which means that whatever happens to interest rates in general, a maximum limit is set to the interest rate that a borrower will have to pay.

Long term or short term

Loans are usually over a period between 0 and 30 years. This range marks the difference between short- and long-term loans but the intermediate area is not defined. Many people consider 1–2 years to be short term, equivalent to the development period for most projects, 2–7 years as medium term and more than 7 years as long term. Overdrafts are technically payable on demand and thus are short-term borrowing, but many companies have an overdraft outstanding almost indefinitely. With a multi-option facility (MOF), a company might technically be borrowing for 3 months at a time. At the end of three months, it repays the original loans and takes out new ones for another 3 months. If the facility runs for 5 years, effectively it has the use of 5-year money by 'rolling over' (Brett 1997).

Recourse, non-recourse or limited recourse loans

If the loan for a particular project or for a particular subsidiary company is guaranteed by the parent, the lender has recourse to the parent, so can claim on the assets of the parent. If the only security for the lender is the project itself as in a pure form of project-based finance and the parent company has given no guarantees, the loan is non-recourse. A non-recourse loan is very unlikely to be granted in practice; banks would generally require the loans to be limited recourse. The parent may have guaranteed interest payments but is under no obligation to repay the loan itself in these circumstances. A limited recourse loan would still depend on the reputation of the borrower and the track record of the company, as well as the quality of the project itself.

In the UK, most property investment loans are non-recourse so that, in the event of default, the lender only has recourse to the subject property and not to the other assets of the borrower; or, if the borrower is a corporate entity, not to the parent company of that borrower. For non-recourse property lending, it is usual for the borrower to place the property asset into a special purpose vehicle (SPV). The SPV's only assets will be the property assets against which the lender is providing debt. So the SPV provides a company over which the lender can establish a legal charge. If the borrowing vehicle is not an SPV, it makes it difficult for the lender who is providing non-recourse finance to ensure its legal charge is not superseded by a third party. This problem can result if the borrowing vehicle owns other assets on which other lenders are providing debt finance and also in the case where a receiver is appointed to manage the borrower's assets (Freeman Publishing 2000). Recourse finance may be required where the security on a property is not deemed sufficient and this may be required, for instance, on development projects or for lending to secondary properties where the lending risk is considered higher.

Domestic or euromarket loans

Loans can be raised in the UK or in the euromarkets. Euromarket loans can be in sterling abroad (eurosterling) or other currencies (eurodollar). A company may well raise monies in the euromarkets in different currencies and then swap to sterling if sterling is not popular at the time of raising the funds. The terms and

Box 3.4   Types of finance

	Equity	**Debt**
Project funding	Unitisation/securitisation Loan with profit share Mezzanine finance Forward funding Venture capital Sale and leaseback	Mortgage Syndicated loans Bank loans Project management fee
Corporate funding	Authorised Property Unit Trusts (APUTs) Shares Warrants Options Futures Convertibles Venture Capital	Bonds (Deep-discounted bonds) Debentures Loan stock Multi-Option Facility Commercial paper Euromarket

conditions of operation in the European market can be different; for instance, euroloans are often unsecured.

3.3   The finance market

The types of finance are shown with examples in Box 3.4 and these are discussed in detail in later chapters. Types of finance and the terms and conditions are going to vary depending on the purpose of the finance. The key areas for finance will be:

- finance for investment
- finance for development
- owner-occupier finance for property
- structured finance based on the corporate structure.

Examples of the terms and conditions for these types of loans follow; note that while these give an indication of the elements of the conditions of the finance, they are not and cannot be up to date as the markets are constantly changing.

Development finance

Amount of loan:	75 per cent total costs, perhaps 85 per cent with profit share
Loan period:	For construction period and void period before letting
Interest rate margin:	1 per cent (pre-let)–3 per cent (speculative) above LIBOR or base rate
Interest rate payment:	Variable, quarterly but rolled-up to end
Repayment of loan:	On sale of project or long-term mortgage
Security:	First charge on property, recourse to borrower

Comments: Speculative finance might be difficult and the lender would be looking for a pre-let. Loan advances are determined by the level of security offered and can be increased to 100 per cent of cost in some cases. Pricing is dependent on the level of security offered, type of building contract and profitability of the scheme.

Investment property finance

Amount of loan: Up to 85 per cent of cost or 75 per cent of value, whichever is the lower

Loan period: Up to 15 years

Interest rate margin: 0.25 per cent–2.5 per cent above LIBOR or bank base rate. Long-term finance is priced off gilts and is available through the insurance companies. A maximum loan would equate to 75 per cent of value.

Interest rate payment: Fixed or variable rate interest payments. Part of the sum can be deferred and paid as a capital sum at the end of the facility.

Repayment of loan: Most facilities are interest only and will require repayment through sale of the asset or by refinancing.

Comments: The quality of the tenant is crucial to these transactions, together with adequate levels of security.

Owner-occupied property

Advance: Up to 100 per cent of cost

Loan period: Up to 10 years

Interest rate margin: Between 0.5 per cent and 3.0 per cent over LIBOR or bank base rate

Interest rate payment: Fixed or variable

Repayment of loan: Full amount at the end of the facility or principal amortised over the term of the loan

Comments: Owner-occupiers are able to obtain a much higher loan to value ratio where it can be demonstrated that they can service the interest charges out of their business cash flow.

Joint ventures

A variety of joint venture partners, including banks, finance houses, insurance companies, pension funds, contractors and other developers, can be accessed in today's market. The structure of the transaction is dependent on what the parties bring to the venture by negotiation. Many financial contacts are passive investors enabling the developer to get on with the job. Joint venture arrangements are discussed in Chapter 11.

Structured finance

More sophisticated finance can be structured to suit particular deals and relate expressly to the deal and its financial management for instance, this can commonly use the following methods:

1 Bonds – which enable interest rates to be rolled up with payment at the end of the life of the bond.
2 Finance leasing – this enables the client to sell a property to a finance company, pay a market rent and have the option to repurchase the building at the original purchase price plus any deferred interest.
3 Off-balance sheet financing – many clients reduce their exposure on their balance sheets by structuring loans outside their group holdings.
4 Capital market instruments including interest rate caps, interest rate floors, interest rate swaps (from variable to fixed interest rates) and swaptions (an option to swap in the future).

3.4   Glossary of financial and property terms

Cap	A means of providing an interest rate ceiling for a variable rate loan by the use of an insurance policy
Collar	Provides a ceiling and floor for interest rate movements for a variable interest loan
Covenant	The financial status of a party involved in a property transaction
Deficit Financing	The financing of a project in such a way that the cash flows in the early years of the project are insufficient to cover the interest on debt payable
Discount	Bonds with below market coupons (interest rate payable) trade at a discount below par (the nominal value).
Finance Lease	This involves the sale and leaseback with a financial institution; there may be tax advantages in such an arrangement without loss of control over the asset.
Gearing	Strictly, this is the proportion of debt capital to total capital, but commonly in property it is used as the ratio of interest-bearing debt to the shareholders' funds; basically it is the ratio of

debt to equity which gives an indication of the financial standing of the company. A highly geared company has a high proportion of debt.

Ground Rent	An annual payment for the land element in a development proposal
Interest Capitalisation	The process of rolling up interest on a project and adding the interest to the costs of the project, the total being shown in accounts as the asset value.
Joint Venture	Two or more parties, working together, sharing the rewards and risks of the project
Loan to Value Ratio	The level of the loan expressed as a percentage of value
Margin	The interest rate payable over a base rate to reflect the risk of the project or the parties involved; commonly used as a margin above LIBOR
Mezzanine Finance	Above a conventional loan to value ratio of, say, 70 per cent, certain lenders will lend additional monies known as mezzanine finance. This is priced at a higher rate than the senior debt (the initial advance) and may include profit-sharing to reflect the increased risk.
Overage	The growth in capital value over the development period that is available to be shared between vendor and developer
Pre-let	The letting of a development before the completion of the project. This reduces the risk of voids and improves the funding position.
Ratchet Basis	Used on profit participation transactions; whereas the overall profit increases, the proportion of profit received can increase or fall.
Recourse	The ability of the lender in a loan situation to have recourse to the assets of the company receiving the loan in the event of default. These assets are in addition to the assets immediately involved in the project for which the loan was made. In a non-recourse situation, the lender can only have recourse to the project and its underlying assets.

Rental Void	The period of time a completed development is unlet and thus not income producing. During this period it is also not usually possible to sell the completed project.
Swap	An interest rate swap is an agreement between two parties to swap their interest rate obligations, normally from a variable interest rate to a fixed one. A swap option is an option to change to a fixed rate in the future at pre-set terms.
Swaption	An option to swap in the future.

References and further reading

Brett, M. (1997) *Property and Money, Estates Gazette,* London.
Freeman Publishing (2000) *Guide to the Property Industry*, Freeman Publishing, London, June.
Ross, S. A., Westerfield, R. W. and Jaffe, J. F. (1993) *Corporate Finance*, Irwin, Boston, MA.
Sharpe, W. F., Alexander, G. J. and Bailey, J. V. (1995) *Investments*, Prentice-Hall, NJ.
Venmore-Rowland, P. (1991) 'Vehicles for Property Investment', in P. Venmore-Rowland, P. Brandon and T. Mole (eds), *Investment, Procurement and Performance in Construction*, RICS, London.

4
Property Lenders

4.1 Sources of finance

The main lenders in the market are financial institutions, overseas investors and property companies. The financial institutions are the pension funds and the insurance companies. Other investors are High Street clearing banks, foreign banks, building societies, merchant banks and finance houses. In their report on the sources of money flowing into property, DTZ Debenham Thorpe and the Central Statistical Office (CSO) provided the figures shown in Table 4.1 for the years 1980–96. This covers the critical years in the 1980s and early 1990s, showing the boom and slump of the property cycle and the contribution made to finance during this period by the banking sector.

Table 4.1 New money into property, 1980–96 (£ million)

	Pension funds	Insurance companies	Banks	Property companies	Overseas	Total
1980	908	855	72	147	100	2,082
1981	843	1,073	469	97	70	2,552
1982	797	1,059	822	263	120	3,061
1983	680	845	934	83	85	2,627
1984	997	744	963	237	65	3,006
1985	590	815	1,691	344	90	3,530
1986	434	821	2,224	737	150	4,366
1987	240	755	3,998	2,300	290	7,583
1988	312	1,102	7,954	761	1,897	12,026
1989	92	1,510	10,622	1,647	3,267	17,138
1990	−491	1,080	7,066	164	3,269	11,088
1991	467	1,483	678	1,352	1,551	5,531
1992	349	600	−1,708	212	1,232	685
1993	299	232	−3,248	2,022	1,514	819
1994	−325	2,708	−2,077	1,848	1,740	3,894
1995	−16	283	−1,093	1,146	1,790	2,110
1996[a]	154	70	−120	261	689	1,054

[a] 1996 first two quarters only.

Sources: Evans (1993), Central Statistical Office or CSO (1994a, 1996), DTZ Debenham Thorpe (1996).

The scale of lending has increased during the late 1990s and grown on a record scale in 2001. In the year to 30 September 2001, commercial property lending grew by £15.8 billion, the largest annual increase recorded according to the Bank of England. This brought the total loans outstanding to property companies to £67.5 billion compared to the peak in the early 1990s of £40.7 billion. Lower interest rates encouraged this growth, leading to a positive differentiation between interest rates and long-term property yields in certain areas of property investment (*Property Week* 2001b).

High Street clearing banks

The big four clearing banks are Lloyds TSB, Barclays, National Westminster (owned by the Royal Bank of Scotland) and Midland (owned by HSBC). These are probably the first port of call for people looking for loans, especially if they have established relationships as account holders. However, they are conservative and may view new transactions related to property in a less than enthusiastic way especially in the light of their overexposure in the last property slump. Smaller banks may be more useful potential funders. The smaller banks are likely to have less of a bad debt problem and may want to increase market share. The larger banks are burdened at the moment by overexposure to the property sector; the emphasis at the present time is on debt repayment rather than new lending. British clearing banks' exposure to the property sector at the critical period to the end of the 1980s, as the property market came into slump, is shown in Figure 4.1.

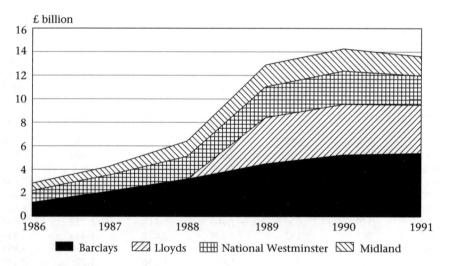

Figure 4.1   British clearing banks' UK property lending

Note: No figures for Lloyds 1986–8.

Source: Scott (1992).

Foreign banks

The foreign banks tend to be more aggressive sources of property finance, or were in the early 1990s, but by 1993 they were showing less interest. They are useful sources of funding, particularly for quality and corporate transactions. The collapse of BCCI in the early 1990s made borrowers more wary of dealing with foreign banks. The collapse of a bank halfway through a development may mean that it could take years to unwind the legal problems and thus would put the borrower's own financial position at risk.

Building societies

The building societies fared badly during the slump in the property market in the early 1990s. In the late 1980s, their inexperience and desire for market share in commercial property lending led to substantial bad debt. They are now putting their respective houses in order with more qualified staff and are likely to be an important source of commercial finance in the future.

Merchant banks

Merchant banks rarely lend their own money but act as advisers and concentrate especially on large corporate transactions. They are unlikely to be interested in ordinary debt transactions because there would be little opportunity to use their expertise and add value to such a transaction.

Insurance companies

The insurance companies are limited providers of funds. They do, however, offer the attraction of long-term, fixed rate funds priced at a margin over gilts (government stock) that can be useful in certain transactions.

Finance houses

In essence, the finance houses have been the principal providers of funding to the secondary leisure and retailing markets, providing finance for the purchase of freehold shops, pubs, restaurants and hotels. Their small trader exposure has made them particularly vulnerable to the recession that resulted in most of them leaving the market in the early 1990s.

Figures for money going into commercial property in the last five years (approximate only) are shown in Figure 4.2, whilst overseas investment in 1998 is shown in Figure 4.3.

Institutional investors

These institutions do not lend money in the market but provide equity and investment funds. Institutions investing in the capital market in the UK are suppliers of finance to companies. These institutional investors include insurance companies, pension funds, investment trusts and unit trusts. The institutional investors are covered in more detail in Chapter 9.

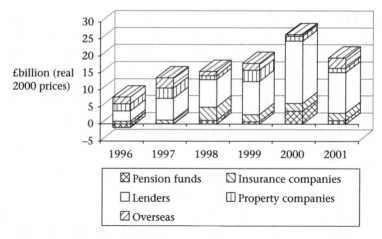

Figure 4.2   Net capital flows into commercial property

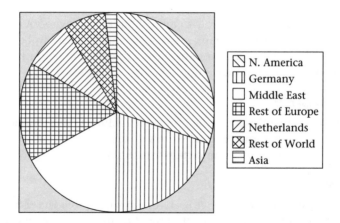

Figure 4.3   Overseas investment in property by nationality (1998 and first quarter 1999)
Source: DTZ Debenham Thorpe (1999).

Summary of sources

In summary, the possible sources of finance can be summarised thus (Freeman Publishing 2000):

1   Debt can be provided by banks or building societies or else by property companies selling corporate debentures. It may also be raised by the selling or the securitisation of a rental income stream (see Chapter 12 for a summary of securitisation).
2   Mezzanine finance could be available from a range of sources but traditionally it is provided by merchant and investment banks and specialist lending houses. As has been discussed earlier in the book, interest rates on mezzanine finance are higher or the lender can take a percentage share of the profits generated.

3 Equity can be raised from property investors or venture capitalists (see Chapter 8). It may be that the investors own equity in the form of a joint partnership or joint venture with other investors. No interest is paid on pure equity, but investors receive a profit share.

Use of debt finance

Debt finance enhances investment returns through the mechanism of gearing. In simple terms gearing reduces the percentage of equity in a project and enhances the percentage profit. This gearing is shown in the example (adapted from Freeman Publishing 2000) given in Box 4.1.

Debt finance will increase the volatility of an investment's return and therefore its risk but by reducing the equity input, the investor's equity can be diversified between projects. Thus, debt finance increases specific risk of the individual property whereas the diversification of equity reduces the portfolio risk. Debt finance can also increase liquidity by releasing part of the capital value whilst the investor can retain some equity to benefit from future increases in capital value. As well as increasing specific risk, debt reduces the investor's control over the investment asset.

4.2 Lending criteria

The cost and availability of lending is a function of the value of any particular project and the amount of cost to be financed. The nature of the development is important as well as the design, mix, location and likely demand. The letting conditions are important, as is whether or not the investment is pre-let or speculative. The quality of the tenant, who will be providing the cash flow to the

Box 4.1 Example of gearing in a property asset

Gross purchase price	£10 million
Initial yield	7.5 per cent
Holding period	5 years
Exit price	£12.5
Senior debt interest	7.75 per cent p.a.
Mezzanine interest	14.0 per cent p.a.

Scenario	Equity input (£ million)	Sum of net rental and sale proceeds (£ million)	Internal rate of return (IRR) (%)
100% equity	10	16.1	10.8
20% equity, 80% senior debt	2	5.0	18.7
10% equity, 10% mezzanine finance, 80% senior debt	1	3.1	20.8

investment, will also be important. Other important criteria are the track record of the developer and the strength of security. Finally, the duration of the loan will be important as well as the details of repayment (for instance, the anticipated regularity of repayments and the size/amount of repayments prior to redemption).

Most lenders look for the same aspects of a lending proposal, which in simplified terms are the four 'Cs':

- character
- cashstake
- capability
- collateral.

Character

This relates to the trading history or development experience of a borrower. In respect of a property developer or an investment company, the lender will want to know whether the borrower has the experience to complete the development, manage the investment or run the business, if applicable. The lender will also be interested in whether the client is respectable and trustworthy. The lender may, if the borrower is not an existing client, question why the borrower's own clearing bank will not lend the money.

Cashstake

This relates to how much equity (the borrower's own money) is going into the transaction. In addition, the bank will want to know where the equity has come from:

1 Is it lent from someone else?
2 Is it from other profitable activities?
3 Is it simply a surplus that has arisen on the revaluation of property?
4 Is it already pledged as security?
5 Is it legally acquired money, not illegal, laundered money?

Capability

Does the borrower have the capability to service the loan: that is, to pay the interest when it arises and the capital as and when repayment is required? Does the borrower have accounts or a business plan to show his/her present financial position and any estimate of future cash flow?

Collateral

The lender will want to know what security will be offered for the loan, its value and its saleability. The lender will want to know who valued the security and on what basis. The lender will need to assess the extent of the loan that would be exposed to the value of that security. Finally, will personal guarantees be given by the borrower?

General criteria

These are the general principles of underwriting but the most important aspect is the borrower's capability to meet loan repayments. Lenders will want the borrower to be a successful, well-respected individual or company who can comfortably afford to repay the proposed borrowing. There is a concern about the quality of the loans in the present market. Quality for the principal property sectors means:

(a) *Development* – profitable schemes pre-let to blue chip tenants with a full guarantee from the developer for cost overruns;
(b) *Investment* – prime investments with blue chip tenants on long, full repairing and insuring (FRI) leases;
(c) *Commercial mortgages* – well-established companies with good quality accounts information that clearly establishes their ability to service the loan.

4.3 Development and investment lending

General loan finance terms

Freeman Publishing (2000) sets out the key loan finance terms as follows:

1 *Loan to value (LTV) ratio.* This is the most important factor and is dependent on the quality of property (location, design and specification), the strength of the tenant (covenant) and the length of the unexpired lease. Senior debt LTV ratios may be 80–85 per cent for prime properties (modern buildings let to excellent covenants with more than a 10-year unexpired term on the lease).
2 *Loan margin.* This is the way the risk of the loan is priced and reflects the lender's perceptions of the property, the rental cash flow profile, LTV and security. The base rate is usually the LIBOR rate but may be a gilt rate. To this base rate, a margin is added to give the overall interest rate. In 2000, rate margins varied from 0.60–2.00 per cent with prime property at 0.75–1.00 per cent.
3 *Loan term.* The loan term is governed by the borrower's preferences and the bank's lending policy. Most lenders require that a borrower will fix the interest rate over the term of the loan, usually through a swap agreement; the cost varies depending on the period over which the interest rate is fixed. If interest rates are expected to fall in the future, then short-term money is more expensive than long term. Terms vary between 1 and 30 years with 5 to 10 years being most common.
4 *Hedging requirements.* The loan's interest rate may be fixed, floating or a combination of both. Most property lenders quote their interest rates as a margin above LIBOR (a floating rate) but will require borrowers to enter into a fixed rate or hedging instrument to protect against rising interest rates. The borrower can either 'swap' its floating interest rate liability for a fixed rate (the swap agreement) or purchase a cap which sets a limit on the floating interest rate.
5 *Amortisation/residual loan.* It is possible to have interest-only loans where the borrower needs only to service and repay the debt in a single bullet payment at the end of the loan term. Many lenders will require the borrower to repay or amortise some or even the entire loan during the loan term. A lender will require amortisation to offset the declining value of the asset on which it is lending. This may result from both building obsolescence and the shortening periods before leases expire, and also to ensure that the residual debt at the end

of the loan term is not too high. The level of residual debt that a lender will accept at the end of the loan term will vary according to a number of factors. The most important factor is the amount and quality of the contracted rental income beyond the loan expiry date. The second factor is the strength of the property's location and reletting prospects and thus its vacant possession value.

Problems related to the residual risk have become more significant. Debt outstanding is growing faster than the growth in capital values from which the debt is to be repaid and this is a problem for the residual risk.

Development lending

Property companies went through a period of re-rating in the early 1990s; this increased their value on the stock market. Thus, property companies went to the stock market to raise new capital and this injection of capital acted as a catalyst to the property market at the time (DTZ Debenham Thorpe 1993). There are, nevertheless, considerable difficulties in borrowing money in the development market as speculative schemes are difficult to fund. However, this should be balanced by saying that if the development were being carried out by any of the principal UK developers, then there are still financial institutions that will look at funding schemes.

Speculative development

Funding is very difficult for speculative funding; however, it may be possible to arrange loans where the following hold:

1 The borrower is very strong and has accounts that prove an ability to repay the loan without any real need to sell assets.
2 The scheme is exceptionally profitable. This usually means that the borrower has been able to obtain the land for little or at historic cost.
3 The borrower is putting in an exceptionally high level of equity, thus ensuring the bank's exposure is kept to a minimum.
4 The borrower can prove that demand for the scheme is undoubted. There is, of course, only one way of proving such demand and that is to pre-let, but substantial evidence of demand may assist this decision.

The bank's view of speculative schemes may be that they are too risky to bother with. The banks had more unlet, unsold, uncompleted schemes on their books in the early 1990s than they knew what to do with and are keen not to get into that situation again.

Pre-let/sold development

Whilst a pre-let or sale makes the job of arranging finance substantially easier, it does, of course, depend who the scheme is pre-let or sold to. If there is a good covenant on the other side of the contract, everything becomes that much simpler. If you have a covenant that no one has ever heard of, you may as well have a speculative development on your hands.

Whilst a pre-let to a good covenant does make life easier, it still does not guarantee funding. The bankers will want to satisfy themselves that the borrowers, and/or building contractor, could meet the completion deadline and the liability for cost overruns, interest shortfalls, or losses on the sale of the investment. Should the scheme be pre-let to anything other than a good tenant, this does not mean that finance cannot be arranged. What it does mean is that the banker will want to investigate the financial strength of the covenant, will probably wish to contribute less towards the overall costs of the scheme and will offer more onerous terms, such as a higher interest rate.

Conclusion

There is varying confidence amongst lenders in this sector but there are possible areas of opportunity, as set out below:

1 Pre-let schemes. Any pre-let schemes that require funding, regardless of whether or not they are let to good covenants or less than 100 per cent pre-let, are possible for funding.
2 Developments which are being undertaken by companies which are not solely developers (i.e., building contractors, who will have other sources of income without being reliant on property sales).
3 Residential developments. Development in the residential sector probably has an upside potential and an increasing number of sources are now considering schemes.

Generally speaking, funding for development properties may be arranged on the following general terms but these circumstances change over time depending on the economic conditions and the nature of the property market, for instance:

Land	70 per cent loan to value
Construction	70 per cent loan to cost

For quality pre-let schemes, in these conditions, it may be possible to arrange the following:

Either

Land	80 per cent
Construction	80 per cent

Or

Land	70 per cent + 25 per cent (mezzanine finance)
Construction	70 per cent + 25 per cent (mezzanine finance)

Mezzanine finance will be explored in greater detail later on. In exceptional circumstances, banks will provide 100 per cent finance under joint venture arrangements. Interest rates for development loans may start at 1.5 per cent above money costs, up to 5 per cent above money costs for a straightforward 70 per cent deal. A mezzanine lender would want a higher return, perhaps 30 per cent to 40 per cent,

Box 4.2 Development funding example

Background
* **Client**
  Newly formed joint venture company owned
  50 per cent landowner (providing an unencumbered site)
  50 per cent building contractor (providing development experience)
* **Planning**

4 × 1 bedroom flats	£232,000
4 × 2 bedroom flats	£260,000
4 × 3 bedroom flats	£338,000
Total	£830,000

* **Costs/value**

Site	£200,000
Construction costs and fees	£420,000
Interest	£40,000
Sales costs	£22,000
Total	£682,000
Profit (22 per cent)	£148,000

Requirement
* The clients already had the land
* Needed 100 per cent of the remaining costs
* Prepared to share in the risks/rewards

Offer
* UK Building Society

75 per cent land, that is	£150,000
75 per cent construction and professional fees	£325,000
* TOTAL	£465,000

* 100 per cent of construction costs, professional fees and interest
* 2 per cent above GDMR (11.95 per cent) at time of offer
* First charge on site
* Mortgage debenture
* Personal guarantees

Note: GDMR is the Gross Domestic Mortgage Rate: see later in the chapter.

whilst a bank entering into a joint venture may want 50 per cent of the scheme's net profit. An example of a development loan is given in Box 4.2.

In terms of the duration of the loan, Naylor (1994) in his research of property development companies found that there was quite a range in the maturity of typical term loans. His analysis showed that 32 per cent of loans were 2 years or less, with 28 per cent being 3–4 years and 40 per cent having maturity dates greater than 4 years.

Investment lending

The most notable change in the investment market, as far as funding is concerned, is the narrowing between the yield and interest rate gap. Rising property yields, and falling interest rates, now mean that many investments are close to self-funding. The difficulty for many funders is that there is not enough investment product to

Box 4.3 Investment funding example

> **Office property**
>
> **Background**
> **Client**
> Newly formed company owned 90 per cent by overseas manufacturer and 10 per cent by London property company. The property company was able to demonstrate a track record of previous successful transactions.
>
> **Requirement**
> * Client had the opportunity to acquire:
>   Newly built Birmingham office investment comprising a floor area of 3,200 square metres let on 25-year term at £300,000 per annum to a blue chip tenant
> * The purchase price was £2.8 million – initial yield of 10.7 per cent
> * Independent valuation of £3 million
> * The client wanted maximum advance at the lowest rate
>
> **Offer**
> * Large British building society
> * 85 per cent advance, that is, £2.4 million
> * 5 year fixed rate (1.6 per cent + 5 year swap)
> * Bullet repayment (full repayment) after 5 years
> * First charge on property
> * Mortgage debenture
> * 10 per cent of loan guaranteed by the London property company shareholder
> * £420,000 (15 per cent) commercial mortgage indemnity

place with the banks, with most of the prime investments being snapped up by the institutions.

From the lenders' view, there is a 'flight to quality' with investment properties. Increasing company failures have left banks with substantial problems in this sector, and they are now suspicious of anything but the highest quality tenants. For any secondary investments, the banks will look very closely at the financial strength of the borrower and probably lend more onerously, reducing the loan to value exposure they are prepared to consider, and pushing up the interest margin they would expect the borrower to pay.

Banks are also looking at the level of interest cover provided by rental income. Previously, banks were happy for rental income to cover interest payable on a ratio of 1:1 or even deficit fund whilst rents were rising sharply. Today, however, banks will require rental cover more in the order of 1:1.2 or 1:1.25, taking the view that there may be little or no rental growth at next review (1:1.2 means that every £100 of interest payable, say, on a monthly basis, will have to be matched by £120 of rental income for the same month). An example of investment funding is shown in Box 4.3.

Conclusion

Examples of two markets that it has been easier to find investment funding in are given below.

1 Investments let to good covenants (well-established firms) where funding is arranged at 85 per cent of the purchase price, at fixed rates of interest from 2 to 20 years.
2 Secondary investments bought on high yields with a good spread of tenants regardless of their covenant strength. In these instances, funds can be arranged at up to 75 per cent of purchase price and again on fixed rates of interest from 2 to 20 years.

4.4 Problems of security

Security is based on the provision of the institutional lease in UK property investment markets; this is commonly a 20-year lease with 5-year rent reviews. However, overseas companies occupying UK premises are undermining this arrangement, especially those companies from the USA who often demand 'break clause' provisions that basically shorten the intended duration of the lease. There is also a move to end upward-only rent reviews that provide security for the landlord against having a drop in income. A solution offered as a compromise is to have upward-only rent reviews for the first 10 years only of the lease. The proposal is designed to satisfy funders' concerns about the security of their investment whilst going some way to meeting occupiers' (especially retailers') worries about inflexible lease conditions (*Property Week* 2001a).

If a company can restrict the security for borrowing to a few assets, there is much more flexibility in the financing strategy. The assets offered as security should make the borrowing cheaper by reducing the interest rates. If the debt is not secured on the company's assets, the investors will probably insist on restrictions on the company's overall level of borrowing.

The disadvantage of secured borrowing is that the company loses some flexibility in its handling of the properties within its portfolio that are charged as securities. You cannot sell the properties with the charge. Some flexibility will normally be built in. This flexibility might be an agreement between the borrower and lender that properties can be substituted from the pool of properties that constitute the security. The substituted property would of course have to be an equivalent property that may be acceptable. The property should be capable of maintaining the income and capital cover of the original portfolio. If, over a period of time, the value of the pool of properties rises, the capital cover for the debt may exceed the stipulated minimum and the borrower will probably be allowed to remove some of the properties from charge, provided the capital and income cover requirements are still met. The alternative is for the borrower to use the excess security for further debt: for instance, in the case of debentures, a further issue of the debenture can be made, identical to the original issue and ranking alongside it. If the value of a property falls, the trustee could insist that the company top it up by putting further properties into the pool. The trustee can call for valuations to establish the value of properties that are charged.

Debentures (loan arrangements) offer good security but the 1986 Insolvency Act compromised this (Brett 1990b). Prior to the Act, if a borrower defaulted on the terms of a debenture with a fixed charge over specified properties, the trustee could sell the properties to recover the loss. With the 1986 Act, creditors with a floating charge have different rights from those with a fixed charge (a floating charge is one over the company's total fixed and current assets). If a company gets into financial difficulties but believes it may be able to get out of these difficulties or at least reduce them in the longer term, it can apply to have an administrator appointed. If this application is granted, then the administrator will provide a plan of action that may involve the continued running of the company or perhaps the selling-off of assets over a period. Thus, the creditor with the fixed charge, although still having a security for the loan, loses control over the security, as the administrator will decide how and when the security is sold. The creditor with the floating charge can appoint an administrative receiver and block the appointment of an administrator by the company and is thus in a more powerful position. Lenders are thus more likely to ask for a floating charge as well as a fixed charge in these circumstances. This approach is less likely to be popular with the borrower as its charge is not limited to specified assets. The alternative may be for the borrower to grant a floating charge over the assets of a subsidiary that owns the properties that would be subject to the fixed charge rather than charging the assets of the group as a whole. Investors would demand a higher yield on a debenture that does not offer a floating charge as well as a fixed one and the difference could be about 20 basis points (0.2 per cent: Brett 1990b).

A White Paper on insolvency reform was published in 2001 following the introduction of the Insolvency Act 2000. Commentators suggest this has further encouraged a 'rescue culture' in this respect. In smaller companies, there will be encouragement for more voluntary arrangements as opposed to the early intervention of secured creditors (D. J. Freeman 2001).

Loan security

In the UK, the vast majority of commercial property investment loans are non-recourse; in the event of default, the lender has recourse to the subject property and not to the other assets of the borrower, or, ultimately, to the borrower's parent company. For non-recourse property lending, it is usual to put the property asset in a special purpose vehicle (SPV). The SPV's only assets will be the property assets against which the lender is providing debt. This provides a 'clean' company over which the lender can place the legal charge that forms its security. If the borrowing vehicle is not an SPV, this can make it harder for the lender providing non-recourse funding to ensure that its legal charge is not superseded by a third party and other interested parties. This problem can result if the borrowing vehicle owns other assets on which other lenders are providing debt finance and also in the case where a receiver is appointed to manage the borrower's assets (Freeman Publishing 2000). Recourse finance may be required where the security on a property is not deemed sufficient.

As well as initial loan covenants or restrictions which apply at the beginning of the loan, most lenders ask for the provision of ongoing loan covenants reflecting the property's value and the income cover (the cover for interest payments from the cash flow of the asset). Loan to value covenants ensure that the value of the property does not reduce to an unacceptable level compared to the loan amount. Loan to value covenants can expose the borrower to the swings in the property cycle: the property may generate enough income to service the interest payment but the downward movement in property values may mean the borrower is in default. In these cases, an income cover test might be preferable; this measures the rental income of the property as a proportion of the loan interest (see Chapter 13 for detailed calculations). The actual level set depends on the strength or security of the rental cash flow but a lender will generally look for a minimum interest cover of between 120 and 150 per cent.

A borrower will be in default if it is in breach of one or more of the ongoing loan covenants. Most loan agreements will, however allow a period of remedy for the borrower in times of economic recession. Lenders do not necessarily foreclose on the loans but may insist that the amortisation schedule (the payback of capital) is accelerated (Freeman Publishing 2000).

Commercial mortgage indemnity (CMI) market

There has been an increase in the use of commercial mortgage indemnity policies since 1980. These top slice policies involve an insurance company taking on the repayment risk on that part of a loan which the bank or building society could not lend. If the bank's normal loan to value ratio is 70 per cent but the borrower needs 85 per cent, then the bank arranges a CMI for the top slice of 15 per cent and lends 85 per cent. In the early years of operation, Eagle Star wrote more business than the rest of the market. The downturn, especially in the residential market in the late 1980s, led to claims to support speculative developers and many insurers suffered. The CMI market is now more cautious and informed and the CMI policy wording needs to be sufficiently broad and flexible to satisfy the banks while the insurers retain certain rights and controls. CMI can take weeks to install whilst the full price and provision is not fully known at the beginning of the transaction. The underwriters are sceptical of highly geared financing where the investor claims to have bought assets cheaply.

Mortgage indemnity charges change over time but, as an example, in the early 1990s when they were commonly used, the charges were 7 per cent on the 15 per cent over 70 per cent loan to value ratio bringing the ratio up to 85 per cent (1990); for instance, on a £10 million property, the premium was 7 per cent of £1.5 million = £105,000, or about 1 per cent of the value.

Underwriting property sales

The two inherent defects of property as an investment are illiquidity and the imperfections of the market. The disposal of property involves risks relating to the price achieved and the timescale of disposal. In a weak market, delays make completion times uncertain. Underwriting Property Services (UPS) was a joint venture company established between the Bank of Scotland and Drivers Jonas, the property consultants. The service in underwriting property sales aimed to remove the uncertainty of the transactions and thus provide a more predictable outcome. The service is aimed at specific clients, for instance:

- investors wishing to change portfolios within a given timescale to maximise growth
- unit fund managers wishing to meet redemptions
- property companies who need to book a profit before the year end
- owner-occupiers needing to raise capital in a given timescale
- public organisations tied to annual accounting and cash limited budgets.

UPS contracted to buy a property if it had not been purchased at the end of a fixed marketing period. It works by granting the vendor an option to sell to the UPS on a predetermined date in the future at a predetermined price. An underwriting contract is entered into by the parties at the outset (Armon-Jones 1992). The underwritten price is in the region of 90 per cent of open market value. The scheme adds liquidity and certainty to sale and thus some stability to the market, although the scale of the operation is obviously limited. *Chartered Surveyor Weekly* estimated to begin with that UPS would stabilise the market at £110 million maximum (*Chartered Surveyor Weekly* 1991).

4.5 Property Lending Survey

Introduction

The Property Lending Survey is a survey of major property lenders that commenced in 1990 and has been carried out on an annual basis since. The survey is a joint project between Chesterton International and the University of Greenwich. The Property Lending Surveys analysed here were carried out from 1990 to 1995. The Property Lending Survey questionnaire was intended to investigate the detailed characteristics of property lending and was distributed to all known lenders. The main issues covered by the questionnaire related to:

1 The provision of a specialist lending division in the respondent's company and the relevant contact names;
2 Details of lending on development property:
   - maximum term of lending
   - types of project
   - loans for speculative development
   - geographic preference
   - maximum loan to cost ratios on land and construction costs
   - maximum loan to value ratios on the completed project value
   - the provision of mezzanine finance
   - maximum/minimum sizes of advance
   - normal margin rate above LIBOR or organisational base rate
   - finance provided on a limited recourse basis
   - capitalisation of interest during the construction period
   - the provision of mortgage indemnity policies

3 Details of lending on investment and owner-occupied property:
   - maximum term
   - type of property
   - geographic preference
   - loan/value ratio
   - interest only periods
   - minimum/maximum size of facility
   - normal margin above LIBOR or organisational base rate;
4 Provision of bridging loans;
5 Loans to single asset property companies;
6 Proportion of lender's portfolio in investment and development property;
7 Loans to overseas investors;
8 Lender's views on property lending over the last 6 months and prospects for speculative lending;
9 Size of lender's loan book and any proposals for change;
10 Key criteria for property lending.

The Property Lending Surveys have provided an overview of the nature and characteristics of property lending in the UK and have provided some key conclusions for the period 1990–95. These conclusions can be grouped in four main areas and reflect the nature of the questionnaire, as outlined above.

The four main areas of study and analysis relate to: (a) the details of lending on development property; (b) the details of lending on investment and owner-occupied property; (c) the size and range of the lender's portfolio; and (d) the criteria for analysing loans. The key conclusions in each of these areas can be summarised as follows:

The details of lending on development property

1 Lending on development property declined over the five years 1990–95 in line with the general decline of activity in the development sector of the property industry.
2 The maximum term for development lending was 25 years but on average it ranged between 6 and 9 years.
3 Speculative lending decreased dramatically from 1990–93 and recovered only slightly up to 1995.
4 Loan to cost ratios declined in the period 1990–95, to around 70 per cent for land costs and 76 per cent for construction costs. Loan to value ratios remained around 70 per cent for the period whilst average development loans ranged between £2 and £16 million and interest margins increased to 2.5 per cent.

The details of lending on investment and owner-occupied property

1 The maximum term for investment lending generally averaged 12 years.
2 Commercial projects were favoured over other types of project by investment lenders.
3 The loan to value ratios are around 73 per cent but could vary between 60 and 95 per cent depending on the lender.

4 Average investment loans ranged between £2 million minimum and £17 million maximum and the average interest margin increased to 2.12 per cent.

The size and range of the lender's portfolio

1 Development lending as a proportion of the lender's portfolio has decreased dramatically from 43 per cent to 15 per cent over the five-year period.
2 Overseas property as a proportion of the lending portfolio varied from 15 to 25 per cent between 1990 and 1995.
3 The size of property loan books reduced to an average of £340 million by 1995.
4 Lenders became much more cautious in 1991 and then relaxed their criteria.

Criteria for analysing loans

1 The most important criteria for lending are cash flow, quality of borrower (becoming less important), quality of tenant (becoming more important), quality of property and track record of borrower. Location of the property has become less important.
2 The criteria for analysing loans have remained static over the period 1990–95.

The detailed data lends itself to further analysis as the time period of the surveys increases. One particular area of study would be to look at interest margins and loan to value ratios as an indicator as to whether property lenders are efficient in their pricing and estimation of risk relative to other indices in the market. The key areas for investigation are the changes in interest rate margins that reflect the profitability of lending and the loan to value ratios that reflect the security aspects of lending. For investment and development property, these are positively correlated. The correlation coefficient is 0.974 for interest rate margins, but lower for loan to value ratios; the problem here is a divergence in the last year of study (1995) but, if this is ignored, the coefficient is 0.992. The relationship between investment and development lending is shown in Figures 4.4 and 4.5.

In order to compare these criteria (interest margins and loan to value ratios) to rates in the market, Figure 4.6 shows details of long-term rates (long-dated government security rates, over 20 years), short-term rates (Interbank 3 month offer rate) and the dividend yield of the FT index of ordinary shares (source: Central Statistical Office 1995b,c). Comparison between these criteria and the returns on the property market can also be examined by looking at Figure 4.7 which provides details of the all property returns and the estimation of the equivalent yield for property for the years 1990–95 (the figures for the end of the previous year have been taken to compare with the incidence of the Property Lending Survey which takes place in January/February of the subsequent year). Finally, the criteria of interest margins and loan to value ratios could be affected by the amount of credit available in the market applied to property and this is investigated in Figure 4.8.

If we look at certain of the criteria examined by the Property Lending Survey a little closer, we can suggest certain relationships. We may assume that development funding should be linked to short-term interest rates and a strong negative

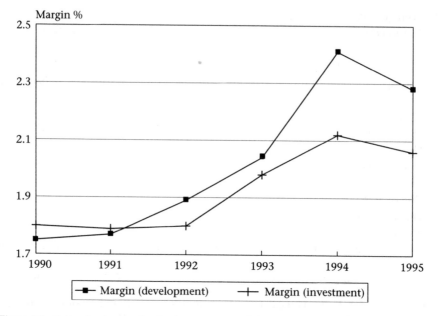

Figure 4.4 Interest rate margins for investment and development lending

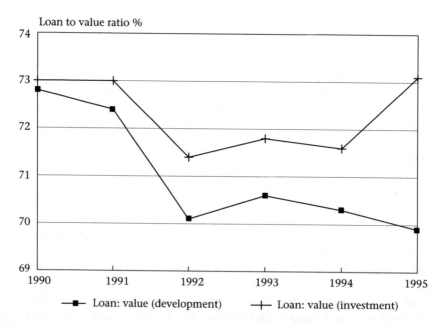

Figure 4.5 Loan to value ratios for development and investment property

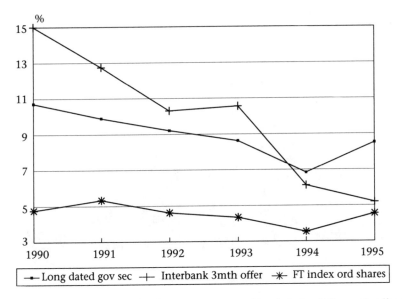

Figure 4.6 Interest rates: long dated government securities, Interbank 3 month offer rate, FT index of ordinary shares: dividend yield

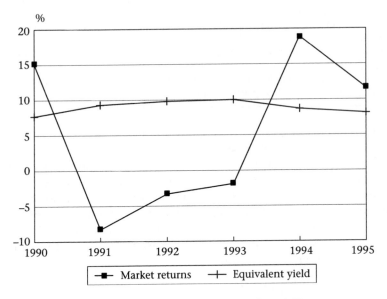

Figure 4.7 The property sector: market returns and equivalent yields
Source: Investment Property Databank (1995).

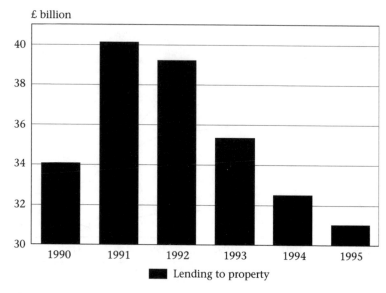

£ billion

Figure 4.8 Bank lending to property companies
Source: Bank of England (1990, 1991, 1992, 1993, 1994a, 1995).

Box 4.4 Results from correlations

Some results: correlation of variables

Interest margins on development property have a strong negative correlation with short-term interest rates (−0.930).

Interest margins on investment property have a strong negative correlation with long-term interest rates (−0.886).

Loan to value ratios on development property show no correlation with overall returns to the property sector (−0.103).

Loan to value ratios on investment property show some negative correlation to equivalent yields in the overall property sector (−0.657).

---

correlation was found here. In terms of interest rate margins on investment property, one would expect that these should relate to longer-term interest rates, and again there is a strong negative correlation. These results are summarised in Box 4.4. In terms of loan to value ratios, it is felt that these reflect risk and security. Some initial analysis has been attempted to correlate loan to value ratios on development property with overall returns to the property sector but no correlation was found. In addition, an attempt was made to correlate loan to value ratios on investment property to equivalent yields in the market; this showed some negative correlation but was not significant.

Other studies of lending policy

DTZ Research found in their report in 2001 that there was some evidence of a relaxation of lending criteria compared to previous studies. They found that average

Table 4.2 Typical acceptable residual value risk levels (%)

	Office	Industrial	High Street retail	Shopping centres	Retail warehouses
Single-let	50	37	50	–	47
Multi-let	47	46	55	54	51

Source: DTZ Research (2001).

LTV ratios on a property asset with 15 years unexpired on the lease was 77 per cent. Whilst this figure is in the range of 70–75 per cent generally thought of as being consistent with prudent lending, it is well below the 85–90 per cent range commonly seen in the 1980s. The spread of responses was found to be quite wide, with High Street banks tending to offer the most conservative LTV ratios (in the region of 70 per cent) whereas insurance companies, building societies and some of the German banks tended to offer 80–85 per cent. With shorter leases of 10 years unexpired, LTV ratios were typically five percentage points lower.

The LTV ratio offered will, to an extent, be dependent on the lender's willingness to accept residual value risk. This is the risk that the value of the debt outstanding on a loan is not covered by the market value of the property when the loan expires. If lenders assume the residual value to be zero and amortise the principal down to zero over the duration of the loan, then the residual value risk is zero. If an asset is assumed to have a positive value when the loan matures (say, 30 per cent of current value), then the loan has only to amortise down to 30 per cent of current value rather than to zero. By allowing more interest to be serviced, the borrower can afford to borrow a larger principal in the first instance. Other things being equal, a higher LTV ratio implies a greater willingness to accept residual value risk. Such risk tends to be assessed on a case by case basis, depending heavily on, amongst other things, the type of property, the location, the expected decay profile and the covenant strength of the tenants. The mean residual value found by the DTZ Research survey was around 30 per cent. There is a tendency for retail banks to accept lower levels of risk (20–30 per cent) compared to building societies and German mortgage banks (up to 70 per cent). Typical acceptable residual value risk levels are shown in Table 4.2.

4.6 Market players

In the 1990s, property came to be regarded as an investment like any other investment and there was a need to compare the characteristics of property with other investments such as government stocks (gilts) or ordinary shares (equities). There was thus a realisation in the property profession that to enable financial specialists to compare these returns, they would need some understanding of property and, in turn, the property adviser would need to be able to analyse returns from other investments. The idea was created, following the deregulation of the financial markets in the 1980s, of a 'one stop shop', where the City security houses could merge with surveyors and the same company could provide property expertise and banking and stock market advice.

The idea of the one stop shop has not really materialised, but the smaller and medium sized surveying practices have been taken over by financial institutions (in the commercial rather than the residential sector). In respect of the latter, there was a major take-out of the private residential estate agents by the financial institutions and building societies; they generally paid expensive prices and, with the slump in the property market, found that returns did not justify the investment. The institutions and building societies sold off many agencies, often to the original owners. The development in the commercial sector has been that financial institutions and financial services in the City have tended to develop in-house expertise on commercial property (Brett 1990b).

Larger estate agencies have set up financial services subsidiaries employing ex-bankers. The banks have now begun to apply the innovative techniques of financing derived from applications to corporate bodies in the trading area and also those techniques introduced from the USA. The traditional institutions (the insurance companies and the pension funds) have become less important as a source of finance for commercial property and the banks have become more important. Traditionally, in development property, the surveyor has been the intermediary between the property developer and institutions. The combination of the factors above has deprived agents and surveyors of their most profitable business: the securities and bank markets.

The insurance companies and pension funds are traditional long-term owners of commercial investments. The life assurance and the general funds both have control of long-term investment monies and, in this respect, property appeared to be a suitable home for it. Both are investing their own funds rather than borrowed funds. So, for these funds, the element of capital appreciation as opposed to income generation is important. There are no problems of an income deficit that may be a problem, for instance, to property owners reliant on borrowed money. In the traditional approach to property development, the property developers relied on bank lenders for short-term finance during the development with a buy-out by the institution enabling repayment of the short-term bank debt. Now the institutions are taking out a much smaller proportion and there has been a change to other, more innovative, forms of finance.

To summarise, the main actors in the property investment market are:

- the financial institutions
- the property companies
- private individuals
- construction companies
- industrial and commercial companies.

The financiers are:

- banks
- specialist property lenders

Table 4.3 Top 5 banks in 1998 and other UK banks appearing in the top 50

Rank	Bank	Country	Shareholder equity ($ million)	Total assets ($ million)
1	Bank of America	USA	45,938	617,679
2	Citigroup	USA	42,708	668,641
3	HSBC Holdings	UK	30,587	475,546
4	Credit Agricole Group	France	26,426	455,782
5	Chase Manhattan	USA	23,838	365,875
19	NatWest Group	UK	14,387	297,411
23	Barclays	UK	13,632	353,296
27	Lloyds TSB Group	UK	12,470	240,033
30	Halifax	UK	11,893	208,687
43	Abbey National	UK	8,995	273,492

Source: *Euromoney* (1999).

- building societies
- insurers and brokers.

In 1999, *Euromoney* published a list of the world's biggest banks. It is interesting to see the scale of these banks and the position of the UK banks in the league. This is shown in Table 4.3. Interestingly, at the time of writing the UK government had just rejected a proposed merger between Lloyds TSB and Abbey National.

4.7   Loans and interest rates

Examples of interest rates that can be applied to the most common transactions are now set out. The example of a mortgage is used but these terms and structures can be applied to other instruments. The interest rates are analysed on the basis of the term, the repayment arrangement and the rates of interest.

Term of loan

Depending on the type of transaction, a client may borrow money on mortgage for terms ranging from 3 months to 30 years. This decision will depend on a number of criteria as follows:

Short-term
(3 months to 2 years)
- The client may only want a bridging loan, pending sale of an existing property.
- The client may wish to turn a property very quickly at a profit, or the scheme may only be a small development.

Medium term
(2 years to 7 years)
- The client may be acquiring a reversionary investment that will be sold after the first rent review.
- The client may have a larger, phased development.

Long-term
(7 years or more)

$\left\{\vphantom{\begin{array}{c}1\\2\\3\\4\\5\end{array}}\right.$ The client basically wants the security of a long-term mortgage facility and has no ambition to move in the immediate future, or the client may have a prime investment that is not intended for disposal, or be an owner-occupier.

Repayment structures

There are also a number of repayment structures that clients may wish to consider:

1   *Bullet repayment* – commonly used in short- and medium-term loans, whereby the client repays interest only for the duration of the loan, repaying the capital in a lump sum at the end of the term. This structure is more commonly used by developers, but is available for investors as well.
2   *Capital and interest* – the most common type of mortgage where capital and interest are repaid over a longer period of up to 30 years. This structure is used by those sectors referred to in the commercial mortgage market and by investors.
3   *Capital holiday* – interest only is payable during the first 2–5 years, after which capital and interest is repayable over a further 15–25 year term. It is particularly useful for investments where rental income will only service interest until first review or for businesses that are establishing themselves.
4   *Deferred interest* – this is where interest is rolled up for an agreed period. It is particularly useful for developers who have no income until sales or lettings are achieved on their scheme. Note that banks are not particularly happy to roll up interest in a depressed market.

Rates of interest

The analysis above relates to loan structures, but the nature of the interest rates also has to be considered. A client may elect to borrow either *floating* or *fixed rate* funds, given the constraints of the loan facility.

Floating rates

Developers and clients borrowing less than £1 million may only have the option to borrow floating rate funds. In the case of the developer, it is impossible to predict with floating rates what the outstanding balance will be at any point in the future, whilst the term of the loan will be governed by the speed at which the scheme is built and sold. For loans under £1 million, the banks may simply find it uneconomic to arrange fixed rate funding. The facility is priced (i.e., the interest rate is agreed at a level over a yardstick rate, which is commonly the base rate and the interest rate is referred to as 'so much per cent over base').

Bank base rate

The bank base rate is simply the minimum level at which any bank may offer floating rate funds to the market as determined by the Bank of England from time to time. Each bank has its own base rate, so you may see documentation that states 2 per cent over Barclays or HSBC base rate. Essentially, each bank's base rate will be that which has been set by the Bank of England, but some secondary banks who are struggling to maintain profitability have, in the past, left their base rates up to 3 per cent higher than the norm! In October 2001, the base rate in the UK fell to 4.5 per cent, its lowest rate since 1964. International terrorism and conflict combined with fears of global recession to force the rate down to this historic low. However, the rate appeared quite high when compared with rates in Europe, the USA (2.5 per cent) and Japan (0.01 per cent). This USA rate was equivalent to zero when allowance for inflation was made.

London Interbank Offered Rate (LIBOR)

This is simply the price at which banks sell money to each other. LIBOR rates are quoted daily by the banks over 3, 6 and 12 months. If the client elects to borrow over 3 month LIBOR, then effectively he fixes his borrowing costs for a 3-month period. At the end of 3 months, the client's cost of borrowing is re-fixed for a further 3-month period, and so on to the end of the loan term. To give you some idea of the difference of LIBOR rates compared with bank base rates, the following are market quotes from *The Times* dated 5 July 2001.

Clearing bank base rate	5.25 per cent
Interbank rates:	
1 month	5.24–5.19 per cent
3 month	5.24–5.19 per cent
6 month	5.35–5.30 per cent
12 month	5.62–5.59 per cent

LIBOR can either be above or below bank base rate, depending on the market's view of future interest rate movements. Twelve months is effectively the longest period of time the banks would be prepared to gamble on fixing interest rates. Whereas LIBOR is the rate at which the banks themselves will lend to one another, the lower rate at which they are prepared to borrow is termed LIBID. The difference between LIBOR and LIBID thus produces the margin or profit on the operation. The middle rate between the two is termed LIMEAN. LIBOR rates are quoted on different terms depending on the length of time from the transaction to repayment (i.e., 3-month LIBOR). Interest rates are usually quoted as being so many basis points above LIBOR or LIBID. (A basis point is one hundredth of a percentage point so 50 basis points above LIBOR is LIBOR plus 0.5 per cent.)

Finance Houses Base Rate (FHBR)

The FHBR is charged by the finance houses, such as Mercantile (Barclays), Lombard (National Westminster) and is a 2-month average of 3-month LIBOR. It tends to lag behind bank base rates and is, therefore, higher as rates are falling and lower as rates are rising.

Gross Domestic Mortgage Rate (GDMR)

GDMR is charged by the building societies and effectively is dictated by the larger societies.

Fixed rates

These rates are usually available to investors and anyone borrowing over £1 million. There are two main sources of fixed rate money, which are the *gilt* and *swaps* markets.

Gilts

Gilts are simply commercial paper issued by the government to finance their public spending programmes. In the 1980s, the government was a net repayer of debt, but more recently it has started to borrow money again. It will, therefore, issue gilts with a variety of maturity (repayment) dates and yields (interest rates). The insurance companies will set aside some funds to invest in the property market and will offer borrowers fixed rates, based on a margin over a rate of return that they would otherwise be able to achieve in the gilt market. Their terms will be anywhere from 5 to 25 years.

Swaps

Given that banks will not offer fixed rate options over 12 months, how can borrowers gain longer terms on fixed rate? The only borrowers who can effectively borrow fixed rate money are large corporations. To do so, they will issue commercial paper or bonds to private and commercial investors at fixed yields (interest rates) with a promise to repay the face value of the bond on a given date.

You will sometimes see the phrase 'convertible (or euro-convertible) bonds' which simply give the investor the option to take shares in the company issuing the bond at a predetermined share price, instead of taking cash. On occasions, it suits the large corporations to offer their fixed rate money to the open market at a premium. So, where they have been able to borrow from the bond market at 10 per cent, they may be able to lend that money to the banks that operate swap options at 11 per cent, thus generating a profit. The banks may then be able to offer that money to borrowers on a further margin of 2 per cent over swap rate. Swaps are actually a little more complicated than described, but this outlines the basic principles by which clients can borrow fixed rate money.

The swaps market is an example of interest rate hedging where interest rates are controlled to an extent to reduce volatility. Swaps and capital instruments that reduce the movement of rates in a floating rate situation are the two common approaches to this. Aspects relating to the use of capital instruments are discussed in the next section.

Advantages and disadvantages of different types of interest rate

In summary, floating rates may fluctuate wildly during the term of the borrowing. The cost of borrowing may, therefore, increase or decrease substantially. Fixed rates give certainty but can prove expensive if borrowing costs drop. Fixed rate finance can also be inflexible with substantial penalties for repayment. Capital instruments (caps) offer the benefits of floating rates with the comfort of fixed rates. They are also flexible and do not penalise the borrower for early repayment. Capital instruments are also tradable commodities and can be sold on the open

Box 4.5 Disadvantages and advantages of variable and fixed interest rates

Variable rate
Disadvantages:
1 Interest rate rise would result in increased costs and mean that the maximum loan amount is reached quicker.
2 The term of the loan generally is shorter and therefore you will need to refinance earlier which will result in increased costs.
3 The value of the property may fall at the time of refinancing and therefore a further cash injection may be necessary.
4 Banks are cautious about rolling up interest and will reduce the loan to 75 per cent value.

Advantages:
1 When interest rates fall you will have to pay less interest.
2 You are able to sell the property at any time without breakage costs (costs on breaking the agreement).

Fixed rate
Disadvantages:
1 When interest rates fall, fixed rate money is more expensive.
2 Should you wish to sell the property and repay the loan, if interest rates fall you will be liable to breakage costs. These costs will equate to approximately £35,000 for every 1 per cent fall in interest rates per year. if interest rates fell 2 per cent with 4 years to expiry of the loan, the breakage costs will be approximately £280,000 (as of 1990).

Advantages:
1 Certain of interest costs.
2 Interest rate is significantly below current variable rates.
3 Banks feel more confident to lend on this basis.
4 If interest rates increase, you would gain a significant advantage and there would be no breakage costs if you sold the property.

market, although their value will depend on the current level of interest rates and the length of term the cap has to remain. Their disadvantage is the cost of the up-front premium. The advantages and disadvantages of variable and fixed interest rates are summarised in Box 4.5.

4.8 Markets and margins

The basic pricing of a loan facility usually involves the following elements:

Arrangement fee

This covers the cost of all preliminary investigations and internal reports and approvals, and a valuation fee if an in-house valuer is used. There is also an element reflecting risk and, if this were higher than may be expected in the circumstances, fees would be higher. Risk and work involved in development and portfolio loans is higher than for single-let properties, for instance. Arrangement fees will also reflect the amount of work the lender is required to undertake in its due diligence process. These fees are generally around 0.3–0.5 per cent but may rise to 1 per cent for development property (Freeman Publishing 2000).

Management fee

This covers the cost of monitoring the project and is usually payable on an annual or semi-annual basis.

Commitment fee

This is usually a fee that recompenses the bank for making the commitment and is charged on the amount of the facility that remains unutilised from time to time. The facility amount will be drawn down in stages over the life of the loan. This fee reimburses the bank that has an obligation to provide the facility amount and therefore cannot utilise those funds for other lending opportunities. Commitment fees are often paid on development loans where the loan is drawn down as required during the development programme. These fees are typically 0.3–0.5 per cent p.a. paid quarterly from day 1 on undrawn amounts (Freeman Publishing 2000).

Interest margin

This margin is above the bank's cost of funds that is charged to pay the bank for its risks in lending the project funds. If the loan is drawn down in stages, any amount undrawn may attract charges.

Repayment/cancellation penalty fee

Some lenders will require the borrower to pay a penalty fee if part or all of the loan is repaid prior to the expiry of the loan term. Often the cancellation fees only apply to the first few years of the loan (say, up to 3 years). If the borrower knows that it is likely to dispose of the asset in the short term, the length of the loan should be structured accordingly. Prepayment/cancellation fees are typically around 0.5 per cent.

Underwriting fees

For large loans over £50–100 million, the total loan amount may be provided by a syndicate of banks. This approach may not be beneficial to the borrower who would have to deal with a number of banks and obtain credit approvals from each of them. An alternative would be that a single bank would underwrite the full loan amount. The underwriting bank then becomes the lead bank with which the borrower will deal. In this scenario, the bank is likely to charge an underwriting fee of 0.25–0.5 per cent of the total loan amount. In turn, the underwriting bank may independently seek to syndicate the loan to other lenders to reduce its overall share. The underwriting fee prices the risk that the lead bank will be unable to pass on part of its loan commitment to other lenders (Freeman Publishing 2000).

* * *

As well as the above, there may be fees for the valuation of the property asset and the payment of the lender's legal fees for reviewing the property title or lease information and preparing the loan agreement documentation. There may be additional fees to provide structural surveys, planning and environmental reports.

Naylor (1994), in his survey of property development companies, discovered a range of fees being charged: First, a *commitment fee* incurred when the lender actually transfers funds to the developer; second, an *arrangement fee* charged for putting the facility to the borrower in place; third, a *prepayment fee* incurred when the loan is repaid earlier than scheduled and so the lender does not receive the interest payment expected; and, finally, even a *back-end fee* charged when the capital sum is repaid.

4.9   Interest rate management and hedging

Hedging arrangements are different interest rate strategies and can include options, futures, caps, floors, forward rate agreements (FRAs), swaps, and so on. Traditionally, bank loans were repaid as instalments of interest and capital in much the same way as a traditional mortgage. The interest rate was calculated at a margin above a yardstick rate based on the minimum cost of borrowing, the base rate or LIBOR rate (described above). New hedging techniques complement new financial approaches and can adjust cash flows to suit the borrower, but they also minimise exposure from the point of view of the lender.

If interest rates change, borrowers need protection from the wider swings of interest rates. This is very important in property where a lot of money is borrowed. Businesses often work on very fine interest margins and cash flows can be severely damaged by unexpected rises in interest rates, so it is possible to fix interest rates in advance, relative to a common yardstick such as LIBOR, but this is still variable. The simplest way to protect against rising interest rates is to borrow at a fixed rate rather than a variable one. The government has been a net repayer of debt rather than a borrower in the late 1980s and 1990s, so there is a shortage of long-dated government bonds, and with a fair bit of competition the prices remain high and the yields low.

Companies take advantage by issuing long-dated bonds at interest rates above those on government bonds but well below the short-term interest rates prevailing at the time. By 1990, long-term borrowing rates had moved right up and looked less attractive. Very long-term fixed interest borrowing may suit property investment companies with revenue-producing properties that they are intending to hold on to indefinitely with long-term borrowing matching a long-term asset. This type of borrowing is not possible for smaller concerns with a less established cash flow.

Fixed rate money has a drawback in that one may lock into a high rate of interest for a long period. For some companies, the best compromise is to borrow short or medium term at variable rates of interest but to 'hedge' the risk that interest rates will rise further.

Interest-only payments

This means that no repayment of capital is made until the end of the period of the loan. This can assist developers who may not have any income arising from the project during the currency of the loan (for instance, where the project is the development of a building which is to be sold on or refinanced at the end of the development period). This is also known as a deferred capital payment or bullet payment.

Deferred interest payment

Rolling up or interest rate holidays means that no interest charges are paid during the currency of the loan or are significantly reduced. The interest thus compounds over the time period before repayment.

Variable and fixed rates

Rates can be fixed at the outset but this is risky in the longer term; otherwise, they can be variable but perhaps changing monthly or quarterly or, even with some home loan mortgages, on an annual basis.

Fully floating rates

These are related to bank base rates or LIBOR rates and can change day to day depending on the change in the yardstick rates. Euromarket issues may be fixed rate or may be floating rate notes (FRNs).

Drop-lock loan

This is a hybrid between the fixed and variable rate. The initial rate is variable but when triggered becomes a fixed rate over the remainder of the loan period. The trigger is usually caused by the fall of the variable rate to a predetermined level, after which the rate is fixed to protect the lender's margin. For example, a loan may be fixed at a margin of 2 per cent over LIBOR; assuming this is (say) 6 per cent at time of agreement, then the variable rate will commence at 8 per cent. If LIBOR falls, the variable rate will fall but perhaps the loan will lock in at, say, 6 per cent to a fixed rate.

4.10   Hedging instruments

Interest rates have been extremely volatile over the last two decades and lenders need to be able to reduce their interest rate exposure. Interest rate exposure arises when:

(a) floating rate financial commitments create uncertainty in respect of future cash flows; or
(b) when assets and liabilities have a mismatch in their maturity or interest basis.

There are three categories of exposure: cash flow, portfolio and economic. Some companies adopt a full hedging policy if they are risk-averse but they are then unable to benefit from favourable movements in interest rates. Active risk management involves selective hedging to minimise costs and hedge costs simultaneously (Mitchell and Peake 1991).

Hedging instruments consist of the following:

1 Forward rate agreements
2 Interest rate swaps
3 Interest rate swaptions
4 Interest rate options
    (a) caps
    (b) floors

(c) collars

(d) floor/swap combinations

5 Futures.

These are covered below.

Forward rate agreements

An FRA enables companies to hedge a future interest payment or receipt, and can be used to change a floating rate to a fixed rate and vice versa. No money is exchanged; the difference between the rates is discounted back to the beginning of the agreed period. A 4 × 10 FRA would start in 4 months and terminate in 10 months (Figure 4.9).

Interest rate swaps

There is a market for trading and exchanging fixed and variable interest rate debt arrangements. The type of loan required by a lender will vary according to market rates, the completion of projects and the cash flow and risk profile of the debt; thus, fixed rate or variable rate funding may be suitable according to the risk–return trade-off. The transaction takes place through a bank. By fixing some money, the lender can minimise exposure to changes of interest rates, especially in volatile periods. They enable balance sheets to be restructured and allow access to a wider range of markets.

The swap is an agreement by two parties to exchange interest payments on a specified principal amount in an agreed currency. The difference between the agreed rates exchanged is settled at the end of each rollover date. Swaps are used to change the floating rate to a fixed rate and vice versa. Companies with a 3-month LIBOR rate could exchange it for a 6-month rate. Companies with investments can use swaps to fix a future rate of return. The maturities of swaps can be up to 10 years and are available in most currencies. A swap is shown in Figure 4.10. Currency swaps also have potential for protecting investors from adverse currency fluctuation in international real estate investment markets (Worzala, Johnson and Lizieri 1997).

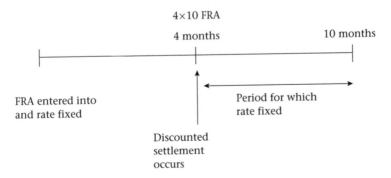

Figure 4.9   Forward rate agreement

Source: Mitchell and Peake (1991), p. 535.

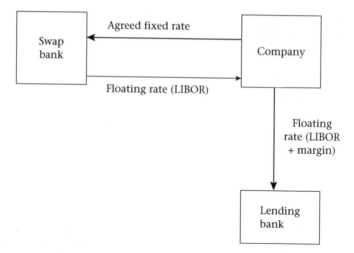

Figure 4.10   Interest rate swap
Source: Adapted from Mitchell and Peake (1991), p. 536.

Interest rate swaptions

An interest rate swaption is an option (see below) to enter into an interest rate swap at an agreed rate exercisable on a certain date in the future for an agreed duration. The option is normally purchased with a view to being exercised for a cash settlement. Theoretically, it may also be exercised into an interest rate swap at the agreed rate. However, as the latter involves a credit exposure for the bank providing it, most swaptions are exercised for a cash settlement. At the end of the option period, if the fixed rate for an interest swap for the equivalent period is higher than the given rate for the swaption, a compensatory payment is due to the purchaser or the purchaser may convert the swaption into an interest rate swap. If the fixed rate for an equivalent interest rate swap is lower, the swaption is abandoned and the premium forfeited. Swaptions have been used as a hedge against the possibility of the election of a Labour government in a forthcoming election on the assumption than such an election victory might lead to a sterling crisis. It is ironic that it was the Conservatives rather than Labour who found themselves in this position in September 1992 (Goldsmith 1992). This type of hedging is useful in:

(a) purchase situations to offset fears of rising interest rates before finance is finalised;
(b) sale situations where a hedging structure is in place, to protect against a fall in interest rate before sale which may lead to additional termination costs arising from the lifting of the hedge;
(c) situations where property companies are negotiating new loans and hedging structure, where a swaption will protect against rising interest costs and a more expensive hedging structure.

Box 4.6 Example of a swaption

Initial swaption:		
	Notional principal	£5,000,000
	Option period	3 months
	Underlying swap duration	2 years
	Strike rate	10.5 per cent
	Interest rate basis	3-month LIBOR
	2 year swap rate on transaction date	10.31 per cent
	Premium cost	£18,000
On exercise date:	Equivalent 2-year swap rate	12 per cent
	Borrower receives cash settlement of	
	£125,000 = net present value of 12 per cent−10.31 per cent for 2 years' duration.	
	If the equivalent rate swap = 10 per cent, the swaption would be abandoned without value (Goldsmith 1992).	

There are two types of swaption based on the difference between US and European style options. European options are exercisable at the end of the option period only; US options can be exercised at any time during the option period. The normal swaption duration is 2–10 years. At the end of the option, one is 'in the money' if the swaption strike rate is below the LIBOR rate it is protecting. If the LIBOR rate is less than the strike rate, the option is abandoned and there is no value (Goldsmith 1992); see Box 4.6 for an example.

Interest rate options

Options in general are discussed in section 6.4. Options give the holder a right to sell or buy shares of common stock at a given exercise price. A call option is a right to buy and a put option is a right to sell. Option features can be found in many areas of finance: for example, in convertibles and warrants, insurance, capital budgeting and currency and interest rate management (as here). Pure options are financial instruments created by exchanges (i.e., stock markets) rather than companies. Where the value of a company's assets falls below the value of its borrowings, shareholders may not exercise their option to repay the loan, but prefer the company to default on the debt (Pike and Neale 1999). Options are the most versatile of hedging instruments as they offer companies the right to 'walk away' if rates move favourably, yet provide protection if rates move against the company.

Capital instruments (caps)

An insurance policy that guarantees a certain rate for a certain period for an up-front premium is commonly called a cap (see Figure 4.11). This places a ceiling on the floating interest rate. This is done by the payment of a single insurance premium paid at the commencement of the loan to protect the borrower against increases. The borrower still benefits from falls in the interest rate. This means that the borrower is benefiting from a partially fixed rate; certainly, if the rate exceeds the capped rate, then it is in effect a fixed rate at the capped rate for

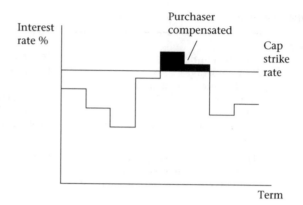

Figure 4.11   Interest rate cap
Source: Mitchell and Peake (1991), p. 536.

as long as this is the case. If a client borrows (say) £1 million at a margin over base rate, that base rate can go up or down. For every 1 per cent the base rate goes up, the client will have to pay an additional £10,000 in interest. Obviously, should interest rates go down, the client would make a similar saving in interest costs. If base rates are 11 per cent and the client believes that they will rise over the next 5 years, the client can effectively fix the base rate at 11 per cent by the purchase of a cap. The cap is effectively an insurance policy that pays out should the base rates rise above the capped level. So, if interest rates rise by 1 per cent, and you have to pay your bank an additional £10,000 in interest each year, the cap will compensate you by the same amount. If, however, interest rates fall, you still get the benefit of lower interest payments. To purchase a cap, the client will have to pay a one-off, up-front premium.

To summarise, the simplest form of interest rate protection is the cap. The cap involves the borrower paying up front a fee or premium for a guarantee that interest will not increase beyond an agreed limit. The fee payable will be determined by:

(a) the interest rate of the cap, relative to the market rate (the lower the rate of the cap, the higher the fee payable); and
(b) the duration of the cap.

The borrower will be recompensed for any difference between the agreed level bought through the cap and LIBOR on the prescribed dates, if on those dates the rate is greater than the level of interest rate bought. The lender on the other side of the guarantee finds counter-parties with opposite requirements to hedge the costs. Caps are quoted against 3-month LIBOR but depend on underlying funding and can be quoted against the base rate. The difference between the base rate quoted and LIBOR is fixed when fixing takes place.

The LIBOR cap is based on the 3-month LIBOR rate and this is checked against the base rate and the difference paid to the borrower. The base rate cap rate is checked daily from the fixing date to compare with the cap rate; the difference is paid 2 weeks after the calculation date. At present, the smaller players are offered no more than the choice between a floating or a fixed rate. Caps for loans of less than £0.5 million are rarely available. The cap thus sets a limit on the borrowing cost so that, if the interest rate rises, the company is reimbursed for costs above the ceiling ('strike rate').

Floor

Let us assume that at the same period as the cap mentioned above, you wanted to fix your base rate at 10 per cent because the investment you were buying would not self-fund at a higher rate. In such circumstances, the cost of the cap is not cheap. Providing that the investment property has a suitably strong tenant, the cap provider may be prepared to purchase a floor from the borrower. This is precisely the opposite of a cap, whereby you guarantee that if base rates fall below, say, 9 per cent, you will compensate the bank for their loss of interest. For this benefit, the bank pays the borrower a premium. Floors thus protect a company if LIBOR falls below the selected rate. Premiums vary according to the rate (see Figure 4.12).

Collar

This has a ceiling and a floor rate between which the floating rate operates. The collar limits the increases and falls in the interest rates, and thus the range of the interest rate is known by the borrower. The combined effect of a cap and a floor is known as a collar, which is effectively a corridor within which the borrower's base rate can fluctuate. Thus, the simultaneous purchase of a cap and the sale of a floor will provide a collar. The company offsets the premium payment for the cap by selling the floor and establishes a band in which interest rates can fluctuate (see Figure 4.13).

A zero cost collar is where the cap premium and the floor receipt cancel one another out. This has a disadvantage in that it is likely that a narrow band would be established in these circumstances. With a stepped collar, the company has

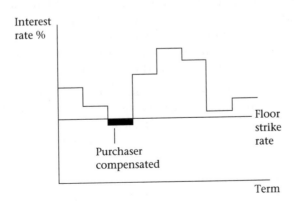

Figure 4.12 Interest rate floor

Source: Mitchell and Peake (1991), p. 537.

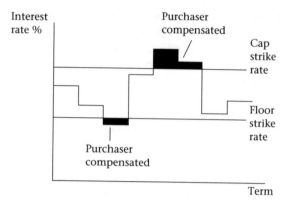

Figure 4.13   Interest rate collar
Source: Mitchell and Peake (1991), p. 537.

a narrow band initially and then it is more flexible. It is possible to have a zero cost for this.

Floor/swap combination

The combined purchase of a swap and the sale of a floor in situations of high interest rates can reduce the costs of hedging.

Futures

A futures contract is a legal agreement between two parties, one to make and the other to take delivery of a specified amount of a commodity or a financial instrument on a certain date in the future at a price fixed on entering the contract. Futures markets are claimed to be the most efficient markets because of their liquid characteristics and standardised investments (Dent and Weeks 1993).

Futures are a less expensive hedging instrument than FRAs or swaps. The disadvantage is that futures are bought only in standard sizes and to match certain dates, and they require the maintenance of a broker. The market involved generally in interest rate hedging by future is the London International Financial Futures and Options Exchange (LIFFE). In May 1991, London FOX (Future and Options Exchange) introduced a property futures market in London, based on four indices:

- commercial property values, using the Investment Property Databank indices
- commercial property rents, using the Investment Property Databank indices
- house prices, using the Nationwide Anglia house price index
- mortgage interest rates, using the London FOX mortgage interest rate index.

Initially, property futures were aimed at developers to hedge their development risk. Futures are a zero sum game with one winner and one loser. A developer who takes out a futures contract would be expected to settle in cash at the end of the contract. This may not be simple as the developer may be illiquid at this stage. Property futures are more suitable for property investors to hedge the risk of portfolio investments (Venmore-Rowland 1991). The problem with London FOX's operation arose from the alleged manipulation of the market, probably to create an impression of volume. The market was trading at low levels and problems arose because the concept was new and had been launched on a market in recession (*Chartered Surveyor Weekly* 1991). The market closed in October 1991; a total of 11,000 commercial and residential contracts had been traded in the market in the 5-month period (Goodman 1991).

Deals were done on the London FOX by 'betting' on the movement of the indices: for example, if the IPD (Investment Property Databank) index stands at 100 and property values move up 20 per cent, then the index moves to 120. Each point of the movement is worth £500 for the capital values contract, so a move from 100 to 101 is worth £500. If you think prices will fall, for instance, then you sell a contract; if the index is at 95, then the cost is £47,500 (£500 per point x 95 points). Assume the index falls to 75 on sale; then profit is 20 points × £500 = £10,000. Thus, on a larger scale, this income could be used to offset the falling value of a property asset you are holding.

So, to bet on a fall in values you sell a contract, to bet on an increase you buy (Brett 1991a). If you are buying or selling where the index is at 95, you do not need to put down the full price of £47,500, but a small deposit of, say, £600 is sufficient. Futures markets thus require only a small proportion of the face value of the contract to be paid up-front. Changes in the value of the contract can be settled on a daily basis. The uses of the market are for speculation, hedging and portfolio management (Richard Ellis 1991).

Derivatives and synthetics

We have looked here at options, swaps and futures as hedging instruments as a means of managing risk in interest rate movements. These can also be used to manage risk in respect of asset price movements and currency price movements and are discussed in this context further in Chapter 12. Derivatives are thus financial contracts whose value is derived from the value of the underlying asset. These are used, as said, in relation to currency, interest rates and commodity prices and thus investors use derivatives to manage risk and uncertainty in investment decisions. Such derivatives may be traded or sold 'over the counter'. Traded derivatives are standardised products with a centralised exchange where prices will vary according to market conditions. An 'over the counter' derivative is a customised product designed by a financial intermediary, such as an investment bank, and is not usually tradable (McAllister and Mansfield 1998a). A synthetic is a type of derivative instrument designed to track the performance of a benchmark index. Synthetics are the main type of derivative associated with the direct property market.

Some advantages of the use of derivatives as against direct property investment can be noted here:

1 *Fast transaction time*
2 *High liquidity*
3 *Low transaction and management costs*

4 *Efficient diversification*: here derivatives linked to a property index allow the investor to track the property market. Potential tracking error (deviation of return from the index) is avoided by eliminating the specific risk (the individual characteristics of a single property).

5 *Enables small funds to invest* where the cost of access to the direct property market may be too expensive.

6 *Ability to sell 'synthetically'*. The derivative market has the potential to allow investors to reduce exposure to the property market by 'synthetically' selling parts of their property portfolio and receiving the returns linked to an alternative investment media. Such an operation would be much quicker than deals with direct property transactions.

7 *Tactical asset allocation*. Using derivatives, investors can easily increase or decrease exposure to the property market and they enable the fund manager to switch easily between asset classes in response to changing market conditions and perceptions of future performance potential (McAllister and Mansfield 1998a).

References and further reading

Armon-Jones, C. H. (1992) 'Underwriting Property Sales', *Journal of Property Finance*, 2(4), 497–500.

Bank of England (1990) *Quarterly Bulletin*, 30(2), May.

Bank of England (1991) *Quarterly Bulletin*, 31(2), May.

Bank of England (1992) *Quarterly Bulletin*, 32(2), May.

Bank of England (1993) *Quarterly Bulletin*, 33(3), August.

Bank of England (1994a) *Quarterly Bulletin*, 34(3), August.

Bank of England (1994b) *Quarterly Bulletin*, 34(4), November.

Bank of England (1995) *Quarterly Bulletin*, 35(3), August.

Berkley, R. (1991) 'Raising Commercial Property Finance in a Difficult Market', *Journal of Property Finance*, 1(4), 523–9.

Brett, M. (1990b) *Property and Money*, Estates Gazette, London.

Brett, M. (1991a) 'How property futures work', *Estates Gazette*, 18 May, 71.

Catalano, A. (2001a) 'No safe haven for small punters', *Estates Gazette*, 27 October, 54.

Central Statistical Office (1992) *Financial Statistics: Explanatory Handbook*, CSO, London, December.

Central Statistical Office (1993a) *Financial Statistics*, CSO, London, September.

Central Statistical Office (1993b) *Housing and Construction Statistics*, CSO, London, September.

Central Statistical Office (1994a) *Financial Statistics*, CSO, London, November.

Central Statistical Office (1994b) *Economic Trends*, CSO, London.

Central Statistical Office (1995a) *UK Economic Accounts*, no. 8, CSO, London, January.

Central Statistical Office (1995b) *Economic Trends*, CSO, London, July.

Central Statistical Office (1995c) *Economic Trends: Annual Supplement*, CSO, London.

Central Statistical Office (1996) *Financial Statistics*, CSO, London, November.

Central Statistical Office (1999) *Financial Statistics*, CSO, London, no. 452, December.

Chartered Surveyor Weekly (1991) 'Editorial: crisis at London FOX leaves futures uncertain', *Chartered Surveyor Weekly*, 10 October, 5.

Chesterton Financial (1993) *Property Lending Survey*, Chesterton Financial, London, February.

Dent, P. and Weeks, C. (1993) 'Is there LIFFE after FOX?' *Estates Gazette*, 9 October, 132–6.

DTZ Debenham Thorpe (1993) *Money into Property*, DTZ Debenham Thorpe, London, August.

DTZ Debenham Thorpe (1996) *Money into Property*, DTZ Debenham Thorpe, London, September.

DTZ Debenham Thorpe (1999) *Money into Property*, DTZ Debenham Thorpe, London.

DTZ Research (2001) *Money into Property*, DTZ Research, London, edition 26, June.

Estates Gazette (2001a) 'Market Indicators', *Estates Gazette*, 22 September, 64.

Euromoney (1999) 'The world's biggest banks', *Euromoney*, no. 362 (June), 209.

Evans, P. H. (1993) 'Statistical Review', *Journal of Property Finance*, 4(2), 75–82.

Freeman, D. J. (2001) 'Security structures, the Insolvency Act 2000 and further proposal for reform', *Property Review*, D. J. Freeman, London, no. 37 (October), 4.

Freeman Publishing (2000) *Guide to the Property Industry*, Freeman Publishing, London, June.

Goldsmith, G. C. (1992) 'Sterling Interest Swaptions', *Journal of Property Finance*, 3(3), 315–18.

Goodman, T. (1991) 'Property futures idea is still alive – just', *Chartered Surveyor Weekly*, 10 October, 11.

Investment Property Databank (1993) *Annual Review 1993*, IPD, London, December.

Investment Property Databank (1995) *Annual Review 1995*, IPD, London.

McAllister, P. and Mansfield, J. R. (1998a) 'Investment property portfolio management and financial derivatives: Paper 1', *Property Management*, 16(3), 116–19.

Mitchell, C. and Peake, J. H. (1991) 'The Management of Interest Rate Exposure', *Journal of Property Finance*, 1(40), 530–8.

Naylor, T. (1994) 'Aspects of senior debt used by and available to property development companies', *Journal of Property Finance*, 5(1), 23–8.

Pike, R. and Neale, B. (1999) *Corporate Finance and Investment: Decisions and Strategies*, Prentice-Hall, London.

Property Week (2001a) 'New model for reviews', *Property Week*, 19 October, 7.

Property Week (2001b) 'Property lending hits £67.5 bn', *Property Week*, 16 November, 17.

Richard Ellis (1991) 'A Look at Commercial Property Futures', *Investment Research Review no. 2*, Richard Ellis, London.

Riley, M. and Isaac, D. (1991a) 'Property Lending Survey 1991' *Journal of Property Finance*, 2(1), 74–7.

Riley, M. and Isaac, D. (1992) 'Property Lending Survey 1992', *Journal of Property Finance*, 2(4), 38–41.

Riley, M. and Isaac, D. (1993a) 'Property Lending Survey 1993', *Journal of Property Finance*, 4(1), 43–8.

Riley, M. and Isaac, D. (1994) 'Property Lending Survey 1994', *Journal of Property Finance*, 5(1), 45–51.

Riley, M. and Isaac, D. (1995) 'Property Lending Survey 1995', *Journal of Property Finance*, 6(1), 67–72.

Scott, I. P. (1992) 'Debt, Liquidity and Secondary Trading in Property Debt', *Journal of Property Finance*, 3 (3), 347–55.

Venmore-Rowland, P. (1991) 'Vehicles for Property Investment' in P. Venmore-Rowland, P. Brandon and T. Mole (eds), *Investment, Procurement and Performance in Construction*, RICS, London.

Worzala, E. M., Johnson, R. D. and Lizieri, C. M. (1997) 'Currency swaps as a hedging technique for international real estate investment', *Journal of Property Finance*, 8(2), 134–51.

Wyles, M. (1990) 'Mortgage Indemnity – A Risk/Reward Arbitrage', *Journal of Property Finance*, 1 (3), 378–86.

5
Project-based Funding

5.1 Introduction

Project-based funding is where the funds are secured against the property being acquired or developed. Project finance is especially important for smaller unlisted property companies to whom stock market sources are unavailable. In these cases, the existing assets may be fully charged against previous loans. The financial status of the companies may also not provide sufficient security for the financier.

Traditionally, project finance was involved in two distinct operations.

1 *Short-term, interim or bridging finance* – This is the finance raised to pay the development costs incurred during the development period for site purchase and payments to the building contractor and fees, for instance.
2 *Long-term finance or funding* – This is required to repay the short-term finance on completion of the project. Long-term financing is not financing for project development but financing the retention of the project as a long-term investment. If the developer sells on completion, then long-term funding is unnecessary as short-term debt can be repaid from the sale proceeds. If the developer wishes to retain ownership or an interest in the completed development that requires funding, then long-term finance will have to be arranged.

Types of finance typically available for project funding are:

- bridging finance
- forward sale
- mortgage
- sale and leaseback
- project management fee
- general funding.

General funding facilities are really based on the asset backing of the company or developer and are discussed later in Chapter 6.

In the past, when the market was more buoyant and funds were more easily available for project development finance, developers would try to observe the rules for seeking finance set out in Box 5.1.

Box 5.1 Ten golden rules for developers seeking finance

1 Never use your own money in a development; try to arrange full external funding.
2 Never give a personal guarantee or personal collateral for any loan.
3 Roll up interest in the development period.
4 Keep as much equity as possible.
5 Fund in the local currency.
6 Avoid 50:50 ventures; someone has to be in control.
7 Avoid tax liabilities; exploit tax relief.
8 Larger projects are more uncertain, so allow for contingencies.
9 Read the funding agreement, and consider the consequences of a worse than expected outcome if conditions change.
10 Secure the funding commitment from the outset.

Source: Adapted from Darlow (1988).

5.2 Equity partnerships

These relate more to a method of funding a development rather than a true joint venture (this will be explored more fully in Chapter 11). These may include arrangements such as participation lending and forward funding. In participation lending, the lender will take a share of the proceeds of a scheme and this may occur where a lender is taking a higher risk, by lending more or at more advantageous rates of interest.

Forward funding is where the purchaser of a development assists the short-term funding of the development; this provides security for the purchaser who has some control as the development proceeds. It may be that the forward funder will fund the development at a lower rate of interest. The subsidy of the interest rate and the reduction of risk to the developer will thus lead to a reduced developer's profit payable and a higher yield on purchase of the completed development paid by the purchaser (because of reduced risk and reduced cost to the developer). Thus, the purchaser purchases at a reduced price.

The problem with equity partnership arrangements is that the interests held by the parties are going to be difficult to resell until the development is complete, so the partners involved have no security to offer to lenders.

5.3 Forward sale

A contract for a future sale can encourage short-term funds because the funder will know that it will get its money back within a period of time. Alternatively, the party providing the future sale contract may also provide bridging finance. If the investment yield for the scheme was 6 per cent, then the forward sale might take place at 6.5 per cent. A forward sale with bridging finance might be 7 per cent.

Pre-funded projects usually involve a forward commitment from the institution to purchase the development on completion. The arrangement would be that the institution advances interim finance at regular intervals at a lower interest rate than the existing market rate. Once construction is completed or when the building has

Table 5.1   Comparison of forward commitment and forward funding

	Forward commitment	Forward funding
Target rent	£20.6 m p.a.	£20.6 m p.a.
Capitalised @	6.5%	7%
Less costs		
Net value, say	£308 m	£286 m
Deduct costs of construction and site	£190 m	£190 m
Interest rate	13%	9%
Finance cost	£44 m	£30 m
Gross profit to developer	£74 m	£66 m
Profit/cost	31%	30%

Source: Orchard-Lisle (1987).

been let, completion of the sale takes place and the institution hands over the purchase price less the total development cost and rolled-up interest (Savills 1989).

The contrast between forward commitment (that is to say, an end purchaser being signed up now, but the purchaser's commitment only being absolute once the present conditions as to the building and its letting have been met) and forward funding, where the fund purchases the site, advances the capital and takes over the completed project with its share of excess profits, can be seen in Table 5.1.

There is no need for the disengagement of the developer from the funder in such an arrangement. By way of a joint venture or a side-by-side lease, where profits are shared, ownership can also be shared. Securitisation (see Chapter 12) offers an ideal way in which to enable the original developer to retain a percentage of income and future benefits. The funder may receive in such an arrangement a pre-agreed share of the overage being the additional return received over the previous maximum estimate in the calculation for cost, return and developer's profit. The share may be subject to the retention of all the overage if the capping of the development return is agreed.

5.4   Sale and leaseback

The developer sells a completed project to an investor and simultaneously takes back a long lease of the development at an agreed rent calculated on the basis of an appropriate rate of return applied to the purchase. The developer then sub-lets the project to occupying tenants and enjoys by way of a profit rent the difference between the rent paid to the investor and that received from the tenants.

In the UK, one of the early major sale and leaseback arrangements was the initial £25 million reserved for Town & City Property by the Prudential. The developers would ask the Prudential to buy a site, pay the building costs and lease it to

Town & City for a return of 6 per cent plus 20 per cent of income growth at the 33-year rent reviews. Thus, a base rent is agreed beforehand; arrangements could be complex and are as for equity partnership situations, (e.g., top slice, side-by-side, etc.). So the freeholder takes a ground rent/base rent and participates in increases in income. Arrangements for payment of the base rent may include:

1 *Lease guarantee*: if the development is not let in 6 months, the developer receives a profit from the fund but takes a leaseback guarantee at the base rent. The guarantee is extinguished on letting.
2 *Profit erosion*: the developer stakes his profit against voids; the guarantee is for 2–4 years and is useful if the developer is weak and unwilling to provide a lease-back guarantee.
3 *Priority yield*: the fund sets the return at 6.5 per cent, target is 7.5 per cent (1 per cent for developer), and the return over target is split 50:50.

History of the sale and leaseback

Sale and leaseback emerged in the 1930s; examples were used by retail trading groups such as that led by Charles Clore (British Shoe Corporation) to raise capital whilst sharing in the revenues of their developments (see Box 5.2). Initially leasebacks had no rent reviews and thus the institutions purchasing the freehold could not share in the growth of the rent and capital value. The income arising from the development was subsequently shared on completion of the leaseback and revised at each rent review. The nature of the sharing was important from the point of view of the overall return, the opportunity for growth and the risk to be taken by the various parties. An income could be sliced at each review, making the top slice vulnerable and risky. If the slicing took place initially, then two options

Box 5.2 Case study: sale and leaseback

An example of a sale and leaseback involved Barclays Bank (Fox 1993). Its portfolio of operational freehold and long leasehold property at the time stood at just below £1 billion. Its property arm, Barclays Bank Property Holdings, wanted a more balanced portfolio. In 1992, it was decided that the large number of secondary, suburban and retail premises which were required for operating needs created an imbalance in the portfolio, so a programme of sale and leaseback of 92 of the properties earmarked was commenced with a target of £40 million for their sale. The details of the sale were (Fox 1993):

Average lot size:	£400,000 in a range between £200,000 and £1.23 million
Leaseback:	20-year lease with 5-year rent reviews. (Consultants had advised that the market would not bear 15-year leases but was indifferent between 20 and 25 years.)
Initial rents:	Current market level.
Methods of sale:	Private treaty and auction for comparison.
Package:	6–10 properties in a package or else individually sold.
Actual sales:	42 by auction, 5 by private treaty, 5 package sales.
Leases:	Standard institutional lease. Open user clause with qualified alienation provisions for assignment and sub-letting.
Yields:	8–10 per cent on the packages, best individual yield 7.9 per cent.

arose at subsequent reviews. The rental could be re-sliced and this could give rise to a geared return to one of the parties (i.e., an increased proportion of total income). However, once the initial slicing had taken place, the proportions to the parties involved could remain stable (i.e., proportional sharing at subsequent reviews). A reverse leaseback emerged where the company leased to the financial institution on a long lease and took a leaseback, leaving a more mortgageable interest to the company.

5.5   Finance lease

A variation on sale and leaseback is the finance lease. This is basically a sale and leaseback to a leasing company (typically Hambros, Abbey National, Lloyds Leasing, etc.). The leasing company, due to the timing of tax payments and efficient use of capital allowances within a building, can reduce the interest element of the rental payment to below bank base rate. This structure only applies to the top 200 UK corporates and non-tax paying bodies.

The basic mechanics

The structure requires a property to be sold to the leasing company which leases the building back to the vendor at a market rent. This rent is fixed for 5 years and is then increased at a pre-determined level. At each fifth year, the vendor would have an option to repurchase the property at an amount that is equivalent to the original sale price plus any capitalised interest. The facility was designed so that at the time it could be off-balance sheet, although the final arbiter of this would be the company auditors (see also Chapter 13 for recent changes in this area).

Outlined below are more details of the structure:

1 The leasing company purchases the freehold or long leasehold of the property for up to 100 per cent of market value.
2 The leasing company then grants the vendor a lease for between 5 and 30 years.
3 The lease will have a break option every fifth year. At this point, the vendor or associate/subsidiary company will have the option to repurchase the property. If the option is not exercised, the property will remain in the ownership of the leasing company and, depending upon the initial yield, the rent may be increased.
4 The rental pattern can be fixed at the outset by the leasing company obtaining fixed rate finance. Initially, the rent can be below the cost of finance and any shortfall will be capitalised and added to the principal which is payable should the option to repurchase be exercised.
5 The lease can qualify as an operating lease and under current accounting rules does not need to be capitalised on the balance sheet. This is subject to the auditors' approval, but leasing companies believe that it can be demonstrated that the risks and rewards of ownership are substantially transferred.
6 Tax relief can be obtained owing to the capital allowances in the building. These allowances can be passed on to the vendor through the rentals paid, or directly. Most new office buildings have between 20 and 30 per cent of their

costs in plant and machinery, and with 25 per cent writing down allowances, a significant reduction in a company's tax bill is achievable.

7 Stamp duty will be charged on the transfer of the property, which will be payable by the vendor.
8 Detailed analyses of tax, accounting and regulatory position will have to be undertaken prior to devising a structure that is suitable for a particular vendor.

Advantages

Leasing company

1 As owner of the building, they can use the capital allowances to offset taxable profits.
2 Leasing companies make money by lending money, and those transactions would be perceived as a good credit risk due to the asset backing and quality of the covenants involved.

The vendor company

1 The market rent is typically below the variable interest rate normally payable.
2 The leasing company will pass some of the benefits back to the company via a lower rent.
3 The company can benefit from any capital appreciation by repurchasing the property at each fifth year.
4 The transaction may give accounting benefits.

Summary

A finance lease is a sale and leaseback arrangement to a leasing company with rental payments linked to the interest rate and level of capital repayment. Other features and benefits that can be incorporated include the following:

1 Option to repurchase at each fifth year
2 May be classified as an off-balance sheet structure (see comments above)
3 Interest rates are charge typically well below market levels due to the efficient use by the leasing company of capital allowances, which reduce interest rates by between 2 and 3 per cent.
4 A non-taxpayer that is unable to use the capital allowances available can pass these to a third party and obtain the benefit.

Target clients for finance leases

1 Non-tax paying bodies
2 Top 200 UK companies
3 Major international companies
4 Major property investors

A finance lease is a real alternative to a straight disposal and can give the vendor an opportunity to repurchase the property and benefit from any capital appreciation. As mentioned earlier, such leases have been subject to changes in accounting rules (see Chapter 13).

5.6   Types of debt

Debt for project financing can be divided up into three types depending on the duration of the loan:

- short-term bridging finance
- medium-term loans and senior debt
- long-term mortgages.

These types are outlined in the rest of this chapter and in more detail in Chapter 7 on debt.

Refinancing debt

Refinancing problems in the market can arise out of problems in the investment market as investment property is the primary security for refinancing. The quality and spread of tenants, the term and review pattern of the leases are all crucial in reassuring a bank that a company will achieve acceptable levels of cash flow from a property in the medium term. Uncompleted or unlet development property is almost unrefinancable unless there are substantial amounts of additional equity available (Clarke 1990).

5.7   Bridging finance

This is up to a 3-year loan. Interest is rolled up until the development is sold and thus the developer must be able to pay the interest and principal on completion of the development. This would be done by selling the scheme or refinancing the bridging finance with long-term loans.

Commercial banks would require:

(a) security over and above project, i.e. other assets which are not charged;
(b) an interest rate of 2–4 per cent above base (LIBOR).

Commercial banks are not interested in an equity stake. Merchant banks may only require the project as security, but will charge 4–6 per cent above base and want an equity share (profits share).

Bridging finance can be provided as a complete funding package, the interim funding being replaced by a buy-out. Interim funding is provided at a rate between the short-term borrowing rate and the investment yield.

Bridging finance is also used in the very short term (i.e., repayable in 6 months or less) to cover the period between buying one property and selling another, or as an equity release pending refinance or sale. This market is dominated by clearing banks and the specialist lenders. As the market for bridging loans grew, several consortium lenders entered the market: Home Bridging plc, Cavendish Group plc and Berkeley Bridging. The collapse of the property market in the late 1980s took its toll on these lenders (Freed 1992).

Types of bridging finance (Freed 1992)

Closed bridging

Here, one property is bought and another sold but the dates do not coincide. Lenders have a first charge on the new property and a second charge on the old, subject to a total exposure of, say, 75 per cent of all value.

Open bridging

This is used when the existing property is unsold before exchanging contracts on the new property. This is useful for 'chain-breaking'. The security is not as good as for closed bridging. There is a lower loan to value ratio (say, 60–70 per cent).

Bridging for acquisition

This is used when there is a need for a rapid acquisition. The bridging loan is used to complete while putting together a long-term loan at leisure. This is popular with developers and property traders where the purchaser expects to effect a sale in the bridging period.

Bridging pending sale

This is used when equity release is required, perhaps for business/accounting reasons. It uses the same principle as underwriting, enabling rapid refinancing.

Bridging for refinancing

This is used when the borrower is in arrears with a conventional loan or unable to release equity with an existing lender. A new long-term lender is found to replace the bridging loan.

Factors in granting a bridging loan

1 The loan to cost ratio or loan to value ratio should be in the range of 60–70 per cent depending on security and the nature of the borrower.
2 The rate of interest to be applied would be 2–5 per cent over LIBOR, whether a fixed or floating rate.
3 The duration of the loan will be a factor (i.e., whether for the whole of the development period or not).
4 Whether interest is to be paid at intervals or rolled up (added at monthly or quarterly intervals to the outstanding loan balance).
5 Whether additional collateral or guarantees are required, such as a personal guarantee.
6 Whether additional charges need to be made by the bank, such as commitment or facility fees or service charges.
7 What monitoring procedures are in place.

5.8   Loan terms and financial agreements

In structuring the financial arrangement, the funder will aim to control certain aspects of the scheme, including:

(a) the criteria by which tenants are selected and leasehold terms agreed;
(b) negotiations conducted and agreements concluded with third parties;
(c) entry by the developer into any legal agreements such as planning gains with the local authority and consequent liability if the developer defaults;
(d) the nature and level of indemnity policies and collateral warranties held or offered by the developer, the professional team, the contractor and sub-contractors, so that in the event of failure, the developer can be dismissed and the funder can assume full authority for the completion of the scheme;
(e) tax implications of the project;
(f) the method of which the final purchase price of the completed project is agreed.

Practical problems may arise from the wording of financial agreements and some are listed below (Ratcliffe 1984).

1 Design documentation attached to the agreement should clearly and precisely set out the objectives of the scheme.
2 A developer is well advised to try to restrict the number of outside consultants whom the funder appoints to act – usually as advisers – on his behalf for the project (a single firm of surveyors should be enough).
3 The need to obtain written approval for the appointment of sub-contractors should be avoided by agreeing a list of nominated sub-contractors.
4 A clear understanding of the definition of the date of practical completion should be established; where possible, the site visits of the developer's architect and the fund's surveyor should be synchronised.
5 The date when the funder finally values the scheme and payment is made should be explicit, and should not depend on the actions of third parties.
6 Access to the site by the funder's surveyors, and facilities to inspect and test materials and workmanship, should be kept within reasonable bounds.
7 A procedure for arbitration should be agreed.
8 It may be necessary for the developer to consider the inclusion of a 'walkabout' clause so that the developer can approach other sources of finance if a top-up of funds is required.
9 Some mitigation should be allowed for delays that extend the completion date beyond that agreed, especially where such delays are beyond the developer's control.

5.9   Syndicated loans

This is where a group of lenders combine on large loans that would be too expensive or too risky for one lender to take on. Thus, the lenders diversify their loan books in respect of a number of loans on various assets to restrict the risk of being too heavily involved in any one. The loan is arranged and then syndicated by the lead banks. The syndicating bank may not be involved in the actual loan but may charge fees for underwriting the loan.

A typical 'syndicated loan' has the following characteristics (Fielding and Besser 1991):

(a) the bank with which the borrower has developed his relationship underwrites the loan and, in most cases, actually lends the monies;
(b) the loan agreement is drafted as an advance syndicated loan agreement, enabling the original lending bank to transfer to other banks tranches of the original loan;
(c) the asset teams of the original lending bank then sells off tranches of the loan in the banking market, the original lender acting as agent bank.

5.10   Mortgages

In the 1960s, fixed interest mortgages were used to finance the expansion of many of the large property companies. Interest rates were low and repayments could be serviced from rents. Because of the difference between cost and value, projects could be 100 per cent financed.

For instance, in a *new development*:

Rents	£100,000 p.a.
Yield @ 6.5 per cent	15.38
Capital Value	£1,538,000
Max. mortgage @ 60 per cent Capital Value	£922,800
Cost of development	£900,000
Mortgage repayments @ 8.5 per cent over 25 years on cost	£88,000 p.a.
Less rental income	£100,000 p.a.
Surplus income to developer	£12,000 p.a.

Note: (i)   Developer has 100 per cent funding;
  (ii) Developer has income surplus from day 1;
  (iii) Developer takes *all* increase on review.

Nowadays, inflation has undermined the use of the mortgage funding. The position is very different now where developers indulge in deficit financing, and where rents do not cover repayments until the first review. Mortgages are generally 10–25 years with an advance of up to two-thirds of the valuation. The interest rate is gilts (government security rate) plus, say, 1.5 per cent.

Repaying a mortgage

There are three common ways of repaying a mortgage and this applies to residential owner-occupier mortgages also:

1 The equal instalments or annualised repayment method, which involves regular repayments comprised of part capital and part interest (see Figure 5.1)

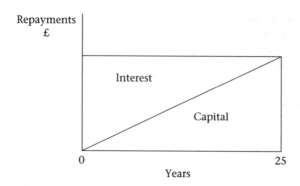

Figure 5.1   Conventional mortgage

2 The capital and interest method, which requires equal annual repayments of capital plus interest on the diminishing outstanding debt. The instalments are higher in the earlier years than in the later ones. The initial net costs are high, allowing for interest relief, but they decrease uniformly over the mortgage period.

3 A non-profit endowment mortgage, which can be taken out so that at the end of the loan period, the amount produced by the policy may be sufficient to repay the original loan. In the intervening period, interest is paid on the debt and regular monthly premiums are invested in the endowment policy. The costs remain high through the duration of the mortgage period as the outstanding capital remains constant, but tax relief may be allowable on the interest payment.

If annual repayments cannot be serviced from income, there may be a number of measures that could be taken:

- interest only payments could be made for a period (no capital repayment in this time)
- interest holiday: the interest is rolled up (no capital or interest payment for period)
- balloon repayment: interest only payment; capital is all repaid at the end of the period
- a variable rate of interest which is stepped up as income increases (say, from rental growth)
- partial capital repayment is made in the period so that most of the repayment is interest
- have a smaller loan and extend the period of repayment
- give equity participation to lender.

5.11   Non-recourse and limited recourse loans

Here, the loan is made solely against the security of a specific project and thus the lender has no rights to recourse to obtain other assets of the borrower if the loan goes wrong. This may be done by making a loan to a subsidiary of a company that holds the single property on its books. This property is the asset over which the lender takes charge. Because the loan to value ratio is less than 100 per cent, the balance is made up by monies provided by the parent company. Limited recourse exists where the lender provides 100 per cent finance but has some additional security or limited guarantee from the parent company. A non-recourse loan limits the liability of the parent company to the project by the extent of a cash investment or the extent of the limited guarantee. Full non-recourse is very rare and lenders will include clauses to cover interest and principal guarantees and obligations to refinance. Thus, the true non-recourse loan is given to a developer who has no other assets than those already committed to the development being financed. The costs of such loans can be 50 per cent or more than that of a recourse loan. The advantages for a larger developer are that the loan may be taken 'off-balance sheet' but these opportunities are restricted by law. By doing this, in theory the debt ratio of the parent company is unaffected, thus enabling it to finance several schemes at once.

A system of limited recourse funding that is off-balance sheet was developed in the late 1980s. The *property* being developed in this case has again become the principal source of repayment, whereas in the past the property loan has been to a *developer but which has been secured on the property*. If the outcome of the development is a successful one, then the bank lender would seek to structure a loan based on a percentage of value (typically 65–70 per cent). It would then undertake to the borrower that it would only seek repayment from the refinancing or sale of the development and not from the borrower. The bank would expect 10–20 per cent of development costs (the difference between the loan amount and the anticipated total cost of completing the project) to be contributed by the developer. The developer would contribute any additional costs incurred in excess of the loan amount in order that the development might be completed and let prior to refinancing. The amount of equity required to be injected by the developer would depend on the level of underlying risk. The bank lender would believe that the 30–35 per cent difference between the completed value and the total loan provides a sufficient cushion for risk.

The structure of a typical limited-recourse bank construction loan is as follows (the basic principles are accepted by all the main property lending banks). The bank will lend a hardcore of the total development costs without recourse to the developer, but committing the borrower or third party, if the developer is not strong enough, to contribute all the other costs. It is prudent to ask for the injection of developer's equity at the start. With a strong developer, it may be possible to put some up at the beginning whilst guaranteeing to put up the rest at the end after the bank facility has been exhausted. There is a need to have some equity at the beginning or the developer could walk away if things get problematic.

5.12 Project management fee

This is not very popular. Here, the fund acquires the site and employs the development team. The developer acts as a project manager for a fee plus a bonus if the scheme is successful. The developer arranges all the finance to be provided from the start and this includes the bonus. The site is handed over to a funding institution which then acquires the site, employs the professional team (with the developer acting as project manager for a fee) and provides all the development finance. The attraction to the developers is that the financial risk is minimised and instead they are paid an attractive fee. The fee will reflect an element of commission or reward for introducing the project to the institution. The developer may also have carried out initial studies, with designs and costings from an architect and quantity surveyor operating on a contingency basis (no deal, no fee) but looking to be instructed by the institution if the development is taken up. There is very little incentive in a scheme like this to encourage the developer to maximise return and thus an additional bonus may be added on (say, a share of rental over the expected level: Darlow 1988). Project management can take many forms and it is outside the scope of this book to discuss these. In many cases, a straight fee rather than an additional bonus is paid.

5.13   Contractor's finance

Construction companies are key operators in the property development process as the companies actually construct the buildings in accordance with the form of contract and building procurement arrangement agreed. Construction companies will also undertake development themselves, usually through a development company subsidiary. Construction companies may also act as a source of finance for the developer. Often joint venture arrangements are organised between the developer and contractor.

References and further reading

Clarke, R. J. (1990) 'Refinancing', *Journal of Property Finance*, 1(3), 435–9.
Cohen, P. (1992) 'Non-recourse Property Funding', *Journal of Property Finance*, 3(3), 319–24.
Darlow, C. (1988) 'Direct Project Funding', in C. Darlow (ed.), *Valuation and Development Appraisal*, Estates Gazette, London.
Fielding, M. and Besser, A. (1991) 'Syndicated loans – *caveat* borrower', *Estates Gazette*, 15 June, 78 and 103.
Fox, J. W. W. (1993) 'Sale and Leasebacks: A Case Study', *Journal of Property Finance*, 4(1), 9–12.
Freed, N. (1992) 'Bridging Finance', *Journal of Property Finance*, 3(2), 187–90.
Orchard-Lisle, P. (1987) 'Financing Property Development', *Journal of Valuation*, 5(4), 343–53.
Ratcliffe, J. (1984) 'Development Financing: Drawing up the Agreement', *Architects Journal*, 22 and 29 August, 63.
Savills (1989) *Financing Property 1989*, Savills, London.

6
Corporate Finance

6.1 Introduction

The two areas of corporate finance relate to debt capital (or loans) and equity capital (or shares). Equity finance is capital paid into or kept in the business by the shareholders, the owners of the business. It is long-term capital and carries the greater risk and attracts the higher returns. Debt finance is money invested in the business by third parties, usually for a shorter period of time than equity and carrying a lower risk and lower return.

Corporate finance is related to the financial structure of the company itself. Choosing the right mix of debt and equity capital that meets the investment requirement of a business is a key financial management decision. There are four strategic issues here (Pike and Neale 1998):

1 *Risk* – There is enormous uncertainty in the business environment. Considerations about risk will cover how the firm would deal with a downturn in business or the economy.
2 *Ownership* – The ownership of the firm is critical; it is important to know who exercises the current control over the company, as a desire to retain control will affect financing decisions. The desire to retain control may mean that borrowing is preferred to raising equity capital.
3 *Duration* – Finance should match the use to which it is put. Finance for investments with no returns in the early years should be raised so there are no payments in these years. One should not raise long-term finance for a short life programme; the firm will be overcapitalised and will not generate sufficient return to repay the finance.
4 *Debt capacity* – The ability to borrow more depends on the existing level of borrowing. This also depends on the type of business and the sector of operation.

The balance sheet model of the firm (see Figure 1.2) can be used to analyse the sources of cash available to the corporate structure. The basic sources of cash for the firm are as set out below:

1 *Shareholders' funds* – The largest proportion of long-term finance is usually provided by shareholders and is termed equity capital. Share ownership lies at the

heart of modern capitalism. By purchasing a portion of or share in a company, almost anyone can become a shareholder with some degree of control over a company. Ordinary share capital is the main source of new money from shareholders. They are entitled to participate in the business through voting in a general meeting of the shareholders and also to receive dividends out of the profits. As owners of the business, the ordinary shareholders bear the greatest risk but enjoy the main fruits of success in the form of higher dividends and capital gains.

2 *Retained profits* – For an established business, the main source of equity funds will be internally generated from successful trading. Any profits remaining after all operating costs, interest payments, taxation and dividends are reinvested in the business (i.e., ploughed back) and regarded as part of the equity capital.

3 *Loan capital* – Money lent to the business by third parties is debt finance or loan capital. Most companies borrow money on a long-term basis by issuing stocks or debentures. The supplier of the loan will specify the amount of loan, rate of interest, date of payment and method of repayment. The finance manager will monitor the long-term financial structure by examining the relationship between loan capital, where interest and loan repayments are contractually obligatory, and ordinary share capital, where the dividend payment is at the discretion of the directors. This relationship between debt and equity is called gearing (known in the USA as leverage). Strictly, gearing is the proportion of debt capital to total capital in the firm.

The three sources of cash mentioned above are matched by three uses of cash in the firm:

1 Cash is used to service (pay returns to) the main sources of finance. Dividends are paid to shareholders; interest is paid to lenders along with any repayment of the loan due. Tax is paid on the profits earned.

2 Cash is invested in long-term assets such as building and plant, to produce goods or services. The investment decisions made in respect of these long-term assets are critical for the success of the company.

3 Cash is also used to pay for materials, labour, overheads and costs incurred in producing the goods or services offered to customers. It is also used to purchase stocks of raw materials, work in progress, finished goods and debtors. In a property trading company, these current assets would also include properties and developments in the process of completion held for trading. Current assets in a firm are offset by the current liabilities that are amounts owing to suppliers of goods and services.

The main ways in which a property company could increase its capital include the issue of:

- debenture stock
- loan stock
- preference shares
- ordinary shares.

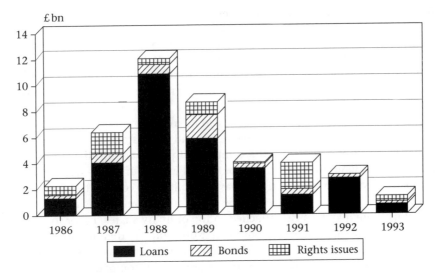

Figure 6.1 Savills Indicator of loans, bonds and rights issues
Note: 1993 to April only
Source: Savills (1993a).

These instruments are described later on. As a general introduction, it is important first to look at issues relating to the difference between debt and equity. Equity investments in a company usually come in the form of share ownership and, in this chapter, types of share, including their issue arrangements, are discussed. In addition, there is a summary of debt approaches related to corporate finance. These sections need to be cross-read with the sections on equity and debt to obtain a more detailed picture. The use of different types of corporate finance can be gauged from the Savills Indicator that relates to the amount of loans, bonds and rights issues over the period 1986–93 (the period of boom and slump in the UK property cycle), as shown in Figure 6.1.

6.2 Equity finance

Equity finance in the form of direct investment and partnership will be discussed in Chapter 8. The distinction between debt and equity is hazy when considered in the context of loans with conversion rights to shares and mezzanine finance, a halfway house between debt and equity. In this chapter, when dealing with corporate finance, the distinction is:

Equity	*Debt*
Ordinary shares	Debentures
Preference shares	Loan stock
Warrants	Bonds
Options	General facilities
Converted stock	Convertible stock

6.3   Ordinary and preference shares

The equity of a company consists of ordinary shares, and shareholders participate in the profits of a company once prior demands have been met; these prior demands for payment will include creditors (trade creditors), holders of debt and preference shareholders. If a company finds that the total of accumulated and retained profits in the company's reserves have grown in relation to issued capital, then a script or capitalisation issue can be made.

Preference shares rank after debentures and loan stock but before ordinary shares in terms of a charge to the company. If profits are insufficient to pay the fixed rate dividend, then arrears can be carried forward if the preference share is a cumulative type. Conversion rights may be available to convert the shares to ordinary capital. This sort of share may be set up if the company is a new company and thus there may be a risk attached to the ordinary shares. If, for instance, the company is a management buy-out or start-up company then it may attract 'venture' capital (i.e., risk-taking capital used to finance new business opportunities). In this case, the investor may wait some years for the company and its cash flow to stabilise before converting the fixed return preference share to an ordinary share. Preference shares are unsecured so, if no profits are made, no dividend will be paid, but if they are cumulative they can carry forward the payment due, as indicated above. The characteristics of preference shares are thus:

- more secure than ordinary shares
- less secure than debentures or loan stock
- return is from a fixed rate dividend payable from profits
- unsecured
- can be cumulative or non-cumulative
- can be voting or non-voting shares (but rarely are voting)
- can be convertible or not convertible into ordinary shares.

The priority of charge against the profits of the company is simply:

(a) debentures and loan stock;
(b) preference shares;
(c) ordinary shares.

6.4   Issues and options

Company shares, together with other securities such as government bonds and stocks and the loan stock of public authorities, are traded on the Stock Exchange. The Stock Exchange arose out of the need to deal in the shares of joint-stock companies that originated in the seventeenth century. By pooling of risk, combination of resources and the development of limited liability, these companies expanded and created the requirement of transferability of capital. Owners of shares or loan capital in the companies required a market to sell their holdings, otherwise the original investment would not have been attractive. The stock market is thus a secondary market for investment in the sense of reselling shares and securities, but it is also a primary market as a source of new funds.

The primary market operates for new issues and, where a company is seeking a listing on the Stock Exchange, it will need to be represented by a broking firm. The broking firm will advise on the company's prospectus and the issue price. The Bank of England controls large issues to programme the timing of such issues. Underwriting is arranged so that if the stock is advertised but not fully taken up, the underwriters take up the undersubscription. This new issue procedure is called a prospectus issue, but other methods exist such as an offer for sale, a placing and a rights issue. In 1983, more than 100 property companies were listed on the London Stock Exchange and at the beginning of 1983 the market value of the 42 major property companies monitored by brokers Rowe & Pitman exceeded £4.27 billion. By the end of 1993, 118 companies were listed by the *Financial Times* in their property section; the Datastream analysis of property companies in their sample had a total market capitalisation in excess of £13 billion. This figure appears to be the same as that quoted by Millman in 1988 (Millman 1988), although the sample may be different. The main features of a property company that would be considered by an investor would be: the quality of assets; the quality of management; sources of income; capital structure and financing. The quality of assets is dependent on the portfolio composition and the location, age and tenure of individual properties within the portfolio. The quality of management is very much a subjective judgement and may in fact be related to the persona of the founder or managing director of the company. Sources of income to property companies vary greatly between investment companies reliant on rent and development companies reliant on the capital gains from the sale of completed developments. Capital structure is important from the point of view of the investor, as a highly geared financial structure is more appropriate for established companies deriving a large proportion of revenue from rental income than for development companies dependent on less secure trading profits.

New public property companies created since the 1960s have rarely gone through the expensive process of obtaining a full listing on the stock market. A quoted property company may emerge from an existing company whose manufacturing or trading activities have declined or been sold off or a company may be bought as a shell into which property assets are transferred. Another alternative, which was popular, was to obtain a quotation on the Unlisted Securities Market (USM); this, however, has been suspended at the time of writing.

The advantages of property shares over direct investment lie in two general areas. First, equity investments generally provide a means of investing in very small units and denominations and thus risk can be spread. Equity investments can also be traded easily in the stock market at low costs of transfer. Thus, beside the liquidity advantage, trading takes place in a market characterised by almost perfect knowledge where share prices are known. The second area of advantage relates to the nature of property itself. The advantages of durability and its effectiveness as a hedge against inflation are clearly seen. As the shares of property companies are based on income arising from rents, these companies are perceived as providing a higher degree of income security than other equities (Debenham, Tewson & Chinnocks 1984).

Raising corporate funds

The aim of this section is to analyse further recent development in the property company sector and to understand why equity capital is important in the present state of the market. Historically, property companies grew in the postwar years because of the ability to obtain funds at low interest rates. It is important to recognise the relationship of low interest rates to higher inflation rates to understand property company growth. Basically, if the cost of a development was, say, two-thirds of its value, then the total cost could be covered by mortgage funds. If the mortgage interest rate was, say, 7 per cent and the yield 6 per cent, it can easily be seen that from the completion of the scheme, using 100 per cent borrowed funds, the developer not only owned one-third of the value but could retain this equity as his return (at 6 per cent) covered his interest payments (at 7 per cent on two-thirds of the capital, say, 4.7 per cent). Further, with growth, the value of the property and the level of rents increase but as interest rates are static, then the return to the developer increases dramatically over time because of the gearing effect. (With a 5 per cent compound growth rate over 5 years, the return to the developer would have increased to 7.66 per cent on the original capital value.)

The purpose of the above analysis is to understand the position of present day development funding. Because interest rates have been high relative to the rate of inflation, it is difficult to finance developments using long-term money. Real interest rates had been positive and over 4 per cent for most of the mid-1980s, a state of events that had not existed for this long since the 1930s (Scrimgeour Vickers & Co. 1986). Thus, in the late 1970s and early 1980s, many developers became 'merchant developers' and 'traders', using short-term monies and selling on the completed development to institutions. This analysis is a simplification of a number of different phases that have been evident in the market as institutional influence increased and property crashed in 1974–75. By 1983, because of the changes in interest rates, a number of established property companies had provided for their financial needs by raising cash from their shareholders by the issue of ordinary shares or convertible stock. Land Securities raised £100 million in 1980 and MEPC raised £30 million of 35-year debenture money (Brett 1983b). After 1983, the debenture market continued to raise large sums, and the latter half of 1985 alone saw £220 million raised with coupons (interest) around the 10.5 per cent mark (Scrimgeour Vickers & Co 1986):

		£ million
July 1985	Evans of Leeds	12
August	Brixton Estates	15
October	Hampton Court	10
October	Peachey	20
November	Haslemere	100
November	Land Securities	40
December	Rosehaugh Greycoat Estates	15
December	Allied London Estates Agency	8
		£220 million

In the late 1980s, there was an ongoing need to raise corporate funds because of a shortage of funds in the markets due to institutional absence. The institutional lack of enthusiasm had been caused by the lack of performance of the property sector compared to equities since 1979/80 and limited evidence of satisfactory growth. Basically, the institutions had bid down initial yields on purchase to unrealistically low levels and the growth of the overall institutional portfolio was insufficient to provide the target return. Thus, there was an institutional oversupply of funds which moved yields to historically low levels because of the scarcity of new buildings (Cadman and Catalano 1983). Study of property prices and yields relative to all shares for the period 1968–86 indicates how the institutions, as well as depressing direct yields, also had the same effect on property share yields. Other research has also shown that the yield of the pension funds' portfolio over the ten years to 1985 had been depressed by the inclusion of property (Graham 1985). By the early 1990s, institutions were still avoiding the property markets.

Whilst institutional finance is still important in the longer term, alternative sources are increasingly providing both equity and debt finance for the construction phase or medium-term finance, perhaps up to the first rent review. Investment trusts, venture capitalists and various corporate entities have provided finance together with short- or medium-term bank debt. Medium- and long-term financing has generally centred upon mortgages or debentures. This finance has been in the form of loans varying in term between 10 and 40 years with fixed rate, floating rate or 'drop-lock' interest options and capital repayment holidays. Traditionally, this form of funding has been applied more to income-producing property rather than speculative development, but in recent years, medium-term mortgage and debenture arrangements have been used to redeem construction loans. The problem of replacing long-term institutional finance in the development buy-out is a difficult one. If there is a shortfall of rent against interest charges, then the developer will need to await rental growth for a positive return.

Issues and options

There are a number of different ways of issuing shares: for instance, a new issue can be introduced to the market (i.e., sold to existing shareholders); this does not create much of an interest to the public at large. As an alternative, there can be a placing where shares are sold privately to a number of brokers. Finally, there can be an offer for sale. Companies are launched on the Stock Exchange, which is the main dealing area. The Unlisted Securities Market that once formed the secondary market is now defunct. A summary of different methods of issuing shares in the UK in shown in Box 6.1.

An option gives the owner of the option the right to buy a share in the future at a price that is fixed at the time of purchase of the option. This is strictly a 'call' option that empowers the owner to do something. A 'put' option gives you the right to sell to someone else at a predetermined price. Options are traded on the Traded Options Market. To purchase an option, you need to take a view on how the value of the asset you have taken an option on will move over a period of time. For example, you may purchase an option for, say, 10p to purchase shares in A,

Box 6.1   Summary of different methods of issuing shares in the UK

Public issue by prospectus – This uses an issuing house as an agent and attempts to persuade investors to buy shares in the shortest possible time. Superseded by the offer for sale method.

Offer for sale – This is used when a large amount of capital is required. The issuing house, acting as principal, offers the shares at a fixed price. A detailed prospectus is issued and the offer is extensively advertised. In the event of an oversubscription, the issuing house allots the available share to the applicants. To ensure that a ready market exists as many applications as possible get some shares, so applications for large holdings usually obtain only a small proportion of shares applied for and small applications are settled in full.

Private placing – This can be used by unquoted companies who require a small amount of funds with the minimum of issue costs. Normally, an issuing house agrees to purchase a number of shares in the company with the intention of placing them with institutional investors.

Stock exchange introduction – This does not raise additional finance but allows the company to obtain a stock exchange quotation.

Stock exchange placing – This is a combination of a private placing and a stock exchange introduction. The company will need both a quotation and a small amount of capital that is raised from institutional investors.

Issues by tender – These are used when there is some uncertainty over the issue price. A minimum price is set and the public bid for the shares. Allotments are made at the price that will just clear all the shares, known as the striking price.

Source: Asch and Kaye (1989).

say, at 120p on the basis that the shares are worth 100p now but you think they will rise to 150p. If the shares do not increase in price, then the option has no value. If the share price rises, then you will make a profit by purchasing under the option and reselling the shares. You would, however, need to clear 130p before making a profit. If the share price does not increase over 130p, then you have lost money. Traded options in the market usually have a life of 9 months.

Options are not created by the company; rather, the market is created by the owners of the shares. A warrant is different because it is issued by the company which issued the shares. Instead of issuing shares, the company may issue warrants giving the rights to subscribe for new shares in the future. Thus, put and call options generally give the holder the right to buy or sell shares at a given exercise price. A call option is a right to buy and a put option is a right to sell. American options can be exercised at any time up to and including the expiration date. European options are only exercisable at the expiration date. The valuation of the option depends on the price of the underlying assets, the exercise price, the expiration date, the variability of the underlying asset and the risk-free interest rate:

Value of share + Value of put − Value of call = Present value of exercise price
(Ross, Westerfield and Jaffe 1993)

Finally, to clarify types of issue, we should distinguish between a new issue (by an offer for sale, introduction or placing) and a rights issue, where a company issues new shares for cash. In the latter case, they are offered first to existing shareholders, perhaps on the basis of 'so many' shares related to their existing holding.

This needs to be compared with a scrip issue. A rights issue will increase the shareholders' funds and the issued capital. A scrip issue or capitalisation issue is an issue of shares from revenue reserves where the existing share capital is small compared to the shareholders' funds. So, accumulated profits have built up in the company and this is a process of distributing them. Note, however, that no new money is involved in the process, because the net asset value of the company is the same; this is merely a redistribution of the capital in the company. Whilst the shares are issued to shareholders free, pro rata on the basis of their existing holdings, the price of the shares will fall to reflect this (Brett 1990b).

Rights issues

For property companies quoted on the Stock Exchange, it is possible to raise extra capital through rights issues, an issue of shares offered to existing shareholders' in proportion to their existing shareholdings. In order to persuade the shareholders to buy the shares, they are offered at a discount to the current market price. Shares that are not subscribed to by the holders to whom they have been offered must be sold on the market for the benefit of those holders.

The concept behind a rights issue can be explained by the following example. Company X has 1 million 25p shares in issue with a current market price of 150p. It makes a rights issue of one new share for every four held at 100p. A shareholder with four shares has an investment worth £6. If the shareholder takes up the rights issue, the ownership is:

4 shares at the original market value	£6.00
1 share at cost	£1.00
Total: 5 shares worth	£7.00

Thus, each share is worth £1.40.

This final price is called the theoretical ex-rights price, since it excludes the right to the next dividend.

Capital issues were very popular with the quoted property companies until the stock market crash in October 1987; the funds raised through such issues were very often used to repay short-term debt. Capital issues over the period 1980–88 increased from around £200 million in 1980 to a peak of £1.6 billion in 1987 and this reduced to around £400 million in 1988. In this period, some property companies financed their short-term debt through the issuance of debenture stock that was attractive to institutions because of the shortage of long-dated gilts. Increases in share prices in 1992 have led to the re-rating of property companies on the Stock Exchange. Property company shares in 1993 were then standing at a premium to net asset value estimated on average to be 21 per cent. This re-rating enabled new capital right issues to be issued, amounting to over £1 billion from March to October 1993. All the well known property companies had been involved in these issues in 1993 including MEPC, Hammerson, Brixton Estates, Slough Estates and British Land (Savills 1993b).

Real options

A relatively different approach to investment theory has been the use of real options. As we have seen, an option is a contract in which the seller of the option (called the writer) gives the buyer the right, for a certain sum of money, to buy from or sell to the option writer a specified amount of assets at a fixed price or exercise price within a specified period. A right to buy is a call option whilst a right to sell is a put option. Decisions related to property investment or development decisions can be considered as options. The development of the theory is best seen in terms of site development or property refurbishment. The site could be developed immediately or left for a period of time, and thus the development of the site could be viewed as an option to purchase one of a number of different buildings at exercise prices which could represent the various construction costs. The parallel can equally be considered for dealing with investment property. This form of appraisal captures the rights and the flexibility associated with decision-making: that is, that value could be enhanced or depressed not just by the nature of the development but also the timing of the decision. The essence of understanding real options is the fact that the approach exposes the value of flexibility in a world of uncertainty and change. The flexibility to commence or delay construction, to abandon or continue development, to expand or contract operations, to buy or sell, to increase or decrease exposure are valuable rights which are reflected in this approach (Ong and Brown 2001). The main hypothesis in real option models is that uncertainty creates option value; if this is correct, then we would expect to observe higher land prices when investment uncertainty rises. The problems, however, lie in the application of real options in practice. Lucius (2001) indicates some of these:

1 There are problems related to the limited divisibility of property and the levels of transaction costs; these issues affect the assumptions of a perfect real estate market.
2 There are difficulties with the heterogeneity of property assets which affect the analysis; in particular, there are problems in the construction of a 'twin' security, which is required in option theory as at the date of the valuation.
3 There are also other additional critical essential differences between financial and real options.

The real options approach recognises entrepreneurial flexibility and risk explicitly. The opportunity to invest is much like a financial call option where a person has the right but not the obligation to invest in an asset at a future time chosen. When investing in an asset, the person then exercises the option. To relate financial and real options, the asset's cash flow needs to be replicable in financial markets.

In general, the practical application of real options is still being developed but the approach certainly leads to some very different conclusions. Lucius suggests that traditional investment theory defines real estate as a triangle of space, money and time. Particular usage is attributed to a defined space that generates an estimated cash flow over a specific period of time. Here, there is a relatively deterministic understanding of real estate, where immobility and inflexibility are features of the analysis. These features give an impression of certainty that appears then to make the analysis suitable for traditional discounted cash flow approaches. However, with uncertainty, the traditional methods become less safe. Traditional valuation methods thus undervalue alternative decision-making whereas the real option view can introduce flexibility and variability. The real option approach supplements the weaknesses of traditional valuation methods by adding an option value to a solely NPV (net present value) based static value of an investment project.

In practice, if we consider the accept/reject decision-making of the NPV approach, we are making a decision to proceed or not with a project but, if rejected, the project will not then disappear. A property developer who purchases a site or an investor who purchases a property that can be enhanced by good management and capital expenditure is not just buying the opportunity for a one-off investment: the purchasers in both cases are buying rights to the investment. For the developer, such a right would be the opportunity to delay construction. As Brown and Matysiak (2000) suggest, a number of further opportunities may arise if construction is delayed:

- rental value and thus capital value of the project may increase
- alternative uses for the site may become feasible and thus add value
- interest rates and construction and other costs may fall, making the project more profitable.

Each of these can be considered a call option and every project will consist of two types of option; one relates to economic changes in the context of the project that will affect financial outcomes, and the second relates to changes in interest rates. The presence of options thus enhances the value of the project as follows:

$$\text{Total asset value} = \text{Net present value} + \text{Value of real option} + \text{Value of interest rate option}$$

6.5 Warrants and convertibles

A warrant gives the holder the right to buy shares of common stock at an exercise price for a given period of time. Typically, warrants are issued in a package with privately placed bonds. Afterwards, they become detached and are traded separately. A convertible bond is a combination of a straight bond and a call option. The holder can give up the bond in exchange for shares of stock. Convertible bonds and warrants are like call options but there are some important differences (Ross, Westerfield and Jaffe 1999):

1 Warrants and convertible securities are issued by companies. Call options are traded between individual investors. Warrants are usually issued privately and are combined with a bond. Warrants can usually be detached immediately after the issue. In some cases, warrants are issued with preference stock, common stock or executive compensation schemes. Thus, convertibles are bonds (debt) which can be converted into shares. Call options are sold separately.

2 Warrants and call options are exercised for cash, but the holder of the warrant gives no cash for the warrant and receives shares for a further cash payment.

So, a warrant is an 'option' giving the lender of the money the right to subscribe for shares at a given price. Although the price of a warrant is a fraction of the share price itself, in combination with the subscription price it will exceed the current market value of the shares. Thus, a premium is being paid for the right to subscribe at a fixed price in the future. Warrants in themselves do not provide capital for the company; they are a trading vehicle for investors (Gibbs 1987). Warrants are not often issued for cash but as a 'sweetener' to some other kind of issue, such as a fixed-interest bond.

Convertibles are basically debentures (see section 6.7) which have a right to switch to ordinary equity shares at a date in the future at a fixed price agreed at the date of sale and normally at a higher price than the market value at the time. The attraction to the lender is that a lower coupon can be attached to the stock. If a convertible element is detached from the stock, it is bought and sold separately as a warrant.

6.6 Debt

Debt can be applied to the corporate structure and can be seen simply in terms of the application of funds in a general funding situation where the criteria for the funding will be based on the status and assets of the borrower rather than for a specific project.

The lender will look at the borrower's accounts and will want to see:

- good quality property assets on modern leases
- a realistic development programme
- a good portfolio mix
- not all the assets pledged
- a healthy proportion of equity.

A general funding facility may be negotiated where the agreed sum is secured on the developer's assets. This allows the developer to have access to predetermined amounts of money over a given period of time. These loans may be 10–15 years in duration with an option to exercise in a shorter period (say, 5 years). This facility may be negotiated on the basis of an agreed interest rate. An example is given below of a drop-lock loan that may be used on such a facility but you are referred to section 4.9 for further information. In a drop-lock loan, the base interest rate is agreed and if the market rate of interest, which is assumed to be above at the commencement, falls to that level, it is locked in as a fixed rate; otherwise it will vary with the market rate. Two other conditions may also be imposed:

(a) if the market interest rate falls below the base rate agreed during the option period, the option can be exercised in reverse and the developer could be obliged to take up a tranche of cash at the rate which is locked for the term;

(b) if the developer takes up the loan before the predetermined base is reached, then the borrower has to pay a variable rate linked to the base rate until it falls to the base rate, when the loan is converted to a fixed rate.

Overdrafts are common for companies; developers will borrow from the bank to finance such short-term requirements as the interim payments to builders in the construction phase of a development. Borrowing from a clearing bank is traditionally on a short-term basis with a variable interest rate tied to a margin over the LIBOR rate. Companies with a large amount of bank finance will be vulnerable to rising interest rates and short-term recall of the funds by the bank. Merchant banks and finance houses are normally willing to lend on specific terms for up to several years but obviously such sources are more expensive (Fraser 1993).

Ooi (2000), in a study of UK property companies reliance on bank loans, found that bank borrowing constituted more than half of the total outstanding debt of the UK's quoted property sector at the time of the study. The research found that company size and credit risk were the prime determinants of holding a greater level of bank debt. In addition, institutional ownership also had a strong positive effect on reliance.

6.7 Debentures

Debentures, which are secured loans, are discussed in Chapter 7 in more detail. They are sealed bonds of a company acknowledging a debt on which interest is due until the principal is repaid. A debenture holder has a prior charge on the developer's corporate assets although in practice property company debentures are secured on specific assets. Interest is paid half-yearly and there are often trustees appointed to look after the debenture holders' interests. Debenture stock can be redeemable, non-redeemable or convertible. The advantages of debentures can be considered as follows (Gibbs 1987):

to developers
- money borrowed is not tied to a single project
- it is a charge against profits before tax

to investors
- it gives a higher rate of interest than gilts
- they are tradable securities
- there may be rights of conversion.

6.8 Loan stock and bonds

These are the same as debenture issues but may not be secured. The coupon (interest rate payable) is generally high but allows smaller developers to raise non-project-specific funds. Interest is paid half-yearly. Convertible loan stock has a slightly lower rate of interest but can be converted to ordinary shares at a fixed price at a stated date. If the right of subscription is detachable from the loan stock, this is a warrant and can be traded separately.

Bonds may have a low or nil interest rate and these are basically loan stock which are tradable; zero-coupon and deep-discounted bond issues are examples.

6.9   Structured finance

Finance can be structured as appropriate to the capital structure, the assets, cash flow and activities of a corporate client. Structured finance could include the following options as an example:

1 Bonds or loan stock, with a cumulative structure, which allows interest to be rolled up with the repayment at the end of the life of the bond;
2 Finance leasing, which enables the borrower to sell a property to a finance company, pay a 'market rent' and have the option to repurchase the building at the original purchase price plus any deferred interest;
3 Off-balance sheet funding which will reduce lenders' exposure on the balance sheet by restructuring loans outside their group holdings;
4 Capital market instruments, including interest caps, floors, swaps, and so on.

These options are considered in detail elsewhere; the intention of off-balance sheet funding is to reduce the level of debt in the company accounts. This improves the gearing, the ratio of equity finance to debt finance in the balance sheet and thus makes the company look more financially attractive. A case study showing the application of deep-discounted bonds in structured finance is shown in Box 6.2.

The use of various financial instruments has been the subject of regular surveys by Savills, the property consultants. After the mid-1980s, the range of financial

Box 6.2   Case study: structured finance

A medium-sized private company has an existing relationship with a clearing bank but no other banking relationships. It sees the falls in value in the property sector as an opportunity to buy high yielding investments but its clearing bank does not wish to increase its exposure to the company.

Financial information:

Various properties: some let/some vacant sites:	
capital value	£54,000,000
income p.a.	£2,900,000
ERV (estimated rental value) p.a.	£3,800,000
Clearing bank loan	£15,000,000
Net worth of company	£39,000,000

Problem

This is one of cash flow; the current income at £2.9 million will only service a loan of, say, £18 million. (The case study assumes rates in 1990.) Company overheads of £0.5 million are not covered by the present income after interest on the existing £15 million loan. Two of the properties are reversionary and thus would be good security for some kind of roll up/deep discount facility.

Solution

On the basis that these reversionary properties account for, say, £30 million of value and about £1.3 million of current income, it should be possible to raise around £20 million of initial loan with the interest shortfall rolled up and borrowings on a 5 year fixed or capped basis. This leaves £1.6 million (£2.9 million income less £1.3 million for the deep discount arrangement) to service overheads and additional debt. Assuming that the new properties purchased yield an initial 10 per cent, the company should have the capacity to borrow an additional £26.7 million and buy a further £31.7 million of property as follows:

Analysis   Available income   £1,600,000
                less overheads   £500,000
                                                                           £1,100,000

Available income + new income = new interest expense
£1.1 million + [0.10 × (*L* + £5 million)] = 0.16 × *L*
L = £26.7 million, where *L* = loan amount; the extra £5 million comes from the extra proceeds of the £20 million loan.

Source: Clarke (1990).

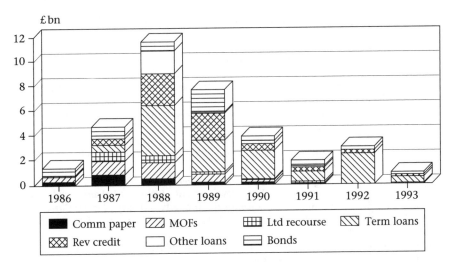

Figure 6.2   Savills Indicator of instrument usage

Note: 1993 to April. Rights issues excluded.
Comm paper = Commercial paper; MOFs = Multi-option Facilities; Rev credit = Revolving credit; Ltd recourse = Limited recourse

Source: Savills (1993a).

instruments used in corporate finance decreased, which was perhaps a reflection of the general state of the market and a move back to funding based on fundamental criteria rather than elaborate derivatives. The graph in Figure 6.2 shows the usage of various debt instruments in the period 1986–93; usage of rights issues was shown in Figure 6.1.

6.10   Hybrids: debt with a profit share

Development projects are funded generally by debt and equity. The senior debt will be 70 per cent of the cost of the project (or may be based on a loan to value ratio); the rest is made up by equity. If there is a shortfall, then this is filled by mezzanine debt, which is risky, or else by profit sharing arrangements. The mezzanine debt may be provided by the same institution as the senior debt or may be supplied by merchant banks or specialist lenders. Mezzanine finance has been discussed elsewhere, as have loans with a profit share. Profit sharing is a complex area looked at in Chapter 7. Quasi-equity is a term given to convertibles and warrants. Convertible bonds and warrant bonds were described in section 6.5. These instruments can be issued in the euromarkets. Another example is the convertible mortgage; this is looked at in section 7.5.

References and further reading

Asch, D. and Kaye, G. R. (1989) *Financial Planning: Modelling Methods and Techniques*, Kogan Paul, London.

Beveridge, J. A. (1991) 'New Methods of Financing', in P. Venmore-Rowland, P. Brandon and T. Mole (eds), *Investment, Procurement and Performance in Construction*, RICS, London.

Brett, M. (1983b) 'Indirect Investment in Property', in C. Darlow (ed.), *Valuation and Investment Appraisal, Estates Gazette,* London.

Brett, M. (1990b) *Property and Money, Estates Gazette,* London.

Brown, G. R. and Matysiak, G. A. (2000) *Real Estate Investment: A Capital Market Approach,* Pearson Education, Harlow.

Cadman, D. and Catalano, A. (1983) *Property Development in the UK – Evolution and Change,* College of Estate Management, Reading.

Clarke, R. J. (1990) 'Refinancing', *Journal of Property Finance,* 1(3), 435–9.

Debenham, Tewson & Chinnocks (1984) *Property Investment in Britain,* Debenham, Tewson & Chinnocks, London.

Fraser, W. D. (1993) *Principles of Property Investment and Pricing,* Macmillan, London.

Gibbs, R. (1987) 'Raising Finance for New Development', *Journal of Valuation,* 5(4), 343–53.

Graham, J. (1985) 'New sources of finance for the property industry', *Estates Gazette,* 6 July.

Lucius, D. I. (2001) 'Real options in real estate development', *Journal of Property Investment and Finance,* 19(1), 73–8.

Millman, S. (1988) 'Property, Property Companies and Public Securities', in S. L. Barter (ed.), *Real Estate Finance,* Butterworths, London.

Ong, S. E. and Brown, G. R. (2001) 'Editorial: What are real options', *Journal of Property Investment and Finance,* 19(1), 6–8.

Ooi, J. (2000) 'Corporate reliance on bank loans: and empirical analysis of UK property companies', *Journal of Property Investment and Finance,* 18(1), 103–20.

Pike, R. and Neale, B. (1999) *Corporate Finance and Investment: Decisions and Strategies,* Prentice-Hall, London.

Ross, S. A., Westerfield, R. W. and Jaffe, J. F. (1999) *Corporate Finance,* McGraw-Hill, London.

Savills (1993a) *Financing Property 1993,* Savills, London.

Savills (1993b) *Investment and Economic Outlook,* Savills, London, Issue 3, October.

Scrimgeor Vickers & Co. (1986) *United Kingdom Research, Annual Property Report,* Scrimgeor Vickers & Co., London.

7
Debt Finance

7.1 Introduction

A company can raise debt capital (loans) or equity capital through share issues. Share capital is basically the issuing of ordinary shares and this is considered in detail in Chapter 8; debt finance is considered here. A large proportion of the bank debt currently outstanding is provided by the clearing banks on small to medium sized properties throughout the country. It is useful as an introduction to consider the debt problems in the property sector in the early 1990s with the property collapse in 1973/4. The banking crises of 1973/4 put the reliance on institutional investment for recovery. The institutions provided attractively priced 100 per cent fund packages for property developments that they would commit to purchase in the future, at a discounted yield on completion. Whilst property provided satisfactory returns during the period of high inflation in the 1970s, property's performance began to look pedestrian compared to the more sparkling returns offered by the equity market during the prolonged bull market and low inflation of the mid-1980s. The problems of finance in property during the late 1980s and early 1990s cannot really be compared with the property collapse in 1973/4, as the new developers are stronger and the lending banks have more expertise. The collapse of 1973/4 was affected by a rise in interest rates and generally the economy appears more sound now (Barter 1988). However, the total debt outstanding in 1992 was, in real terms, three times that of 1974 and the surge of inflation that assisted in the debt repayment of the 1974 crash did not occur in the 1990s. There was also a distinct difference in institutional attitudes. In the 1970s, institutional portfolios were weighted towards property: insurance companies commonly had 30–40 per cent exposure and pension funds were acquiring property to build up portfolios to around the 20 per cent level. The proportion of property in institutions was much lower in the 1990s, at around 7 per cent (see Chapter 9), and thus the institutional take-out was less likely (Scott 1992). The banks are, however, heavily involved in the property sector: in June 1989, Debenham, Tewson & Chinnocks found that property formed the most important lending security for banks, and facilities secured against property accounted for some 35–40 per cent of total loans. The number of banks offering property loans had grown to 140 in

1989 and the combined property debt of the overseas banks accounted for 40 per cent of loans. Corporate facilities may account for 50 per cent of the loans to property companies outstanding at this time, with specific development funding another 30–35 per cent and investment lending around 20 per cent. Finally 35–40 per cent of total loans to property companies could be on a limited recourse basis (Debenham, Tewson & Chinnocks, *Banking on Property 1989*, quoted in the *Journal of Valuation* 1989).

In the late 1980s, the investment and development boom in property was funded by debt capital. British and foreign bank loans grew by an average of 51 per cent per annum. Bank lending to property companies reached £40.7 billion in 1991, a peak of 8.72 per cent of total bank lending. In 1992, the figure was £39 billion but, if loans to the construction sector are included, this reaches £55 billion or 12.2 per cent of bank lending (Scott 1992).

The debt finance market was difficult in the 1990s. To reiterate, the banks' exposure in the property sector peaked in 1991 at over £40 billion, and this represented more than 8 per cent of the total exposure of the banks, the highest since 1973/4. Bank lending problems were not just confined to the property sector and it is this fact that made financing arrangements very difficult. There were major problems with retailers, leisure operators, construction and manufacturing industries and banking itself. This made it difficult for banks to lend at all without an improvement in economic conditions. There was a major problem to do with refinancing debt because debts outstanding sometimes exceeded the value of the property; banks had the option of taking equity in the project or else foreclosing on the loans and realising the property asset.

There are two important aspects of the problems of the debt market: one is that the banks need to lend money to make money. A bank that loses £1,000 may need to lend £50,000 for one year to make up that loss. The banks have written off a large amount in the early 1990s and thus need substantial activity to recoup this. The second aspect is that, as finance becomes more difficult to obtain, so the importance of intermediaries grows as they provide the contacts.

By 2001, the lower cost of debt finance actually encouraged more private investors into the market. In what was called 'the year of leverage' (Danaher 2001), large amounts of debt at historically low rates enabled private investors (private property companies and individuals) to become involved in larger deals that were previously the domain of the larger institutions. For instance, a £246.5 million deal to purchase the Daily Express building in London's Fleet Street (subsequently occupied by Goldman Sachs) was based on an equity arrangement half-financed by a company called Green Property and half by a consortium of Irish investors. It is thought that, with the low cost of borrowing, 15–20 investors clubbed together, providing as little as £750,000 each. The deal was then heavily geared at 85 per cent with senior debt of £210 million. The security of the income stream is crucial to such a highly geared deal but banks at this time, especially German banks, were eager to lend. Such an arrangement would normally involve a single-let building on a long lease to an AAA grade covenant such as a bank or financial institution. A side effect of this easy credit is that, in the investment markets, many UK institutions – prevented from borrowing by their deeds – have been forced into acquiring less-prime investments.

In 2001, there were a number of reasons for increased demand for loan finance beside lower interest rates. There was a technical reason suggested by DTZ (DTZ Research 2001): the fact that borrowers were benefiting from the 'distortions at the long end of the yield curve'. This meant that as government was reducing its borrowing, so the supply of gilts on the market was drying up. This was coinciding with an increased demand for gilts, for instance because of restrictions imposed on pension funds through regulations related to the minimum funding requirement. Thus, gilt yields in the market fell because of this increased demand and the cost of funding, which was priced off long-dated gilts, also fell. Other structural changes also increased the demand for debt; financial institutions were drawn into geared vehicles to share the increased returns. Another cause was the trend towards outsourcing of real estate and real estate management to focus on the core business which meant that companies used highly geared outsourcing vehicles so that their own credit ratings were not affected. In the stock market, the poor ratings for some UK property companies forced them into the debt market to raise funds. Privatisation and securitisation led to a raising of the required rate of return in unsecuritised property; companies, worried about deteriorating credit ratings resulting from new loan stock issues, resorted to the use of bank debt. Finally, overseas investors changed strategy: instead of long-term equity investment, their cash inflows became more opportunistic and highly geared and, by borrowing in local markets, they reduced their exposure to exchange rate risk. For banks, real estate lending became more profitable relative to other areas of activity. For borrowers, the positive and widening yield gap between property yields and finance costs made property self-financing for a highly-geared investment.

Sources of debt finance

The usual sources of debt finance are:

- High Street and clearing banks
- foreign banks
- building societies.

At the end of 2000, there was £81 billion outstanding to the property sector, and DTZ Research (2001) indicates that this specifically includes debt from:

- banks authorised under the Banking Act 1987 to take deposits in UK branches
- banks not authorised under the Act
- building societies
- insurance companies
- debt securitised by lending institutions.

The important thing in this analysis is that the statistics provided by the Bank of England actually mask the full extent of bank exposure to property. The main component of debt, which is monitored by the Bank of England, is that advanced by banks authorised by the Financial Services Authority to accept deposits from

UK residents in branches established in the UK. In addition to domestic retail and investment banks, official data includes lending by authorised foreign banks with UK branches. However, the Bank of England figures have three main exclusions:

(a) they exclude lending to property company subsidiaries of parent companies in non-property business sectors;
(b) they exclude lending to enterprises incorporated outside the UK and in UK offshore islands;
(c) the figures only include institutions authorised under the Banking Act 1987 but other institutions, as mentioned above, account for around 27 per cent of the debt outstanding to UK commercial property as at 2000, and this group of institutions is becoming ever more important in the market.

7.2   Corporate versus project-based debt

Debt finance can be project-specific or generally tied to the assets of the borrower. Project-specific and asset-based funding and the distinction between the two has already been considered. The principle of asset-based debt finance is that the borrower borrows a sum of money against a company's assets in return for which the company undertakes to make a 'bond' to pay interest on the loan until the principal is redeemed. The difference between corporate bond issues and traditional bank finance is that borrowers are free to use the loans however they see fit and the loans are thus not project-specific.

Types of debt finance

Project-specific:
- project finance
- mortgages
- long-term loans
- convertible loans

Corporate finance:
- commercial paper
- multi-option facility
- debentures
- loan stock
- bonds
- deep-discounted bonds
- junk bonds
- euromarket.

The types of debt used can be seen from research carried out by Savills as shown in Figure 6.2.

Overdrafts

An overdraft occurs when a customer of a bank draws an account into negative balance. Company overdrafts may be for any size, provided that the bank is satisfied by the asset backing and the credit risk of the company involved. The main disadvantage of an overdraft facility is that repayment may be called for without the bank giving any length of notice and could therefore come at any time (when the liquid reserves of the lender are very low, for instance).

Bank loans, syndicated loans and term loans

Since 1986, bank lending to property companies has risen dramatically, and sophisticated lenders have enabled property companies to reduce the cost and risk associated with interest rate and exchange rate fluctuations. Syndicated loans have returned to prominence, which means the loans are syndicated or spread around a group of banks so that the risk of the loan is also spread. Term loans provide a company with a facility to draw down a certain amount of borrowing from a single bank or a syndicate, and the rate and timetable of the drawing down can be previously agreed. Additional charges may be made if the timetable is not adhered to or if the facility is not taken up. Term loans will specify the dates and manner by which the loan is to be repaid. Term loans can also carry an option to convert into a limited recourse loan where, for instance, the funds are for a project that will produce income soon after completion. Interest rates may fall once the property has been pre-let. Term loans cannot be called in before the pre-agreed date for repayment, unlike overdrafts. In their 1989 survey, Savills found most term loans were for less than £100 million, although loans up to £300 million were not uncommon. Maturities were between 1 and 7 years but the 2–5 year range was most common (Savills 1989).

Debt to equity swaps

Debt to equity swaps increase liquidity in the market and have been tried on occasions; property companies such as Imry and Randsworth in the early 1990s were effectively controlled by their banks by such mechanisms. Much of the current debt outstanding in 1993 may be considered de facto equity because the loans will not be serviced and the choice will be between the banks taking equity and foreclosure (DTZ Debenham Thorpe 1993).

7.3 Long-term loans

In the early postwar period, long-term mortgages on commercial property were usually fixed interest and provided by insurance companies. In the 1970s, insurance companies and pension funds provided long-term finance. In the 1980s, there was a decline in institutional interest in the property sector and borrowers had to rely on traditional short-term bank finance, which led to a massive expansion of bank lending and the development of complex and sophisticated financing arrangements. By the end of the 1980s, only a few insurance companies offered debt arrangements to property but in the 1990s, this group became more and more willing to lend in the sector. In the year 2000, non-personal loans to non-residential property by insurance companies increased by 21 per cent to a total of

£10 billion by the year-end. This represented an increase of 50 per cent from 1992 (DTZ Research 2001).

The main types of debt finance available at the moment which relate to long-term finance are:

- commercial mortgages
- mortgage debenture issues
- equity participation or convertible mortgages
- multi-option facilities
- deep-discounted bonds.

These types of loan are summarised below.

Commercial mortgages

Interest is paid currently or capitalised. The principal is either amortised over the term of the loan or capitalised. The interest rate can be fixed or variable and other capital market instruments can be used for the management of the interest rates:

- caps prevent interest rises over a certain rate
- floors prevent interest rates falling below a certain level
- collars restrict the movement of rates between the cap and floor level.

By minimising interest rate fluctuations, you reduce risk and more accurately determine the cost of finance. The length of the loan varies but for banks it is usually a maximum of 5 years; insurance companies and building societies may lend up to 25 years.

Mortgage debenture issues

This is a traditional way of raising corporate finance. The loan is raised against a debenture issue that is secured against the property or other assets. The issue yields either a fixed or index-linked return.

Equity participation or convertible mortgages

This structure allows the lender to share in the uplift in the value of the property for a reduction in the interest rate payable.

Multi-option facility

In this structure, a group of banks agree to provide cash advances at a predetermined margin for a certain period.

Deep-discounted bonds

This is a method of raising long-term finance with a low initial interest rate (see Figure 7.1). Interest payments can be stepped to accord with rent reviews and there are tax advantages. Bonds can be placed with institutional investors. They are debentures on which the annual interest payable is less than the market rate.

In order to make up for the interest shortfall, the bond is issued at a discount to its nominal value (the amount to be paid at the end of the term). The combination of the difference between the amount initially raised and the amount paid at the

Cash flow to investor

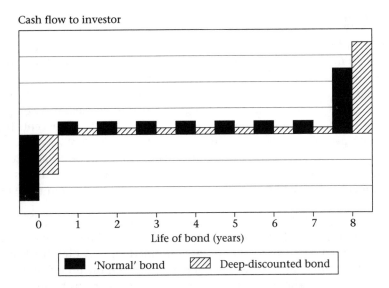

Life of bond (years)

■ 'Normal' bond   ▨ Deep-discounted bond

Figure 7.1   Deep-discounted bonds

Box 7.1   Example of servicing a loan

Loan amount £450,000		
Company's last audited accounts indicate:		
Net profit after tax		£217,000
Add back rent saving		£19,000
		£236,000
Deductions from cash flow:		
Bank overdraft interest	£55,000	
Hire purchase interest	£20,000	
£450,000 loan @ 9%	£40,500	
Future finance costs	£115,000	

Ratio = 2.07:1 thus within guidelines.
But note other costs involved: arrangement fee (0.5–1% of advance), independent valuation of property (0.125–0.2% value) and also lender's legal fees.

end of the term, together with the interest, is equivalent to the market interest that would have been payable.

Servicing a loan

In order to service a loan, it must be possible for the business to create cash surpluses from its trading activities, not only for the repayment of the loan but also for other payments, such as tax. As a rule of thumb, the net profit figure shown in the accounts should be twice the amount of all interest charges (to include bank borrowing, factoring, overdraft charges, etc.). However, where, for example, a rented property is being replaced by a freehold property using the loan, the rental saving should be added back to the net profit figure (Jones and Isaac 1996). An example is shown in Box 7.1.

7.4   Commercial mortgages

Fixed rate institutional mortgages are advanced generally between 66.6 per cent and 75 per cent of the value of the property. In the early 1990s, the ratio was likely to be at the lower end. The lender will require that the income produced by the investment will service interest costs at the start of the mortgage. The rate of interest attached to the loan is priced off the gross redemption yield of a comparable gilt security. Savills in 1989 quoted this margin as 1.25–2.25 per cent. Interest is normally payable half-yearly in arrears. Institutions are unlikely to consider advances less than £250,000. The maturity dates vary between 5 and 20 years. It is possible to get a forward commitment to a mortgage so that funds can be made available on completion of the project or when a pre-let is in place (Savills 1989).

Banks are still attracted by the commercial mortgage market, which is not considered as property lending. In most instances, commercial mortgage applications will be supported by historical accounting information, providing the bank with the comfort of knowing that they do not have to rely on the underlying property asset for repayment. The commercial mortgage market offers the financial services market the largest single growth opportunity because of its very scale and variety. See Box 7.2 for an example.

Box 7.2   Example of a commercial mortgage

Status:
Owner-occupier

Background:
Client was originally a buy-out from an institutional investor
  – is a provincial manufacturer
  – completed first year of trading at the end of 1991

Requirement:
Needed to expand (£4 million turnover)
Clearing bank would not lend further
Clearing bank was owed £600,000 (mortgage) £200,000 (overdraft)

Client's assets:
2,000 square metre factory   £1,000,000
Plant and machinery   £500,000
Debtors   £300,000
Client wanted another £200,000 to refurbish factory

Offer:
French bank
80 per cent mortgage   £800,000
80 per cent debtor facility   £240,000
Loans at 2 per cent above 3-month LIBOR
First charge on factory
Mortgage debenture

The advantages and disadvantages of commercial mortgages can be summarised:

Advantages
- ease of arrangement
- low set-up costs
- low interest rates offer a cash flow advantage
- no tax risk

Disadvantages
- on balance sheet
- increased gearing, thereby reducing financial flexibility in the future
- additional equity may be required if valuations are less
- large equity input required through cash or added security (Jones and Isaac 1996).

Research into the mortgage market indicates that default rates are important in determining the price (interest rate) for the loan. However, the pattern of expenses, the term and the size of loan can be more important, particularly in the last 20 years or so. The cost of default is small as a percentage of loans outstanding (Booth and Walsh 2000). Recent problems in the equity market related to low returns have meant that many perceive problems in the use of endowment mortgages, where the endowment fails to repay the amount of loan outstanding at the completion of the loan term. Booth and Rodney (2000) suggest this may be a 'money illusion', as any shortfall would be matched in full by a fall in mortgage interest in a low inflation economy. Lower interest rates will not reduce the costs for repayment mortgages as much during the term as an endowment mortgage, as the debt outstanding is larger with an endowment mortgage.

7.5   Convertible loans and mortgages

This is a loan, bond or debenture in which the lender of the money has a right to switch the holding into ordinary shares (equity) at a stated date in the future at a fixed price. This price is normally higher than the current share price. The advantage to the lender is that they can partake in decision-making and the growth of the company, whilst the advantage for the borrower is that they can attach a lower interest rate to the loan coupon. Also, the cost of capital is lower as the conversion rights are seen by the lender as advantageous. If the convertible element is 'detachable', it can be bought and sold separately as a warrant. This is considered under equity finance.

The conventional mortgage is the usual way of debt financing in the long term (more than 10 years). The lender usually takes first charge on the property being mortgaged and thus the position of the borrower is secure. No more than two-thirds of the value is usually lent (the loan to value ratio). The problem is that for the borrower, the rental income from the property may not cover the interest repayments under the mortgage. The borrower is thus deficit financing because the cash flow from the property may not cover the outflow. The borrower will still want to hold on to the property because in the long run there may be rental growth from rent reviews and, at that stage, the reviewed rent may amply cover the interest repayments; however, in the short run there is obviously a problem. If the borrower has income from other sources, such as income-producing assets that are not indebted, then this could make up the shortfall, but if there is no additional income then the borrower will need to roll up the interest deficit. The borrower may not wish to do this (it was unpopular with lenders in the 1990s). A possible solution to the problems may be a convertible mortgage. The convertible mortgage may be secured on one or more buildings. A lower interest rate is charged in return for participation in the equity of the building or in the rents received.

7.6 Corporate debt

Replacement of institutional funding by debt

A revised system of debt funding has been developed to replace the traditional approach. The emphasis is on limited recourse and off-balance sheet funding where feasible. The key point is the property being developed being the principal source of repayment, as opposed to the traditional position in the past where the loan has been to a developer, which is then secured on a property.

The basis of the loan arrangement is that the bank will agree a loan to value ratio on which it will lend. Typically this may be 65–70 per cent. It then undertakes to the borrower that it will only seek repayment from the refinancing or sale of the development and not from the borrower. The bank would expect two types of contribution from the borrower:

(a) an amount of equity from the developer, probably in the region of 10–20 per cent, being the difference between the loan amount and the anticipated total cost of completing the project;
(b) payment in respect of any cost overruns not budgeted for.

Thus, the loan to the bank reflects perhaps 80 per cent loan to cost but 65–70 per cent loan to value. The essential point is that the bank will lend the main element of development costs without recourse to the developer but will also commit the developer or a third party, if the developer is not strong enough and requires a guarantor, to contribute all the other costs. Figure 7.2 shows a typical finance structure for a development project.

Examples of short-term corporate finance

Floating rate

The LIBOR rate is a different rate for 3 months, 6 months and 1 year. The finance house base rate is the average of 3-month LIBOR and is reviewed every 6 weeks. The building society base rate is another measure.

Fixed price money

This is usually obtained from insurance companies and is priced off gilts. This can also be obtained from swap markets in the form of mortgages.

Example of a project with a value of £10 million,
million with a bank funding 70% of the value:

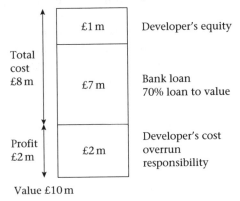

Figure 7.2 Development finance structure
Source: Wolfe (1988).

Mortgages

These can be interest only with a bullet repayment or repayment of capital and interest. It can also be on the basis of part repayment and part interest only leaving an amount payable at the end, known as a 'balloon'. The interest can be fixed or variable and the interest can be deferred.

Revolving credit facility

This is mainly available for larger companies and is generally secured on assets. The minimum size is approximately £30 million. This is an ideal form of finance for many property developers and traders.

A line of credit

Large companies can borrow money from a bank within certain parameters (i.e., if income covers interest or the loan is less than 65 per cent of value, etc.).

Syndicated loans

Where large sums are involved, it is common for such loans to be spread amongst a syndicate of banks where one bank is taking the lead. Syndicated property loans have become increasingly frequent with banks keen to share both the risks and the rewards involved in large-scale property development.

Tender panel facility

A tender panel is a method of raising short-term floating rate finance to a long-term facility with a fixed interest margin. At present, it is only available to established quoted companies. What makes it different from other forms of finance is that although the maximum interest margin over the money rate is fixed (say, 1 per cent over LIBOR), the actual rate paid by the borrower may be less than the maximum. The banks underwriting the transaction guarantee the borrowing bank that it will not have to pay more than the fixed margin but the actual cost of funds will be determined by the banks participating in the tender panel who bid for the opportunity to lend money to the company. Money is usually borrowed over a 3–6 month period and, should the tender panel fail to raise the required amount at the maximum margin or cheaper, the underwriting banks make up the shortfall to the maximum margin. At the end of each period, the exercise is repeated until the term of the facility requires. This is discussed further in section 7.8.

Equity kicker or earn out

This is a facility where a profit share or agreed figure is paid at the end of the facility in payment for a reduction in the effective rate of interest.

Why developers use debt

They are able to take all the rental growth over the development period. There is greater flexibility, greater speed, and greater control. Debt is especially used when the development product is not prime.

7.7 Commercial paper

Commercial paper is a form of IOU note. The issuer sells the paper to investors who are looking for a short-term investment. Bank lending has traditionally provided short-term finance but commercial paper is a means of tapping the money markets direct. Paper is issued in sterling or in dollars. There is currently a lack of investor confidence in the market and prospective borrowers need to have good quality rated names. Security markets have virtually been untapped by the UK property sector in the period to 1991; better sterling pricing was achieved by issuing in US dollars and swapping to sterling (Beveridge 1991). The sterling commercial paper market (sterling CP) was launched in April 1986 to provide an alternative method for companies to raise short-term finance, which was previously restricted to bills of exchange, syndicated loans, advances and overdrafts (Savills 1989). Commercial paper was initially restricted to use by large stock market listed companies but restrictions were relaxed in the 1989 Budget (Brett 1990b) and medium-sized companies were allowed to join the market.

Commercial paper does not bear interest but is sold at a discount rather like the sale of gilts by the government. For example, £95 will purchase, say, £100 nominal value of commercial paper; thus, £100 will be repaid in 3 months, the interest rate being £5 ÷ £95 for 3 months. If the money is then reinvested, the annual interest rate can be calculated on the basis of a quarterly reinvestment of funds (i.e., $(1 + i/4)^4 - 1$, where $i/4$ is the quarterly interest rate). The interest rate is quoted relative to the LIBOR rate.

The sterling CP market suffers from competition from the Bank of England eligible bill market. There is no secondary market for the paper; sterling CP issuers prefer the issues to be placed with investors to be held to maturity. Financial institutions, banks and other companies invest in commercial paper, usually for a maximum period of 1 year although, after the 1989 Budget, this could be a maximum of 5 years. The average period of a commercial paper loan is 40 days but the minimum is 7 days. A commercial paper programme can be set up which effectively lengthens the life of the loan. The programme makes commercial paper into a medium-term source of finance because as one issue of commercial paper falls due for repayment, so there is a further issue and thus a rolling programme of issues is established.

To get into the money market, a bank will need to set up a programme for the company involved. The maximum amount of paper that the company may have outstanding at any one time is £50 million. The banks will act as intermediaries between the issuers and potential investors. The issuer will also need an agent to deal with the redemption of the paper and the banks provide this function. The commercial paper market is not for small issues or investors; the minimum denomination for sterling commercial paper is £100,000.

Commercial paper is unsecured and thus the financial standing of the issuer is very important. The original market was restricted to larger known firms, but now there are less familiar names in the market. The issuer therefore looks for an independent credit assessment for the paper being issued. Rating services can be provided by Moody's or Standard & Poor's (see section 7.11). These credit ratings assist investors, who do not know the market, in assessing the risk.

The procedure for issuing commercial paper is as follows (Brett 1990b):

1　The bank that is arranging the issue will prepare an information memorandum to be circulated amongst investors. Some companies will have a constant amount outstanding in the commercial paper market; other companies will become involved in the market when rates become competitive. The traditional approach to this form of financing is through bills of exchange and acceptances; these are used to finance trade transactions and thus are not applicable to property. However, bills of exchange therefore provide the main competition for commercial paper.
2　If conditions in the commercial paper market are unattractive for future issues at the time of redemption of the paper, then smaller borrowers may have a fallback facility for the renewal of their debt by a line of credit or a multi-option facility (MOF) as a committed facility. A committed facility is where a group of banks have arranged to make a specified amount of funds available at a pre-arranged rate over LIBOR if the borrower cannot raise the finance more cheaply elsewhere. A MOF frequently provides backing for a commercial paper programme.
3　The borrowed money is spread in terms of pricing from LIBID (the lower rate to LIBOR at which banks are prepared to borrow rather than lend) to 12–13 basis points over LIBOR for small property companies, with medium-sized companies somewhere in between.

Very large property companies are not confined to borrowing in the sterling commercial paper market as there is a larger and longer established domestic commercial paper market in the USA for those wanting funds in dollars or who are prepared to borrow in dollars and swap into sterling. This can provide cheap finance, but an appropriate credit rating will be required for the borrower and a fallback facility for the borrower will be essential. There is also a euro-commercial paper market tapped by some larger property companies. This euro-commercial paper market (ECP or euro CP) was started in 1983. There is a small secondary market. Swaps play an important part in the ECP market (Savills 1989).

7.8 Multi-option facility

The newer financing techniques are usually applied initially to the larger corporate borrower. The MOF is a flexible method of tapping the money markets for short-term funds. As with commercial paper, money is borrowed for relatively short periods but can be rolled over to provide the equivalent of a medium-term loan. As one 3-month loan falls due, another is taken out to replace it. It is possible to arrange a multiple option facility in excess of £25 million, and large and medium-sized property companies have taken advantage of this.

The MOF should provide cheaper funds because it encourages banks to compete to provide the finance. The MOF can take a number of difference guises. The most common form is in two parts: a guaranteed or committed facility which ensures that the company will get its money when it needs it, and an uncommitted facility which may allow a company to borrow at more advantageous terms.

If a company requires a MOF, it will need to go through several stages. It will need to involve a bank to set up the facility. If the MOF is for £50 million, then this means that the maximum outstanding at anyone time is £50 million. The arranging bank talks to other banks who put together a syndicate of banks who agree that jointly they will provide up to the amount (£50 million) required if called on to do so. The interest rate is agreed at this point not as an absolute amount but as a margin over LIBOR. The agreed margin might be, say, 15 basis points or 0.15 per cent over LIBOR, so the borrowing costs will go up and down with the LIBOR rate but the maximum percentage margin over LIBOR remains constant. Note that this rate represents the maximum amount, but is not the real rate. The second stage of the MOF is for the arranging bank to put together a tender panel; the bank will arrange to add some additional banks to the original syndicate that agreed the committed facility. When the company wants to borrow, the tender banks are invited to bid to provide the finance. Those offering the cheapest rates will make the loans. If the banks in the tender panel do not bid the amount, the company will need to draw down funds under the committed facility instead. Either way, it is sure of getting its finance.

The advantage of the system is, in theory, the competitive element of the tender panel. Banks that have a lot of money available can bid to put up the cash required. Others who have limited funds may not wish to bid. This part of the facility is thus uncommitted, and the cost of the uncommitted funds will normally be lower than for the committed facility because the tender panel banks are not entering into an undertaking to supply funds. The limit on the uncommitted facility may be the same as the committed. Sometimes, the uncommitted facility will be larger, although a company may organise a committed facility of £50 million and an uncommitted facility of £100 million. This means in real terms, although the maximum it can borrow is £100 million, it is not guaranteed more than £50 million. Recently, the tender panel mechanism has become less effective as the banks have been more aggressive on the profitability of such transactions. In these cases, the borrower has been thrown back on the committed facility. The multi-option in the facility refers to the fact that the company is able to raise its funds in more than one form. It can thus pick the loan that suits its requirement at the most reasonable price. The facility may also include bills of exchange facilities (i.e., acceptance credits). Bills of exchange are short-term IOUs, based on trade transactions and thus not available to property investors, but there may be facilities to offer other forms of short-term IOUs and raise loans in other currencies. The commercial paper programme may be included in the MOF or backed by a MOF (a committed facility).

To calculate the cost of an MOF you need to allow for fees as well as the interest rate margin on funds borrowed. There are arrangement fees for the bank for setting up the committed facility and this may be an annual rate over the life of the MOF. There is an annual indemnity fee for the banks that provide the committed facility. This ensures that the funds will be available when required. The general hope of the borrower is that the tender panel will provide finance at a cheaper rate and thus he or she will not need to draw heavily on the committed facility. There is a utilisation fee if the company does not draw down more than a contracted percentage of the committed facility (say, 50 per cent). If a company's credit rating falls, then the tender banks will not provide funds and the company will need to rely on the banks underwriting the committed facility (Brett 1990b).

Example of a multi-option facility (Gibbs 1987)

Company:	Wates City of London
Facility:	£56 million
Guaranteed ceiling:	LIBOR + 30 basis points
No. of banks in tender panel:	19
Bids:	over 3–6 months, lowest bidder gets business

If the tender panel fails to raise the required amount at the maximum margin or cheaper, the underwriting banks make up the shortfall. This exercise is repeated until the facility expires.

The advantages to the borrower are:

- fine pricing
- loan can be unsecured
- option to receive cash or notes (commercial paper)
- can be in currency (cash) or in promissory notes ($US).

An underwriting fee and arranging fee must be paid. The MOF offers a variety of financing options in one package including facilities such as commercial paper and multi-currency arrangements. The loan sizes of MOFs in the 1989 Savills survey were between £50 million and £300 million, with an average of £120 million.

Maturity dates were between 2 and 10 years, with 7 years the most popular (Savills 1989).

7.9   Loan stock

Loan stock is the same as standard debenture issue. If the loan stock is unsecured, the lender has no guaranteed security other than the previous track record of the borrower. Thus, the coupon (return) is very high but it does allow smaller developers to raise non-project specific finance. Also, loan stock can have a call option giving the borrower the right to repurchase the stock before maturity. The use of options in loan stock is evidenced by convertible loan stock that gives the holder a combination of a straight loan arrangement or bond combined with a call option. On exercising the option, the holder exchanges the loan for a fixed number of shares in the borrowing company.

7.10   Debentures

A debenture is a tradable 'IOU' similar to gilt-edged securities (gilts) issued by the government. There is a different terminology in the UK and the USA. US debentures are unsecured borrowing but in the UK the borrowing is secured on the assets of the company. This thus differs from similar unsecured loan stock or bonds issued in the euromarket which are generally unsecured. The mortgage debenture is the longest term and most traditional way of raising finance by a security issue (Brett 1990b).

A debenture is the sealed bond of a corporation or company acknowledging a sum on which interest is due until the interest is repaid. A debenture is thus the description of a financial instrument, whilst debenture stock is the description of a debt or sum secured by an instrument. The lender holding a debenture has by right a prior charge on the developer's corporate assets, although in practice property company debentures are typically secured on specific assets. Properties up to 150 per cent of the value of the loan are put up as charges in the event of default. Interest on the loan is normally paid half-yearly and independent trustees are often employed to look after the debenture holders' interests.

A company can also issue debentures as convertible securities (secured or unsecured) containing an option entitling the holder to convert the debt at specific times to ordinary or preference shares at a pre-arranged rate. These can be issued at a low rate of interest because of the conversion rights. Debentures may also be issued with subscription warrants attached that are the options to acquire ordinary shares in the company (Savills 1989).

Debentures are advantageous to borrowers because:

- borrowers can do what they want to with the money
- the interest paid is a charge against profits before tax
- debentures can be a contract between single investors and the company or by a public issue or placing on the stock market (private arrangements are more frequent).

Debentures are advantageous to lenders because:

- they are able to obtain a marginally higher rate of interest than for the equivalent gilt-edged stock
- debentures are legitimate tradable securities and therefore can subsequently be bought and sold at varying prices dependent on the prevailing market cost of capital
- debentures are sometimes accompanied by rights of subscription or part conversion (see convertibles).

Issues relating to the Insolvency Act 1986 have already been considered in section 4.4. This Act restricts the trustee's powers of enforcing the security. Most large debenture issues are listed on the Stock Exchange and can be traded in the same way as government stocks. Smaller issues are placed with a limited range of investors; this is called a private sale. Because a debenture is a debt security rather than equity, issuers are under no obligation to offer new issues to existing investors. In the domestic market, issues are available in the registered form (i.e., the owners are registered with the company which knows who owns the stock). In the euromarket, the stock is likely to be in bearer form, so the stock certificate is the proof of ownership. Debentures may be issued in a part-paid form, so that the price is paid in instalments over a period of time, as with some share issues.

7.11 Deep-discounted bonds and junk bonds

A 'bond' is basically another term for a debenture or secured long-term loan. These are long-term borrowing facilities with the interest either rolled-up or phased at a substantially lower rate than the market would expect (i.e., lower than the gilt rate which is the rate on government securities and which is risk-free). The stepping-up of the interest rate (coupon) can correspond to actual rent reviews. Thus, these bonds pay less as a coupon/interest but make up for it by paying a higher redemption figure. A zero coupon bond, for instance, pays no interest but the redemption figure should be sufficient to allow for this, so that, when interest is analysed over the period to redemption together with the redemption sum, a realistic yield will be obtained. In order to borrow on a deep-discounted bond, a company will need to provide a strong covenant. This facility has been used so far by owner-occupiers seeking to develop property and for whom property is not their main business. An example of this approach was the issue by Safeway Ltd (Gibbs 1987):

> *Safeway Limited Deep-Discounted Bond Issue*
> Issue: £100 million
> Date: 1986
> Purpose: Property expansion programme for owner occupation
> Redemption: 20 years with a defined 5-yearly uplift pattern.

The attraction of the deep-discounted bond is that it compensates for the reverse yield gap, so money can be raised at low rates comparable to initial yields on a

Box 7.3   Example of a deep-discount bond refinancing

A joint venture company has successfully developed and let a property but has failed to sell it. How can it realise some cash and hold on to the property until the investment market recovers without substantial commitments to interest shortfall?

Solution:

Existing income (p.a.)	£3,800,000
Estimated rental value (p.a.)	£4,750,000
Capital value	£48,000,000
Maximum loan at maturity	£43,200,000
Reviews through load period	5 years
Interest rate	13.5 per cent p.a. fixed
Initial drawdown (approximately)	£37,000,000

Notes: After the initial drawdown, the balance of the loan will be used to meet the interest income shortfall for the 5-year loan period. The estimates for rent passing during the period are based on appraised estimate rental value assuming no growth. The bank benefits from a CMI (mortgage indemnity) from an insurance syndicate on the first £7.2 million of the loan, while the additional cost to the borrower of £430,000 is paid on first drawdown.

Source: Clarke (1990).

prime property. The phased uplifts are usually structured to ensure that the effective equated yield enjoys a clear margin over the prevalent gross redemption yields on gilts. These are tradable instruments. Box 7.3 shows an example.

Deep-discount, zero-coupon and stepped bonds are referred to generally as DDBs. The main characteristics can be summarised as follows:

1 The debt may be secured or unsecured;
2 The value at redemption should exceed that on issue;
3 The interest rate is defined by reference to a coupon and this is usually priced off a floating rate LIBOR and the margin is known;
4 The repayment date is a fixed, one-off date where the principal sum or nominal value needs to be repaid;
5 The discount may be likened to a rolling-up of interest and this has a compounding effect, creating a higher effective rate than the coupon, which is charged on the outstanding value of the instrument;
6 The bond has a discount to nominal value at the time of issue;
7 A coupon is paid on an annual or some other periodic basis.

ZCBs (zero coupon bonds) are the same as deep-discount bonds except that the discount is greater and there is no coupon paid out. All interest is effectively in the discount that grows until the date of redemption when it is paid out. Stepped coupon bonds (SCBs) have a coupon that rises at fixed intervals by fixed amounts during its life. There can be variations such as a zero coupon bond for three years then a fixed coupon (see example in Figure 7.3: Shayle 1991).

Term to maturity	9 years	Initial roll up period	3 years
Coupon	10%	Coupon payable/roll up on a	
Amount on issue	£2.0 m	semi-annual basis	

Value at the end of year 3: £2,680,200*
Coupon payable:

year 3.5 = £134,010}   Annual payment £268,020
year 4.0 = £134,010}   Annual equivalent rate 13.4%

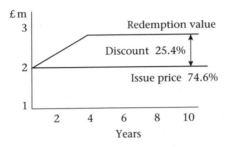

Figure 7.3 Example of a complex deep-discount bond

Note: *Found by using the formula: $p(1 + r)^n$ where p = issue price, r = coupon rate, n = number of periods to be rolled up.

Source: Shayle (1991), p. 12.

Junk bonds

Junk bonds are not very relevant to property funding at the present time but they do provide a case study in the use of derivatives. They experienced a period of popularity then notoriety in the USA, and are linked to very risky investments; they are also highly geared and unsecured but may offer a high reward commensurate with the risk taken. They have been issued as a defence against takeovers in some instances by companies.

The growth in junk bond financing can better be explained by the activities of one man than by a number of economic factors. While a graduate student in the 1970s, Michael Milkin observed a large difference between the return of high-yield bonds and the return on safer bonds. Believing that this difference was greater than would be justified by the extra default risk, he concluded that institutional investors would benefit from purchases of junk bonds. His later employment on Wall Street, at Drexel Burnham Lambert, allowed him to develop the junk bond market. Milkin's salesmanship simultaneously increased the demand for junk bonds among institutional investors and the supply of junk bonds among corporations. Corporations were particularly impressed with Drexel's vast network of institutional clients, allowing capital to be raised quickly. However, with the demise of the junk bond market and with Michael Milkin's conviction on securities fraud, Drexel found it necessary to declare bankruptcy.

Junk bonds were important in their use to finance mergers and other corporate restructuring. Whereas a firm can only issue a small amount of high-grade debt, the same firm can issue much more debt if low-grade financing is allowed as well.

Therefore, the use of junk bonds lets acquirers effect take-overs that they could not do with only traditional bond-financing techniques (Ross, Westerfield and Jaffe 1993).

Bond ratings

In American texts, the junk bond is defined as a speculative grade bond rated 'Ba' or lower by Moody's or 'BB' or lower by Standard & Poor's, or an unrated bond. The junk bond is also referred to as a high yield or low-grade bond. The bond ratings are very important to the status of an issue and thus the amount that can be raised. Firms in the USA frequently pay to have their debt rated and the two leading bond-rating services as mentioned above are Moody's Investor Service and Standard & Poor's. The debt rating will depend on:

- the likelihood that the firm will default
- the protection afforded by the loan contract in the event of default.

Bond ratings are important because bonds with lower ratings tend to have higher interest costs. In the 1980s in the USA, a growing part of corporate borrowing has taken the form of low-grade bonds (high yield or junk bonds: see Table 7.1). Bond ratings are set out in Table 7.2.

Table 7.1 Growth in junk bonds in USA, 1985–91

Year	Par value of bonds outstanding ($billion)
1985	59
1986	93
1987	137
1988	159
1989	201
1990	210
1991	209

Source: Ross, Westerfield and Jaffe (1993).

Table 7.2 Bond ratings

Bond rating	Standard & Poor's	Moody's
Very high quality	AAA	Aaa
	AA	Aa
High quality	A	A
	BBB	Baa
Speculative	BB	Ba
	B	B
Very poor	CCC	Caa
	CC	Ca
	C	C
	D	D

Note: Junk bonds are speculative grade or below.

Source: Ross, Westerfield and Jaffe (1993).

7.12   Euromarket lending

Larger companies can raise long-term unsecured loans in the international market. The international market or euromarket is a market of 'stateless' money; this is money held outside its country of origin. For instance, deposits of US dollars in a German bank are eurodollars; pounds sterling held in Holland are eurosterling. The market in eurocurrencies is not subject to the controls of any one domestic financial authority. London is the main centre for eurocurrency dealing but British banks are not the main players in the market, which is dominated by American and Japanese banks. There is no central marketplace; deals are arranged over the telephone and funds can be borrowed in most of the world's currencies. The eurocurrency markets provide a parallel for most of the products and facilities available in the domestic financial market.

Thus, money can be borrowed very short term, called euro-commercial paper, and very long term (a 20-year eurobond). The borrowing can be in the form of bank loans as well as security issues. There are fundamental differences between the euromarket and the domestic market (see below):

1 Euro-borrowing is generally unsecured and thus, without security, the reputation and standing of the borrower is all-important. Thus, major internationally known corporations have no trouble in tapping the market but it is not accessible to smaller companies known only in their domestic markets.
2 Domestically, property investment companies have always been regarded as exceptionally secure because of the strength of their assets. In the euromarkets, investors are looking more at the cash flow and are less familiar with those British property companies which may not be rated so highly; thus, it will normally be the large companies that tap the euromarkets.
3 With changes in the rules for the issue of domestic sterling bonds, the distinctions between domestic and euromarkets have largely broken down for sterling issues. The euromarket is more an issuing and trading technique than a totally separate market. Most British banks and security houses will deal almost interchangeably in domestic and euro-issues of sterling bonds. Eurobonds are normally listed on a stock exchange (probably London or the lightly regulated Luxembourg market); most dealing is between traders rather than through exchanges.

The euromarket is not restricted to fixed interest money or long-term money. Bonds on the market can be issued with a life of just a few years or, instead of a fixed interest bond, a company might issue a floating rate note (FRN) where the interest payment changes with a movement in a benchmark interest rate (usually LIBOR). Traditionally, eurobonds in sterling denominations have not done well in the market but it has been possible to issue long-dated sterling eurobonds at maturities of 15/20 years and this has been done over the life of the market. The bonds are usually at a fixed rate, and if sterling is not popular at the time of issue, it is possible to issue in an alternative currency and then swap to sterling subsequently. In 1990, MEPC issued two separate Luxembourg franc issues and one euro-yen issue and subsequently both swapped into sterling at satisfactory levels. The issue of the bond can thus be linked to a swap subsequently (Beveridge 1991).

An example of a eurobond issue was the £100 million issue by Hammerson, a major property company, in 1989. The bond was issued at £99.888 for £100 nominal stock at a 10.75 per cent coupon. The bond was repayable in 2013. The bond was issued in denominations of £10,000 and £100,000 bearer bonds, so the owners were not registered with the company. A feature of the bonds was that UK income tax on interest paid was not deducted at source (Brett 1990b).

7.13   Securitisation of debt

The securitisation of property loans (for a wider analysis and understanding of securitisation, see Chapter 12) by banks or their conversion into mortgage-backed bonds is a solution to the problems of loan turnover. Lenders can raise new funds by the sale of these financial assets which can then bolster lending capacity. There is a problem here that relates to the risk of default by the borrowers. This is because, if the seller of the securitised debt continues to provide a guarantee or security of the debt, then that debt may still need to be shown in the bank's accounts (DTZ Debenham Thorpe 1993). Another problem is that buyers of secondary debt can demand a high level of discount against the original value of the loan. Despite these difficulties, the secondary debt market developed into a million-dollar industry in the USA in the early 1990s when, for instance, Bank of America and First Chicago disposed of $3 billion of real estate loans.

Recent moves by the Bank of England suggest a growing support for innovations in trading in debt including debt for equity swaps, property-backed bonds and securitisation. The object is to break the logjam in property loans and inject liquidity. The traditional financing approach of funding the development during the development period with loans that could be refinanced on completion and letting has meant that when these short-term loans become repayable, in many cases the level of debt outstanding exceeds the value of the property. The borrower at this point would normally be required to put further equity in, to take out the debt. As this is not possible in depressed markets, banks are faced with the choice of taking an equity stake in the project or foreclosing the loan, realising the property asset and making provisions to cover the loss incurred. As has been said earlier, much of the debt outstanding in the early 1990s could be considered already as de facto equity (Scott 1992).

Debt securitisation involves the parcelling-up of loans and using them to issue bonds. Borrower's interest payments on the loans cover the coupon paid by the lender to bond investors plus the set-up costs. The difference between the two rates of interest represents the lender's profit margin on the securitisation. This financing tool is useful for financiers seeking to expand their loan books but constrained from doing so by internal lending limits. By securitising part of their loan books, lenders are able to advance more loans without having to syndicate them to other banks. Securitisation removes the debt from the lender's balance sheet (and consequently from the official Bank of England data on bank debt outstanding) and provides the lender with reserves against which it can issue new debt. Despite being off-balance sheet, the associated property-specific risk exposure remains;

lenders rely on interest payments paid by borrowers to pay the coupon on the bond. This form of financial instrument is becoming increasing popular in the USA and the volume of commercial mortgage-backed security (CMBS) issuance was $50 billion in 2000. The market has been slower to develop in Europe but German banks especially have been keen to securitise their loan books. However, the European market in 2000 was dominated by issues in the UK. Morgan Stanley continued its programme of securitisation in 200 with ELOC 3 raising £254 million and ELOC 4 raising £462 million. The second of these bond issues is unusual in being backed by just one loan to a single borrower, namely the joint venture established by MEPC and Westfield to purchase six of MEPC's shopping centres (DTZ Research 2001).

One of the benefits of securitisation is that the asset-backed paper is immune from 'event' risk, where an unforeseen event such as a merger or takeover can reduce credit quality overnight. Securitised assets are ring fenced and are usually well protected from corporate changes that could impact on a company's credit rating. By securitising property, however, the asset cover on existing unsecured debt falls. Other things being equal, this had the effect of increasing the risk of holding existing bonds and decreasing their liquidity, thereby cutting their price (DTZ Research 2001). This is shown in British Land's securitisation of the Broadgate estate, completed in April 1999. Between January 1998 and May 1999, the spread (margin over the benchmark gilt) on its senior unsecured bonds, due 2016, increased by 90 basis points. Over the same period, spreads on Land Securities unsecured bonds, due 2020, increased by 6 basis points.

References and further reading

Barter, S. L. (1988) 'Introduction', in S. L. Barter (ed.), *Real Estate Finance*, Butterworths, London.

Beveridge, J. A. (1991) 'New Methods of Financing', in P. Venmore-Rowland, P. Brandon and T. Mole (eds), *Investment, Procurement and Performance in Construction*, RICS, London.

Booth, P. and Rodney, B. (2000) 'The Repayment of Mortgages by Endowment Assurances in a Low Interest Rate Environment', *Real Estate Finance and Investment Research Paper*, no. 2000.01, City University Business School, November.

Booth, P. and Walsh, D. (2000) 'Cash Flow Models for Pricing Mortgages', *Real Estate Finance and Investment Research Paper*, no. 2000.02, City University Business School, November.

Brett, M. (1990b), *Property and Money*, Estates Gazette, London.

Brett, M. (1991b), 'Property and Money: Mortgages which convert into property', *Estates Gazette*, 17 August.

Clarke, R. J. (1990) 'Refinancing', *Journal of Property Finance*, 1(3), 435–9.

Danaher, T. (2001) 'The year of leverage', *Property Week*, 16 March, 12–13.

DTZ Debenham Thorpe (1993) *Money into Property*, DTZ Debenham Thorpe, London, August.

DTZ Research (2001) *Money into Property*, DTZ Research, London, edition 26, June.

Gibbs, R. (1987) 'Raising Finance for New Development', *Journal of Valuation*, 5(4), 343–53.

Jones, T. and Isaac, D. (1996) 'Finance for the Smaller Building Contractor', in D. Isaac (ed.), *Construction Management: Issues and Perspectives*, Greenwich University Press, London.

Journal of Valuation (1989) 'Market Data', *Journal of Valuation*, 8(1), 87–9.

Ross, S. A., Westerfield, R. W. and Jaffe, J. F. (1993) *Corporate Finance*, Irwin, Boston, MA.

Savills (1989) *Financing Property 1989*, Savills, London.

Scott, I. P. (1992) 'Debt, Liquidity and Secondary Trading in Property Debt', *Journal of Property Finance*, 3(3), 347–55.

Shayle, A. (1991) 'The Use of Deep Discount and Zero Coupon Bonds in the UK Property Market', *Journal of Property Finance*, 2(1), 11–17.

Wolfe, R. (1988) 'Debt Finance', in S. L. Barter (ed.), *Real Estate Finance*, Butterworths, London.

8
Equity Finance

8.1 Types of equity finance

An equity investment is a financial interest in an economic venture where the return to the investor is residual in character and entirely dependent upon the financial profitability of the venture. The returns to equity are thus variable, volatile and insecure. The distinction between debt and equity is that, in comparison, debt is based on borrowing. The borrower offers the lender a guaranteed money return, expressed in fixed terms, usually over a finite period. The investment return is not related to the financial success of the company and is usually secured. Apart from the risk of default by the borrower, the investment return is therefore quite precisely predictable in money terms and is comparatively secure.

Up until 1991, property development expanded on the back of bank finance had grown to £37 billion or, with committed loans, to around £40 billion; this reduced after that date. At the same time, the amount of new equity into property was around £2–3 billion per annum. The sources of equity have relied on institutional purchasing of buildings; in the past few years this equity has mainly been from overseas: institutional take-up of debt (mainly debentures and eurobonds) and small amounts of directly subscribed capital. At this rate, it takes many years to replace the bank debt outstanding and thus banks are committed to 'rolling over' their current and outstanding positions. UK property has been financed too much by debt and has tended to be starved of equity for many years (Beveridge 1991).

8.2 Sources of equity

In the market, the main sources of equity are:

- long-term institutions (pension funds and insurance companies)
- property companies
- private investors
- others.

Institutions and property companies are examined elsewhere. This chapter will concentrate on private investors and others, who can be owner-occupiers, overseas investors and construction companies.

Private investors are excluded from participation in many areas of the property market because of the large sums involved in purchase and transaction costs. Some funds have been established for groups of investors with a single specific purpose. Authorised unit trusts are one means of access and are discussed later. In the lower end of the market with high yielding secondary and tertiary property, individuals do play a part; this is a significant sector. However, generally the role of the private investor in the property market in the UK is smaller than elsewhere. Catalano (2001a) suggests that there are few opportunities for the small investors in property due to a lack of securitisation of property equity (see Chapter 12 for a further discussion on this). The scale of direct investment means that small investors have to be involved in indirect investment, but the collective investment vehicles available for this are inappropriate because:

- quoted property company shares suffer from double taxation, discounts to underlying values and problematic management (see Chapter 10)
- authorised property unit trusts are tax-efficient but are dogged by restrictions that hamper their operational freedom: by 2001, only two specialising in commercial real estate had been set up.

Tax transparent vehicles that avoid double taxation, such as limited partnerships, are limited to large investors and the other example, unauthorised unit trusts, is only available for tax exempt institutions such as pension funds.

Other sources of finance may be owner-occupiers. Commercial owner-occupiers are in operation to earn a profit and therefore will compare rental payments with the opportunities for owner-occupation. The benefits of purchase mean that the asset base of the company is extended and, if the cash flows have been worked out correctly, there may be net savings in occupation costs. However, if the company has to borrow to purchase the property, the debt will need to be shown on the balance sheet. In the 1960s and 1970s, there were a number of sale and leasebacks where owners disposed of their freehold interests in land and took on occupational leases. There appears to be a reversal of this in recent years because of the disadvantages of the standard institutional lease. These disadvantages are:

(a) the length of lease and difficulties of assignments (privity of contract previously meant liability for the full term whether assignment takes place or not);
(b) because of regular rent reviews that may have been upward only, no equity can be built up in the property asset;
(c) lease terms, besides the rent review terms and length of lease, can be onerous in terms of repairing, use and other obligations and damaging to the cash flow (Mallinson 1988).

A survey of private property vehicles in the UK carried out in 2001 showed the market to be dominated by limited partnerships, controlling £14 billion of real estate and accounting for 12 per cent of the UK direct institutional market (see

Chapter 11 on joint ventures). The main vehicles in the market in order of size (value of investment) were as shown below:

1 Limited partnerships
2 Private property companies
3 Unauthorised property unit trusts
4 Managed funds
5 Authorised property unit trusts

Property unit trusts together have approximately £9 billion of real estate invested in them (Catalano 2001b).

Construction companies may also provide equity; this is likely to be short-term finance and may be provided as a package to the developer to ensure a building contract. Some construction companies will participate over a longer period as partners or in joint ventures, but these interests are usually held in property company subsidiaries.

Overseas purchasers are generally institutions, property companies or construction companies. They tend to deal in London and are cautious small players, often seeking partnerships with UK developers. The scale of overseas investment is estimated at £1.5–2 billion for 1993 (down from £3 billion in 1989/90). The overseas investment is concentrated in central London. In the early 1990s, German investors led the market with Middle Eastern and Asian investors following (DTZ Debenham Thorpe 1993). Figure 8.1 shows overseas investment in property and the rapid increase in the late 1980s.

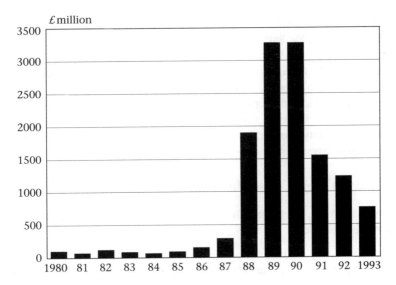

Figure 8.1 Overseas direct investment in property, 1980–93

Note: 1993, first two quarters only.

Source: Evans (1993), p. 81.

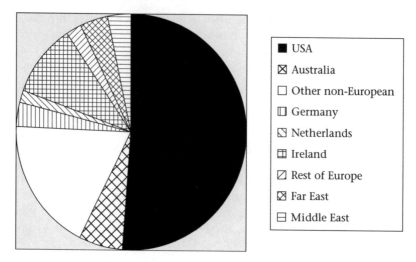

Figure 8.2   Overseas direct investment in property, 2000 and 2001 (Quarter 1)

In the fifteen months from January 2000 to March 2001, overseas investment in UK amounted to £8.9 billion. On an annualised basis, this represents twice the total of 1999 and is 50 per cent higher, after allowing for capital value inflation, than the previous highest annual total of 1997. The contribution of overseas investors to the liquidity of the market is shown by the fact that over this period they accounted for 25 per cent of all reported transactions exceeding £1 million in value. The investor base is diversified but activity has become increasingly dominated by fewer nationalities, particularly those from Germany, the Netherlands, Ireland, the USA, the Far East and Australia. US capital dominates inflows of foreign direct investment in the UK, accounting for more that two-thirds of all real estate projects initiated by foreigners in the UK. From January 2000 to March 2001, half the investment from overseas was from the USA. In particular, US investment has targeted the acquisition of UK property companies to obtain local expertise as a platform for expansion. Overseas investors include high net worth individuals, institutional funds, property companies, opportunity funds and trust investment vehicles. The make-up of overseas investment is shown in Figure 8.2 (DTZ Research 2001).

8.3   Equity in project-based funding

If equity finance is project specific, it can take a number of forms, including the following (Isaac 1996):

1 Finance from the developer's own cash and resources;
2 Partnership funds where another party joins in to share the risks and rewards of the enterprise;
3 Financiers providing equity against which collateral or debt can be raised. The money is thus not used in the development and neither is a joint company formed, but a form of guarantee is provided;

4 Forward funding by an institution. The institution may meet the costs of development including the acquisition costs of the site, construction fees, interest and letting fees. The institution may provide these monies at a lower interest rate but may require purchase of the completed development at a lower rate.

8.4 Equity in corporate funding

The types of equity share and issues have been dealt with elsewhere. This section will concentrate on an overview. If the maximum debt gearing available to a certain project is 70 per cent of cost or value (whichever is the less), then there is a substantial shortfall to make up with equity. In a development situation, the offer from a lender may only be, say, 70 per cent of the site cost plus the prime building cost which may only perhaps equate to 60 per cent of overall cost. In addition, such a level of funding may assume that a pre-let or pre-sale is in position at the outset. If a lender agrees a 70 per cent loan to cost ratio, this may include interest and thus effectively the loan reduces to perhaps 50–60 per cent of cost (Berkley 1991).

The balance can be funded in a number of ways, and typically in the present market it may be funded from any of the following:

1 The lender's own resources;
2 Collateral security, but even with this the maximum gearing of, say, 70 per cent applies;
3 A commercial mortgage indemnity (CMI) taking the loan to value ratio up to 85 per cent (CMIs have been discussed in Chapter 4). This additional 15 per cent cover is often used to service a shortfall on rental income until a review or to purchase a 'cap' to limit the interest charged by the lender to a figure that equates with the rental income;
4 Issues of shares, if the company is a public limited company;
5 Equity/mezzanine participation finance.

Mezzanine finance is discussed in detail in section 8.7. This mezzanine finance can come from the supplier of the prime debt but usually is provided by a specialist lender. The loan above the 70 per cent level will attract a higher rate of interest than the prime debt because of the additional risk; alternatively, a single fee may be charged. This mezzanine debt many be used by borrowers to take the loan up to 85 per cent of value where a cap is not available. The return reflects a share in anticipated profits. Some lenders take shares in the borrowing company; others prefer a second charge on the subject property and collateral security ranking behind the prime debt (Berkley 1991).

8.5 Authorised property unit trusts

The use of unit trusts to encourage investment in property has already been discussed, as well as the difficulties related to setting up an authorised unit trust. On 15 July 1991, the Securities and Investments Board issued regulations enabling authorised property unit trusts (APUTs) to invest directly in property. Thus, APUTs allow investors to enter the commercial property market in exactly the same way as unit trusts offer investors exposure to shares. Prior to the change in regulations, unit trusts were not permitted to invest directly in property. This meant that unauthorised property unit trusts were only open to exempt funds such as pension funds and charities.

There are tax advantages in investing in an APUT; corporation tax at the time was paid at the base rate level of 25 per cent on net income instead of the full rate of corporation tax at 33 per cent. A distribution made by an APUT to its unit holders will be treated for tax purposes as dividends. Individual unit holders received a tax credit of 25 per cent on those distributions and will only be liable for higher rate personal tax. Corporate investors who, at the time, paid corporation tax at the small companies' rate of 25 per cent also have the whole of their liability to tax arising from APUT covered by the tax credit. An APUT, in addition, is entirely free from capital gains tax arising on the disposal of property. Unit holders will, however, remain subject to any capital gains tax arising from the disposal of their units unless, of course, they are tax exempt. Set against these tax advantages, APUTs will have to comply with many regulations imposed by the Securities and Investment Board (SIB) to protect non-institutional investors from the risks involved in property investment. These problems include the lack of liquidity of property, a unit price based on possible subjective valuations, changes in values and the actual market for the units themselves (Baring, Houston & Saunders 1991; Ryland 1991).

The regulations as at 1991 were as shown below.

Structure

The structure of an APUT is similar to existing unit trust schemes with a trustee and a manager. The manager is responsible for the day-to-day management of the scheme with the trustee and manager owing a fiduciary duty to the unit holders.

Investment characteristics

1 A fund must attain a value of £5 million within 21 days. Thereafter between 20 and 80 per cent of its funds must be invested in property or property related securities. These investments can be in EU member states and a number of other countries, such as the USA and Canada.
2 Up to 10 per cent of the portfolio may be invested in unlisted property shares.
3 Between 20 and 30 per cent may be invested in cash or near cash (government securities or quoted property company shares).
4 A fund can only invest a maximum of 15 per cent of its value in any one property. This maximum value may increase to 25 per cent once the property has been included in the portfolio. No more than 20 per cent of the gross rental income may come from the tenant and only 25 per cent of the fund may be invested in vacant or development properties.
5 APUTs may borrow against properties, up to a maximum of 30 per cent of each property's value or 15 per cent of the whole portfolio.

Valuation

The value of an APUT is strictly controlled with a full independent valuation once a year, carried out by a qualified surveyor in accordance with the Royal Institute of Chartered Surveyors (RICS) guidelines. In addition, to keep unit prices current, there will be an 'armchair' valuation at least once a month to review the last full valuation. Any new purchases must not exceed 105 per cent of the valuation.

Redemptions

Units will normally be redeemed within four business days after the valuation following the request for redemption. In certain circumstances, a manager may suspend redemption rights for a period up to 28 days subject to trustee approval and the SIB being advised.

Potential

APUTs offer a good opportunity of gaining exposure to the property investment market. By the end of 1991, only two APUTs had been established, as substantial commitment is required from the institution or funder to establish an APUT. The APUT has achieved more acceptance in the market than securitisation vehicles (see Chapter 12) but APUTs are not a direct alternative to these vehicles since they invest in smaller-sized properties which already have a broad market appeal among investing institutions rather than in large illiquid properties (Sexton and Laxton 1992).

8.6   Investment trusts and unit trusts

Investment trusts are companies that own shares on other companies; they suffer from the problems of discount on net asset value, which are described in the context of property companies in Chapter 10. As an example of a property investment trust, Banque Paribas announced in October 1993 the setting-up of a £50 million property investment trust on the Stock Exchange. The trust was called the Wigmore Property Trust and concentrated on the shares of small companies with a market capitalisation of less than £250 million. The trust invested in mainly quoted ordinary shares and focused on investment companies. It aimed to have up to 20 per cent of its net asset value in special situations that could mean finance for corporate restructuring and acquisitions (Catalano 1993). The trust is a quoted company and closed-ended, unlike a unit trust. (For an explanation of closed- and open-ended trusts, see section 10.1.)

Exempt property unit trusts (PUTs) are designed for non-tax paying investors, such as pension funds and charities. The market in these units is illiquid. They are valued at the underlying net assets value with no discount. Exempt PUTs are open-ended.

APUTs, as discussed in the previous section, are also open-ended; the manager has to be in a position to liquidate part of the trust's investment at any time to redeem units that investors wish to sell. The market price of APUTs is again the net asset value without discount. The experience of Rodamco in Holland has shown the shortcomings of open-ended funds that invest in illiquid assets; this is treated as a brief case study in Box 8.1. There is a liquidity problem with APUTs (Venmore-Rowland 1991).

Box 8.1 Rodamco, a case study of an open-ended trust

The principle

Rodamco was established in 1979 as an open-ended fund. Rodamco forms one of the main investment vehicles within the largest Dutch investment fund management group. To investors, the vehicle appeared a safe and highly liquid exposure to direct property; it attracted the interest of institutional and private investors who formed, initially at least, 80 per cent of the shareholders. Such companies expand by issuing new shares when demand exceeds supply but as the company stands in the market it also has to repurchase shares when no other buyer can be found. The shares were thus considered a low risk investment. Stock market transactions took place at prices close to the net asset value of the company and the net asset value was recalculated each day. This situation requires the company to maintain substantial cash balances but at the same time there was little dilution of assets or earnings per share from share issues; this enabled the company to expand without the need for increasing bank debt to any significant level.

The reality

The fund grew rapidly by way of share placings in 1980. This expansion led to a series of acquisitions especially in the UK and US, in 1986 Haselmere Estates were acquired in the UK and Hexalon Real Estate in the USA. In 1988 it mounted a bid for Hammerson but was outbid by Hammerson's major institutional shareholder. The downturn in 1990 in the US and UK markets led to investors selling the Rodamco stock. This was easy for investors to do as the company stood in the market and bought in the shares offered at the daily quoted net asset value price. The company's shares were suspended in September 1990 and the company changed to being 'close-ended': that is, to having a fixed number of shares in issue. On being relisted the share price fell sharply (around 20 per cent) prompting additional selling of the stock before settling at a more normal, in UK terms, discount to net asset value.

Source: Paribas Capital Markets (1993a).

Australian PUTs and US real estate investment trusts (REITs) are close-ended trusts. The REIT market is a useful comparison for developments in unit trusts and securitisation. The REIT market started in the USA in 1960; the laws allowed certain companies (REITs) to own property and mortgages and to pay dividends without prior deduction of corporate taxes. Of the REITs in existence in the USA in 1993, 50 per cent were mortgage REITs and 40 per cent were equity REITs (which derive their income from rent); the remainder were hybrids. There were some mistakes in the issues during the period 1985–86 which affected confidence in the market, but now there is better gearing in these companies and management is better trained to deal with investment decisions, especially in the specialist investment areas (Jennings 1993).

A property unit trust could be used with securitised property (SPUTs; see Chapter 12 for developments in the area of securitised property).

Real Estate Investment Trusts

A US REIT is a real estate company or trust that has elected to qualify under certain tax provisions to become a 'transparent' entity (for more discussion on tax transparency, see Chapter 12). This means that it distributes almost all of its earnings and capital gains. The REIT does not pay tax on its earnings but the distributed earnings do represent dividend income to its shareholders and are taxed accordingly. To qualify as a REIT for tax purposes, the trust must satisfy certain requirements. These include:

- at least 75 per cent of the value of a REIT's assets must consist of real estate assets, cash and government securities
- at least 75 per cent of the gross income must be derived from rents, interest on obligations secured by mortgages, gains from the sale of certain assets, or income attributable to investments in other REITs
- distribution to shareholders must equal or exceed the sum of 95 per cent of REIT taxable income.

(Hoesli and MacGregor 2000)

In investment terms, it is usually shown that the income return component of US REITs is correlated with that of direct property investments but that the capital return components are highly correlated with that of common stocks.

8.7 Mezzanine finance

Mezzanine debt represents the additional finance that has to be put between the senior debt and the equity to complete the development costs. Senior debt is assessed as a proportion of loan to cost or loan to value (cost here being the total development cost, whilst value is the gross development value on completion). If the loan to value ratio is 70 per cent and the gross development value is £10 million, then the equity required is £3 million. If the developer can only come up with £2 million, then mezzanine finance will be required for the additional £1 million. This is riskier than the senior debt and thus should attract a higher interest rate, or an alternative would be to offer rights to convert into equity. The lenders can thus be provided with a profit sharing arrangement, or options for equity, or they may get an additional proportion of the surplus profit. Possible returns are set out below.

Returns on debt and equity

	Percentage of cost	Gross return
Senior debt	0–70	17%
Mezzanine debt	70–90	30–40%
Equity	90	40+%

An example of the application of mezzanine finance is shown in Box 8.2.

8.8 Venture capital

Venture capital is a specialist area but is related, especially to the situations discussed previously in mezzanine finance. Venture capitalists invest in risky start-up operations or restructures. These would generally be in respect of commercial

Box 8.2   Example of mezzanine finance

Residential example

Development of 40 residential units.

Appraisal:	£
Net sale proceeds	3,490,000
Less total cost	2,600,000
Projected profit	890,000
Return on cost	34 per cent

Funding:

	£
Prime debt finance (70 per cent of site and prime building costs)	1,400,000
Equity funds from borrower	500,000
Mezzanine finance required	700,000
Total finance @ 100 per cent of cost	2,600,000

Profit share:

	Profit	Split	Return
Borrower	£534,000	60%	107%
Mezzanine	£356,000	40%	51%

Source: Berkley (1991).

companies but may overlap with properties in two areas at least:

- where the company is trading in the property or construction sector
- where the company has large property assets or where the cash flow is very dependent on its property assets (leisure, housing, medical).

Venture capitalists will introduce risky equity and use this perhaps to gear up or assist in restructuring a new venture. Restructuring may take place by a reverse takeover or an import of management skills or assets or technology. The common types of equity investment for venture capitalists are:

- management buy-outs (MBOs)
- start-up companies
- restructuring of companies
- purchase of bankrupt operations
- pump-priming for new developments or infrastructure
- development of new technologies.

Needless to say, besides private sector monies, this equity may involve quasi-public sector monies (trusts or funds which are provided at subsidised rates) and public funds (development agencies). In the November 1993 budget, the Chancellor of the Exchequer introduced a Venture Capital Trust to encourage venture capital investment with tax concessions. The Venture Capital Trust Scheme will give tax-free dividends and capital gains for pooled investment schemes in unquoted trading companies.

In the same budget, an Enterprise Investment Scheme was introduced to follow on from the Business Expansion Schemes which gave 20 per cent tax relief on £100,000 invested in qualifying unquoted companies per year. Income tax and capital gains relief are available on losses. Property related investments are specifically excluded from the Enterprise Investment Scheme.

References and further reading

Baring, Houston & Saunders (1991) *Property Report*, Baring, Houston & Saunders, London, November.

Berkley, R. (1991) 'Raising Commercial Property Finance in a Difficult Market', *Journal of Property Finance*, 1(4), 523–9.

Beveridge, J. A. (1991) 'New Methods of Financing', in P. Venmore-Rowland, P. Brandon and T. Mole (eds), *Investment, Procurement and Performance in Construction*, RICS, London.

Catalano, A. (1993) 'Paribas trusts in the upturn', *Estates Gazette*, 23 October, 52.

Catalano, A. (2001a) 'No safe haven for small punters', *Estates Gazette*, 27 October, 54.

Catalano, A. (2001b) 'Limit to LP's attractions', *Estates Gazette*, 3 November, 61.

DTZ Debenham Thorpe (1993) *Money into Property*, DTZ Debenham Thorpe, London, August.

DTZ Research (2001) *Money into Property*, DTZ Research, London, edition 26, June.

Evans, P. H. (1993) 'Statistical Review', *Journal of Property Finance*, 4(2), 75–82.

Graham, J. (1985) 'New sources of finance for the property industry', *Estates Gazette*, 6 July.

Hoesli, M. and MacGregor, B. D. (2000) *Property Investment: Principles and Practice of Portfolio Management*, Pearson Education, Harlow.

Isaac, D. (1996) *Property Development; Appraisal and Finance*, Macmillan, London.

Jennings, R. B. (1993) 'The Resurgence of Real Estate Investment Trusts (REITs)', *Journal of Property Finance*, 4(1), 13–19.

Mallinson, M. (1988) 'Equity Finance', in S. L. Barter (ed.), *Real Estate Finance*, Butterworths, London.

Paribas Capital Markets (1993a) *European Equity Research: Rodamco*, Banque Paribas Nederland NV, October.

Ryland, D. (1991) 'Authorised Property Unit Trusts', *Estates Gazette*, London, 9 November, 163–4.

Savills (1989) *Financing Property 1989*, Savills, London.

Savills (1993b) *Investment and Economic Outlook*, Savills, London, Issue 3, October.

Sexton, P. and Laxton, C. (1992) 'Authorised Property Unit Trusts', *Journal of Property Finance*, 2(4), 468–75.

Venmore-Rowland, P. (1991) 'Vehicles for Property Investment', in P. Venmore-Rowland, P. Brandon and T. Mole (eds), *Investment, Procurement and Performance in Construction*, RICS, London.

9

Institutional Investment

9.1 Introduction

The financial institutions consist of the insurance companies and pension funds, the two principal channels for the nation's savings. Because of the nature of the real property market, individual investors generally have withdrawn from the market, and because the channelling or collectivisation of savings into financial institutions is more tax effective than direct saving, savings have tended to go into those institutions.

The institutions dominated the funding of development properties in the early 1980s. The traditional approach to development finance was to obtain short-term finance to complete a development and then arrange a buy-out by an institutional fund; this dominance has declined since. After 1985, the important new money into commercial property has been from banks, property companies and through overseas investment (Evans 1992). The growth of financial institutions that was fuelled by the collectivisation of savings and the decline of personal sector saving, and evidenced by the expansion of development activity in the postwar period, has now abated. This has resulted in a significant move away from property investment and funding by institutions (Woodroffe and Isaac 1987). The decline of the institutions in the commercial property market has been matched by an increase in indirect investment in property companies by way of bank advances. In the critical period between 1985 and 1993, outstanding bank loans to property companies increased from £5 billion in 1985 to just over £40 billion in the second quarter of 1991; this declined only slightly to £36.8 billion at the beginning of 1993. Over the period between 1986 and 1992, institutions' purchases have generally exceeded their sales but their net property investment has been a declining share of the total. Institutional net property investment is shown in Table 9.1 and Figure 9.1 for 1985–93, which represents the period of the recent boom and slump in the UK property cycle.

From 1984, there was a noticeable fall in the availability of long-term institutional funding and the reaction of the City to the shortfall was to turn to innovative financing methods. Out of necessity, developers turned to alternative finance sources to complement institutional finance (Richard Ellis, 1986). Money flowing

Table 9.1 Institutional net property investment, 1985–93 (£ million)

	1985	1986	1987	1988	1989	1990	1991	1992	1993[a]
Insurance companies:									
Life funds	803	789	726	1,008	1,090	946	1,493	668	95
General insurance	12	32	29	94	420	134	−10	−68	−21
	815	821	755	1,102	1,510	1,080	1,483	600	74
Pension funds	509	434	240	312	92	−491	467	349	134
Property unit trusts	−5	−101	−516	99	31	−61	19	−12	7
Total	1,319	1,154	479	1,513	1,633	528	1,969	937	215

[a] First quarter 1993 only.

Source: Evans (1993).

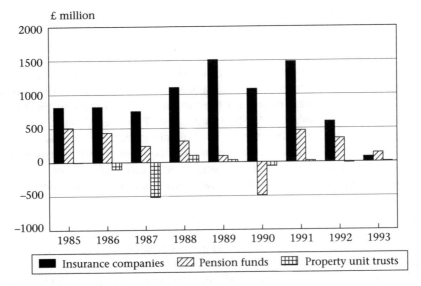

Figure 9.1 Institutional net investment in property, 1985–93

Note: 1993 first quarter only.

Source: Evans (1993), p. 76.

into property during the early 1980s increased from £2 billion to £4 billion in the period from 1980 to 1986. Between 1986 and 1989, there was a rapid increase to £14 billion. It then tailed off to £8 billion, £4 billion and finally £0.5 billion in 1992. The pension funds' involvement had been relatively static but had decreased in the late 1980s. The insurance companies have been more stable investors with an increase in investment in the period 1989–91. The Stock Exchange has not been a significant contributor except in 1987, 1989 and 1991. Banks rapidly increased their involvement between 1986 and 1991 but this has since decreased quite dramatically (see Figure 9.2).

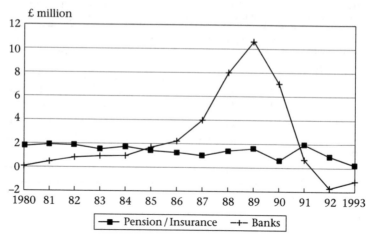

£ million

Figure 9.2 Institutional investment and bank finance in property, 1980–93

Note: 1993 first quarter only.

Source: Evans (1993), p. 76.

Property as a proportion of overall institutional investment has been falling in recent years. The Investment Property Databank Annual Review for 1993 suggests that the best end of year figures for the proportion of property in institutional portfolios as at December 1992 showed a fall to 7 per cent from the figure in December 1991, which was 9 per cent. The bulk of the drop can be explained, however, in terms of the differential price movements between the different asset classes held in the portfolio. Net property investment by institutions is still positive, but at the lowest recorded level since 1980 (Investment Property Databank 1993).

9.2   History

In the early postwar period, the insurance companies in particular played an important role in property financing by lending long-term fixed interest funds. This approach was useful immediately after the war when inflation was low and thus the returns were not eroded. Financial arrangements between developers and property companies were encouraged because of the shortage of supply of commercial space, the heavy demand and the resultant rental grown and capital value gain. When inflation established itself, the fixed interest approach was no longer attractive to the institutions, and insurance companies, which had previously had financial arrangements with major developers, broke these and moved into providing funds for sale and leaseback or situations where they could obtain some share in growth. Eventually, the institutions carried out direct development, funding the developer in an arrangement whereby the developer received a project management fee with some additional incentives.

The good performance of equities in the 1980s was matched by a poor performance in property. The demand for development sites by the institutional funds increased land values and capital values of completed developments. The level of income arising from the developments in terms of rentals was overexaggerated and thus the yield was poor. The insurance companies had been more firmly established in the development markets and the decline in activity affected them less. The pension funds, except for a few larger ones, cut back their portfolios quite drastically. As has been said, new purchases were still made but marginal or poorly performing properties were removed from portfolios. In 1990, the property holdings of the insurance companies (life and general companies combined) reached £42 billion, with pension funds having holdings of £22 billion (Brett 1990b).

9.3   Partnership arrangements

The larger insurance companies and the very large pension funds have extensive property departments, capable in many cases of actually carrying out development as well as advising on the purchase and management of completed investment properties. Smaller funds may choose alternative approaches to investment in property (by indirect investment in unauthorised property unit trusts, for instance).

Conventional mortgage finance was replaced with direct development by institutions in the 1980s as mentioned previously; alternatively, the institution would find a sale and leaseback, which involved the sale of the freehold of the property to the institution and the taking back of a long lease by the developer. The developer then sub-let the development to occupying tenants on conventional 25-year occupational leases. Early deals had no provision for rent reviews but, in the late 1960s and early 1970s (as shorter and shorter review periods became the norm), these interests provided an appropriate inflation-proofed equity investment while at the same time minimising any management problems (which were taken on by the developer). Equity-sharing sale and leaseback arrangements are extremely complex and relate to the balance of risk and return of the parties involved. They have been discussed in other chapters, including Chapter 8 on equity.

9.4   Direct versus indirect funding

Long-term savings institutions, the pension funds and insurance companies are the main sources of equity finance. The history of the involvement of institutions has been a move towards direct funding of property development and property investments. Smaller institutions wanting to take a stake in commercial property but lacking the size of resources to invest direct can use indirect routes into property (see Figure 9.3); the main indirect routes are (Brett 1983b):

- property company shares
- property bonds – unit linked life assurance schemes
- exempt unit trusts and managed funds
- mortgages and debentures.

The property company differs from the other indirect routes in that it is a corporate body whose shares can be quoted on the Stock Exchange. The value of its

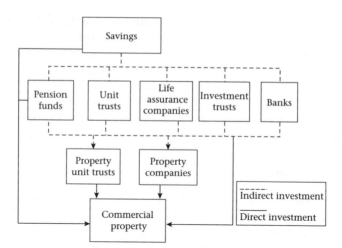

Figure 9.3   Direct and indirect investment in property
Source: Brett (1983b).

shares will bear some relation to the underlying property assets held in the portfolio of the company but the link is not a direct one. Property bonds and unit trusts work on a different principle. The value of the unit is directly determined by the value of the properties in the fund. Funds that operate on the unit principle are 'open-ended' in the sense that the number of units can increase or decrease with the purchase or sale of assets, whereas the share capital of a company is fixed apart from new issues of shares or capital reductions requiring legal permission.

9.5   Criteria for investment

Institutions such as pension funds and insurance companies are long-term savings institutions. They invest in equity to support products that have a long duration and could have open liabilities (i.e., products such as pensions or insurance policies for which the pay-out is not fixed in money terms and so is prone to inflation). Because the liabilities of these institutions extend over long periods, the risks and uncertainties of the returns being affected by inflation are accentuated (Mallinson 1988).

The needs of long-term savings institutions in terms of their equity investment relate to the certainty of return. The institution will wish to minimise risk in an investment of course, and associated with this will be the aspects of difficulties of management that may accentuate problems of the certainty of return. Also, to avoid risk, the institution will require a diversity of interests to avoid putting 'all the eggs in one basket'. Finally, in terms of return, income is required at the present time rather than capital growth.

Research by Rydin, Rodney and Orr (1990) has pointed out that, although surveyors and property analysts like to extol the values of property investment and complain that too small a proportion of institutions' portfolios is taken up by property, the proportion of institutional portfolio in property assets remains well below 20 per cent and fell to 11 per cent in 1987. This has fallen further, as indicated in the beginning of this chapter. Around 20 per cent has historically been seen as an appropriate percentage for property in investment portfolios.

The results of this research showed that the main reasons and disadvantages were perceived as follows:

Reasons for including property in portfolio	*Disadvantage of property*
Long-term return	Poor liquidity
Low level of long-term risk	High unit costs
To achieve a balanced portfolio	
Lack of short-term volatility	

Less important	*Less important*
Low level of short-term risk	Management costs
Inflation hedge	Problems of property as a specialist area
Short-term returns	(i.e., tax, lettings, valuation)

The reasons for including property are consistent with the historic patterns of returns from property investment with a low variability of returns, low correlation between property and equity or gilts returns and relatively low beta coefficients (indicating risk) for property (Rydin, Rodney and Orr 1990; Barter 1988).

9.6   Future for institutional investment

A survey in 1993 of over 50 major insurance companies and pension funds indicated that the planned purchases of property assets for 1993 would be at least 100 per cent over 1992, and this indicated the start of a recovery in institutional investment. The institutional investment sector as a whole has a gross investment potential of some £7 billion over the 12–18 months to the end of 1993 and 1994. Disposals by institutions rose over this period since the lack of liquidity in the market since 1990 had prevented the restructuring of investment portfolios (DTZ Debenham Thorpe 1993). The survey covered what the institutional investors saw as the attractions and disadvantages of property investment as well as their investment intentions into the future; these are set out in Table 9.2 and should be compared with the results of Rydin set out previously. A survey by Chesterton Financial (November 1993) confirmed the renewed interest of institutions in the property market. The interest in schemes for forward commitment and forward funding was high (94 per cent and 83 per cent respectively); the sectors of most interest were offices and industrial property, followed by retail warehouses. Retail was the least popular sector (Chesterton Financial 1993).

In 1997, the government abolished the dividend tax credit for pension fund shareholders. The changes introduced have had an adverse effect on pension funds' dividend income and significantly increased the disadvantage for pension funds to hold property investments via a company structure. Rental income, though, from property investments held directly by the pension funds still has no deduction of tax. The maximum amount receivable by a pension fund from £100 of pre-tax profits, rents and interest from investments in property, industrial and commercial companies was reduced from 83.75 per cent to 69 per cent after the July 1997 budget (Brett 1997).

In 2000, institutional investors increased their exposure to directly held UK real estate by £6.1 billion. This represented an increase of more than 100 per cent on 1999 and was the highest annual total recorded. The net investment was dominated by the pension funds, which committed £3.7 billion to real estate. At the beginning of 2000, the average weighting of the UK insurance companies investment portfolio devoted to property was 8.1 per cent whilst the equivalent pension fund figure was 7.1 per cent. Both percentages were expected to increase in the following year. For the financial institutions in 2000, limited partnerships were the most popular vehicle for indirect investment in property, with 90 per cent of indirectly held property being held in this form by insurance companies. This proportion was lower for the pension funds which had a higher exposure to property unit trusts. Overall, property's share of new institutional investment rose from 4.5 per cent at the end of 1999 to 10.1 per cent by the end of 2000, boosted by unprecedented levels of purchasing from the pension funds. This reinforced the upward trend seen since the mid-1990s. Throughout the 1980s the bullish outlook

Table 9.2   DTZ Debenham Thorpe survey of institutional investors

(i) Attractions and disadvantages of property investment in order

Attractions	Disadvantages
Income security	Illiquidity
Performance outlook	Management costs
Spread of risk in portfolio	Indivisibility
Heterogeneity	Research information
Inflation hedge	Performance outlook

(ii) Investment intentions

1993 Activity	% Response for: Purchases	Sales
greater than 1992	75	57
same as 1992	15	23
less than 1992	10	20
1994 Activity	% Response for: Purchases	Sales
greater than 1993	34	32
same as 1993	38	36
less than 1993	28	22

Source: DTZ Debenham Thorpe (1993).

for equities, combined with the abolition of restrictions on international cash flows (which enabled funds to diversify using overseas equities), was detrimental to property investment. The improved and relatively stable performance of property since the mid-1990s, combined with the poor return on equities and low bond yields by 2000, led to property having a higher share of institutional investment (DTZ Research 2001).

References and bibliography

Barter, S. L. (1988) 'Introduction', in S. L. Barter (ed.), *Real Estate Finance*, Butterworths, London.

Baum, A. E. and Schofield, A. (1991) 'Property as a Global Asset', in P. Venmore-Rowland, P. Brandon and T. Mole (eds), *Investment, Procurement and Performance in Construction*, RICS, London.

Brett, M. (1983b) 'Indirect Investment in Property', in C. Darlow (ed.), *Valuation and Investment Appraisal*, Estates Gazette, London.

Brett, M. (1990b) *Property and Money*, Estates Gazette, London.

Brett, M. (1997) *Property and Money*, Estates Gazette, London.

Chesterton Financial, Internal uncirculated reports, Chesterton Financial, London.

Chesterton Financial (1993) *Property Lending Survey*, Chesterton Financial, London, February.

DTZ Debenham Thorpe (1993) *Money into Property*, DTZ Debenham Thorpe, London, August.

DTZ Research (2001) *Money into Property*, DTZ Research, London, edition 26, June.

Evans, P. H. (1992) 'Statistical Review', *Journal of Property Finance*, 3(1), 115–20.

Evans, P. H. (1993) 'Statistical Review', *Journal of Property Finance*, 4(2), 75–82.

Investment Property Databank (1993) *Annual Review 1993*, IPD, London, December.

Isaac, D. (1996) *Property Development; Appraisal and Finance*, Macmillan, London.

Mallinson, M. (1988) 'Equity Finance', in S. L. Barter (ed.), *Real Estate Finance*, Butterworths, London.

Richard Ellis (1986) 'Development Finance', *Property Investment Quarterly Bulletin*, Richard Ellis, April.

Rydin, Y., Rodney, W. and Orr, C. (1990) 'Why Do Institutions Invest in Property', *Journal of Property Finance*, 1(2), 250–8.

Woodroffe, N. and Isaac, D. (1987) 'Corporate Finance and Property Development Funding', Working Paper of the School of Applied Economics and Social Studies, Faculty of the Built Environment, Polytechnic of the South Bank.

10
Property Companies

10.1 Introduction

Property business is defined as extraction of value from land and buildings such that the landlord takes a creditor's view rather than an equity holder's view of the occupiers. In March 1988, the quoted property company sector (this refers to quoted property companies: i.e., ones that are listed on the Stock Exchange) owned property valued at £17 billion, market capitalisation of shares worth £13 billion and net assets of £14 billion. This could have been compared at the time with the market capitalisation of BP (£15 billion) and the commercial banking sector (£16 billion). Seventy per cent of the shares at that time were owned by institutions (Millman 1988). The total book assets of the sector increased up to 1990, when they reached a peak of nearly £30 billion, but decreased in 1992 to £25 billion (S. G. Warburg Securities 1993). Debt has continued to rise in the balance sheets of the property sector, although less rapidly to 1992. Table 10.1 shows a summary of asset values and borrowings in the balance sheets of property companies for the period 1986–92.

In 1993, there was a dramatic re-rating of property companies because of a major shift in confidence. In the first half of 1993, equity and convertible issues raised by property companies totalled around £1.3 billion. Capital issues raised subsequently showed a rapid expansion (see Figure 10.1). By the end of 1993, share prices had risen so strongly that they were no longer trading at a discount to net asset value. Property companies were, at the end of 1993, in the rare position of being able to raise money without significant dilution of net asset value or earnings. However, the situation in 1993 was marred by the continued fall-out from the consequences of overlending, overdevelopment and much reduced property values (Evans 1993). A number of property companies had huge write-offs. For example, London & Edinburgh Trust (LET), a subsidiary of the Swedish company, SPP, had a 1992 pre-tax loss of £449 million against a loss of £138 million in the previous year. SPP bought LET in 1990 for £491 million. Table 10.2 gives a sample of the main quoted property companies on the Stock Exchange in 1993, while Table 10.3 gives a simplified updated list of the property sector in 2001.

Table 10.1 Quoted property companies: balance sheets, gearing and financing

Year	Total book assets (£ million)	Total borrowings[a] (£ million)	Cash (£ million)	Debt[b] as a % of book assets	Short-term borrowings (£ million)	Short-term borrowings as a % total
1986	11,298	3,087	437	24.4	1,075	34.8
1987	15,172	4,254	722	24.4	1,506	35.4
1988	19,862	4,988	1,407	19.4	1,748	35.0
1989	27,055	6,939	1,716	20.6	2,648	38.2
1990	30,933	8,590	1,453	24.2	3,642	42.4
1991	27,992	10,132	1,223	32.7	4,374	43.2
1992	25,462	11,130	1,278	38.7	5,218	46.9

Notes
Short-term borrowings are less than 5 years and also include convertible loan stocks and bonds.
[a] Total borrowings include convertible loan stocks and bonds.
[b] Debt is net of cash.

Source: S. G. Warburg Securities (1993).

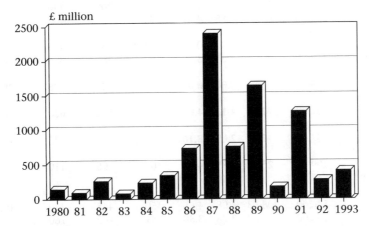

£ million

Figure 10.1 Net capital issues by property companies

Note: The 1993 figure is first two quarters; the second quarter had £445 million of issues.

Source: Bank of England/Evans (1993), p. 82.

Quoted property companies have been re-rated since the beginning of 2000, and their share prices have benefited from intense corporate activity, disenchantment with new technology stocks and the good performance of the underlying asset class. The real estate sector discount to net asset value per share (see later in the chapter for a detailed analysis of this benchmark) narrowed from 35 per cent in February 2000 to 16 per cent at the end of March 2001. The real estate sector accounted for 1.5 per cent of the value of the market at the end of March 2001 compared with 1.3 per cent at the beginning of 2000, despite subsequent equity withdrawals, from the market (DTZ Research 2001). These equity withdrawals, in conjunction with a clear preference to raise debt in the sector, have led to

Table 10.2 Major quoted property companies (1993)

Company	Price 29 Oct. 1993 (p)	Mkt cap (£ m)	Yield (act) (%)	Yield (prosp) (%)	Est'd current NAV (p)	Historic book NAV (p)	Forecast book NAV (p)	Discount to f'cast book NAV (%)
Asda Property	132.00	103.7	2.12	2.08	92	80	95	(38.5)
Bilton	670.00	290.4	3.76	3.64	740	739	740	9.5
Bradford Property	235.00	338.0	3.06	3.19	175	170	185	(27.0)
British Land	401.00	1205.8	2.33	2.40	330	294	365	(9.9)
Brixton	239.00	553.8	4.66	4.11	189	168	195	(22.6)
Burford Holdings	88.00	163.5	1.74	1.99	60	52	63	(39.7)
Capital & Regional	184.00	55.0	0.80	1.02	160	145	165	(11.5)
Cardiff[a]	230.00	5.9	1.39	1.30	215	232	215	(7.0)
Chesterfield[a]	583.00	109.1	2.52	2.57	445	398	475	(22.7)
Compco[a]	300.00	6.2	5.76	5.40	470	461	475	36.8
Derwent Valley	633.00	73.7	1.81	1.78	550	501	565	(12.0)
Frogmore	486.00	243.9	4.39	4.37	417	409	440	(1.05)
Great Portland	228.00	695.5	5.85	4.39	182	170	195	(16.9)
Greycoat[b]	27.00	23.7	0.00	0.00	33	33	n.a.	n.a.
Hammerson 'A'	369.00	905.3	3.61	3.39	393	385	395	6.6
Hemmingway Props.[a]	36.00	34.1	0.00	0.00	27	25	28	(28.6)
Land Securities	737.00	3720.4	4.13	4.07	575	504	620	(18.9)
London & Associated[a]	37.00	25.7	2.09	2.16	41	37	42	11.9
London Merchant Securities	109.00	260.2	4.89	4.82	102	95	110	0.9
MEPC	536.00	2080.3	4.98	4.66	450	445	450	(19.1)
PSIT	168.00	203.9	3.28	3.38	151	142	160	(5.0)
Scottish Met.[c]	107.00	103.9	1.87	1.93	85	82	100	(7.0)
Slough	259.00	995.5	4.17	3.91	260	245	265	2.3
Southend Properties[a]	85.00	78.4	6.67	3.53	100	94	105	19.0
Tops Estates[a]	223.00	102.8	1.26	1.23	200	189	210	(6.2)
Water City[c]	91.00	109.2	1.13	0.00	82	73	85	(7.1)

Notes

n.a. = not available

NAV = net asset value.

[a] Paribas Ltd is a broker to these companies.

[b] Subject to financial reconstruction proposals.

[c] Adjusted for right issue.

Source: Paribas Capital Markets (1993b), p. 4.

Table 10.3 Selected companies from the property sector of the Stock Exchange, 5 July 2001 (*The Times* 2001)

Company	Share price	Yield %	Price:earnings ratio
Asda	270	1.5	19.8
Br Land	501	2.3	20.1
Brixton	225	4.6	15.8
Canary Wharf	525		
Cap & Regnl	232.5	2.4	25.2
Cardiff Properties	500	1.0	5.6
Chelsfield	335.5	1.3	37.6
Estates General	136.5	2.4	81
Gt Portland	284.5	3.4	24.1
Grantchester	194.5	0.7	44.5
Hammerson	481.5	2.9	20.6
Helical bar	867.5	1.4	12.5
HK Land	127.25	5.0	
Land Securities	870.5	3.7	20.0
Mountview	2870	2.8	
Pillar Properties	371	2.0	
Slough Estates	340.5	3.6	13.3
UK Land	167.5	4.4	

Note: Entries in bold are in the FTSE 100 index.

a significant increase in the average gearing ratio of the quoted sector in this period. Bond issuance continued to be the favourite vehicle for raising capital throughout 2000. Unsecured debt issuers included Hammerson, Rodamco and Slough Estates. In June 2000, Canary Wharf completed a £975 million long-term financing. This innovative deal provided for £475 million of long-term funding with a final maturity up to 30 years; it also allowed for £500 million of revolving short-term notes that may be drawn on when further properties are added to the portfolio. Part of the proceeds were used to finance some existing loans and the balance was retained by the group for general corporate purposes. The group's weighted average cost of debt at the end of June 2000 was 7.2 per cent compared with 7.5 per cent a year earlier. Investor interest in corporate bonds has increased in recent years, underpinned by a number of factors:

1 UK government borrowing has fallen, reducing the supply of government bonds.
2 An ageing UK population has contributed to increased cash flows into pension funds thereby increasing demand for investment assets such as corporate bonds.
3 Bondholders benefit from an economic environment of lower inflation risk due in part to economic policy and improved public finances.
4 An increase in the tax burden on dividends from 1999 in the UK has provided pensions funds with a stronger incentive to invest in bonds rather than shares (DTZ Research 2001).

Features of property companies considered by an investor

The property companies listed on the Stock Exchange offer potential investors a range of different opportunities. The main features of a property company to be considered by an investor are as set out below:

1 The quality of assets in the portfolio: the age, location and tenure of individual properties and their relative importance in the portfolio, different types of property and the proportion of overseas investment.
2 The perceived quality of management in the company, which is very subjective and is often about single individuals in the company.
3 The sources of income of the company. These will vary between well established property investment companies relying on rents, and property development companies whose income arises from selling on completed developments.
4 The capital structure and gearing of the company. A highly geared financial structure is more appropriate for established companies deriving a large proportion of revenue from rental income rather than for development companies dependent on less secure trading profits. The nature of debt is also important.

The summary for a successful property company from an investor's viewpoint is shown in Box 10.1. As an example of the problems that a property company may face, it would be useful to look briefly at the case of Olympia & York. In May 1992, Olympia & York Development Ltd, owners of Canary Wharf in London Docklands and, at the time, the largest privately owned real estate development in the world, filed for bankruptcy protection in Canada, the USA and the UK. Over the previous 35 years, several successful real estate projects, funded from the world's largest banks and global real estate appreciation in the 1980s, had contributed to the company's rise. When property values declined in the late 1980s, financial problems ensued. Poor use of free cash flow, failure to limit cross-subsidisation and to provide adequate information to lenders, and the composition of the company's Board precipitated the crisis (Ghosh, Guttery and Simons 1994). Ghosh, Guttery and Simons's study of the crisis that caused Olympia & York's demise considered the effect on US and foreign banks' common stock prices. It found that exposure to Olympia & York was a significant factor affecting a bank's stock prices.

Box 10.1 Criteria for a successful property company

1 Ability to understand and forecast external influences
2 Reputation, track record, style
3 Links with other developers/investors
4 Links with financiers
5 Exploitation of competitive advantages
6 Efficient use of resources
7 Management structure
8 Market leaders rather than pack followers

Funding of property transactions by property companies

There are a number of indirect routes into investment in property. The main ones are: property company shares; property unit linked life assurance schemes (so-called 'property bonds'); exempt unit trusts and managed funds; mortgages and debentures. Within this scheme of things, shares are generally available to a wide range of investors, whereas bonds are an investment medium for an individual. Exempt trusts and managed funds, on the other hand, often provide an indirect investment vehicle for pension funds and charities. The property company, unlike the other indirect routes, is a corporate body with its shares quoted on the Stock Exchange. The value of its shares bears some relationship to the value of the property it owns and the income it derives from property operations, but the link is not a direct one. Property company shares will fluctuate on the market depending on the value of property owned, but the stock market will also tend to discount expected economic and financial events before they happen. An investment trust is a company that holds a portfolio of shares.

Property bonds, exempt property unit trusts and managed funds work on a different principle: the value of the unit in the fund is determined directly by the valuation of the property portfolio of the fund. Thus, the value of the portfolio is divided by the number of units held in the fund and, after allowing for the fund's expenses, this value becomes the unit price of the fund. The managers of the fund then operate the market at this price by the sale of units whose owners wish to dispose of them and by issue to new investors. There is obviously a margin between offer and bid prices to cover costs of transfer of the units and there is also a need for some liquidity in the system, as sales will not equal purchases in the short term. If demand exceeds supply, then new monies can purchase new investments that are added to the fund. If sales are not matched by new demand for units, then assets have to be disposed of.

Funds operating on the unit principle are 'open-ended' in the sense that the number of units in existence can increase or decrease. Share capital is fixed (the company is 'close-ended') apart from new issues authorised by shareholders or capital reductions. Direct and indirect reductions in capital are closely governed by statute and case law, and the doctrine of share capital maintenance distinguishes between the income and capital of a company. There are two basic forms of funding: corporate finance and direct project funding. In the 1980s, because of the exempt or partially relieved tax status of the principal financial institutions, and the landlord and tenant system established in this country (which encouraged the investor rather than the owner-occupier), the long-term funding of most property projects was usually project-based rather than through the stock market or the company share medium.

One avenue of property finance was the Business Expansion Scheme. This scheme provided tax concessions involved in development but, as an opportunity for investment with tax relief, this avenue was closed by the 1985 Budget which excluded certain property development companies from the scheme, and further by the 1986 Budget which excluded high asset-back activities and effectively closed a loop-hole previously exploited by several property based activities.

It is difficult to analyse precisely the proportion of new development attributable to property companies, as it is difficult to distinguish between investment funds used for existing and new development. From statistics available, it is possible to distinguish broadly the amount of funds available for direct and indirect funding by institutions. Studies in the mid-1980s (Woodroffe and Isaac 1987) show that in 1983 around £1,498 million was invested in property (other than house mortgages) by the institutions; banks advanced £969 million to property companies. However, as will be shown in the next section, new development represents a small proportion of the overall investment and the major problem related to funds is how much of the direct and indirect funding relates to new property. At the beginning of 1983, the total market value of the 42 major property companies was in excess of £4,274 million. Again, it is difficult to analyse the amounts of internal capital available for corporate funding of property but the figures produced by Rowe and Pitman at the beginning of 1983 show a total retained profit of the order of £65 million. Looking globally at these figures it was evident that property companies are playing a significant role in property investment and funding. Using the outline figures mentioned earlier, it may be shown that in 1983 property company investment was running at 70 per cent of institutional funding (there were £969 million of bank loans to property companies together with £65 million retained profit, compared to institutional investment of £1,498 million).

Investment in existing stock compared to development projects

Whilst the precise percentage of the total investment market effected through corporate funds is unclear, from the previous section it can be clearly seen as a major contributor. The property companies' funds consist of corporate capital and loans and it should be recalled that the institutions do provide these funds alongside banks, investment trusts, unit trusts, charities, individuals and other corporate investors. Despite the variety of funds, the role of the company in channelling the monies into property developments or investments is a key one.

However, the actual proportion of new to existing development in the market is small. A study of the proportion of new floorspace constructed in 1981/2 showed that it represented less than 2 per cent of the total commercial floorspace in England. New buildings in that period contributed less to the increase in floorspace than extensions and changes of use, but the total gross increase was only 3.5 per cent of the total stock. Thus, the development market relative to existing stock would appear small.

Investment by property companies

The re-rating of property companies meant that in 1993 they were able to raise new capital and look at investment and development programmes again. The Gallup survey commissioned by *Chartered Surveyor Weekly* (*CSW*) in the middle of 1993 indicated that 36 per cent of the major property companies and institutional investors were planning fresh speculative development over the two years from August 1993. The investment value of the planned schemes aggregated to £1.94 billion (Kynoch 1993). The main results are shown in Figure 10.2. This indicated

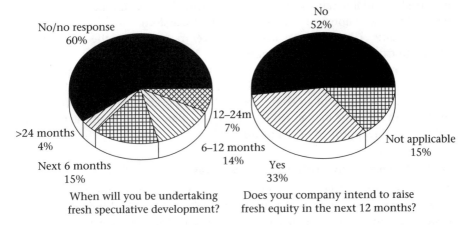

Figure 10.2 Gallup/*CSW* survey August 1993

Note: >24 months includes those saying yes but not stating a date.

Source: Kynoch (1993), p. 19.

a revival of fortunes in the property development market beyond 1995 that has taken place, but not to the extent of the 1980s.

10.2 Property shares

Property companies hold all or most of their assets in property; shares are thus a surrogate for property. There should be a close correlation between share prices and property value. Shares are more favoured than direct property because of the general rising share market, because of gearing which can increase returns to equity, because of the benefits of stock selection, and because of the perceived dynamic management of property companies (Barter 1988). The drawback of share ownership against direct property investment is the incidence of tax, which affects the returns compared to direct property investment as the shareholder is in effect double taxed (as shown later).

Thus, property company shares offer the investor four main features, as described below:

1 *Management* This takes away the direct problems of management and offers specialist management and entrepreneurial skills.

2 *Gearing* Gearing (debt/equity as a percentage is used here which is common in the market but, as mentioned earlier in the book, debt/total capital is usually used in economic texts) of the larger quoted companies varies quite dramatically; for instance, at January 1993, Speyhawk (before its demise) had a negative equity of £105 million, Stanhope had a gearing of 600 per cent, and Bradford & Warnford had no borrowing. Land Securities had a gearing of 54 per cent (S. G. Warburg Securities 1993). As well as the level of debt, the type of debt is important (whether

it is fixed or variable rate, or short- or long-term). Gearing can increase the equity return (but see Chapter 1 for a more detailed discussion).

3   *Liquidity* The market in shares has a central price and there is a speed of entry and exit in and out of the market.

4   *Other participants* Liquidity exists because there are other participants in the share market; institutional investors hold a high percentage of shares. Usually the shares are held as part of an equity, rather than a property, portfolio and thus are managed in the more market-led style of equity shares rather than the more asset-led style of direct property (Mallinson 1988).

Tax inefficiency of investing in property shares

There is an innate inefficiency in investing in property shares; this was more marked when there was a wider differential between personal income tax at the basic rate and corporation tax rates. The tax inefficiency can be shown thus (Woodroffe and Isaac 1987):

Assume base rate tax is 30 per cent and	
using corporation tax @ 52 per cent	£
Taxable profit	100,000
less corporation tax @ 52 per cent	52,000
Profit after tax	48,000
Assume all profit is distributed as dividend:	
Net dividend is	£48,000
ACT paid by company	
($\frac{3}{7} \times$ £48,000)	£20,571
Amount received by investors:	
Net dividend	£48,000
Tax credit (= ACT)	£20,571
	£68,571

ACT is advance corporation tax and the dividend payment made by the company consists of a net of base rate tax to shareholders. The tax payment is at the rate of 30 per cent on the gross dividend or $\frac{3}{7}$ on the net dividend (i.e., the gross dividend of £68,571 @ 30 per cent tax is £20,571).

If the net dividend is less 30 per cent tax = 0.7 gross dividend, the $\frac{3}{7}$ is a grossing-up factor for the net dividend as $\frac{3}{7}$ will be 0.3 of the gross. (The formula is $t/(1 - t)$ where t is the tax rate, here $0.3/(1 - 0.3)$ is $0.3/0.7$ or $\frac{3}{7}$).

If the shareholder is an individual and is not liable for tax, then he/she can claim back the tax credit. If there is a liability for a higher rate of tax than the 30 per cent, then the taxpayer will receive a further tax bill. The ACT paid by the company is deducted from the total tax liability of the company (£52,000 in the example) and the remainder paid as 'mainstream tax'.

Thus, a gross fund (a pension fund not liable to tax) would receive £100,000 if it invested directly but here it received £68,571 or 68.5 per cent.

If we take a more updated example where the differences between the corporation tax rates and the personal basic rate tax has lessened, then this will look like:

	£
Assume base rate tax is 25 per cent and using corporation tax @ 35 per cent	
Taxable profit	100,000
less corporation tax @ 35 per cent	35,000
Profit after tax	65,000
Assume all profit is distributed as dividend:	
Net dividend is	£65,000
ACT paid by company ($\frac{25}{75} \times$ £65,000)	£21,666
Amount received by investors:	
Net dividend	£65,000
Tax credit (= ACT)	£21,666
	£86,666

This is still inefficient but our gross fund here would have obtained 86.6 per cent, increasing the proportion as the differential between the basic income tax rate and the corporation tax rate lessened from 22 per cent to 10 per cent. See also Chapter 9 for tax changes on gross funds.

There may also be a disadvantage in terms of capital gains taxation. Owning investment properties through UK companies or groups has been systematically disadvantageous since 1972 relative to direct ownership of the same properties by UK taxpayers, gross funds and by non-residents (Millman 1988). An example of this is shown in Box 10.2.

10.3   Discount on net asset value

Property investment companies, as opposed to trading companies, are valued on the basis of their net assets rather than the income produced. A feature of the market in property investment shares was that they traded at a discount to the net assets held. This may not be true in cases of a very bullish market and over longer periods for exceptional performers, but generally this discount appeared to be around 20 per cent (see Figure 10.3).

The discount is measured as:

$$\frac{\text{net asset value per share (NAV/share)} - \text{share price}}{\text{NAV/share}} \times 100\%$$

This means that the underlying assets were undervalued and three reasons were commonly given for it:

- problems of possible loss on the forced sale of the company's assets
- tax liabilities, capital gains tax on disposal of properties and the tax inefficiencies of holding shares as opposed to direct investment
- disquiet over the valuation by surveyors of the underlying property assets.

Box 10.2   Capital tax disadvantages of the corporate structure

Capital gains tax: disadvantage of ownership through a corporate entity

A property was purchased in 1965 for £4 million, had £6 million spent on it and was sold in 1982 for £40 million. Consider the different tax position of direct ownership against purchase by a UK holding company, which is sold after sale of the property to put its shareholders in funds:

	£million
Sale proceeds	40
Cost	(10)
Gain	30

	Holding company	Direct ownership
Gross gain	30	30
Tax on capital gain	(9)	
Available to shareholders	21	

	Tax on capital gain	Net proceeds	Tax on capital gain	Net proceeds
UK gross funds	–	21	–	30
Non-resident	–	21	–	30
UK tax-payer	6.3	14.7	9	21

Source: Millman (1988).

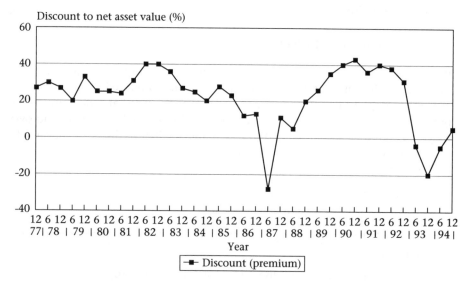

Discount to net asset value (%)

Figure 10.3   Average discount on net asset value 1977–94

Note: As at December and June. Projected figures for December 1993 and 1994.

Source: S. G. Warburg Research (1993), p. 5.

Recent research is inconclusive but this situation has an effect on financing and activity in the sector. Assets are undervalued and this discourages the growth of property companies through equity expansion and forces them into borrowing to expand. This leads to companies being highly geared (having a high ratio of borrowed capital to total capital). It discourages takeovers within the sector because takeover situations raise share prices and narrow the discount. Subsequently, the share price will tend to fall to a realistic discount as perceived by the stock market. On the other hand, property investment companies could be vulnerable to takeover by firms from other sectors where there are no discounts (Woodroffe and Isaac 1987). Lack of liquidity is an essential element in this analysis and liquidity has to be considered as the tradability in the investment market of an asset which does not lead to a discount in the net asset value.

Contingent capital gains tax on a property investment company prior to the 1988 budget (which moved the base date for capital gains tax forward from 1965 to 1982) probably amounted to about 20 per cent of net asset value; subsequently this fell to probably 10 per cent. An argument was made for valuing property investment companies by net net asset value (NNAV) which takes into account the contingent liability for capital gains tax. On this basis, the discount would be narrowed (Millman 1988). Investment trusts are companies that hold investments in shares; they also suffer from discount on net asset value in respect of their ownership of property investment company shares, but are not liable to capital gains tax.

Hoesli and MacGregor (2000) suggest that the discount is due to asset management fees, taxation effects, agency costs, excess volatility from stock market 'noise' because of uniformed trading in shares and the stock market's lack of confidence in the management of the property company concerned; this is taken from the work of Barkham (1995) and Barkham and Ward (1999).

10.4   Corporate finance structure

Capital structure

The question of an optimal capital structure for a particular company is a question that has aroused much debate. The problem is the choice of the best mix of debt (loans, debentures) and equity (ordinary shares, reserves and retained profits). The following factors ought to be considered, but assessing the weight to be given to each one is a matter of judgement.

Cost

The current and future costs of each potential source of capital should be estimated and compared. The costs of each source are not independent of one another. It is generally desirable to minimise the average overall cost of capital to the company.

Risk

It is unwise to place a company in a position where it may be unable, if profits fall, to pay interest as it falls due or to meet redemptions. It is equally undesirable to be forced to cut or omit the ordinary dividend to shareholders.

Control

Except where there is no alternative, a company should not make any issue of shares that would have the effect of removing or diluting control by the existing shareholders.

Acceptability

A company can only borrow if investors are willing to lend to it. Few listed companies can afford the luxury of a capital structure that is unacceptable to the main institutional investors. A company with readily mortgageable assets will find it easier to raise debt.

Transferability

Shares may be listed or unlisted. Many private companies have made issues to the public so as to obtain a listing on the Stock Exchange and improve the transferability of their shares (Isaac and Steley 2000).

Cost of capital

A company cannot always choose the cheapest source of capital because of the need to pay attention to the factors indicated in the previous section. The costs of each potential source of capital should be estimated to reduce the average cost of capital. The costs of issuing capital need to take into account any tax benefits (for instance, the interest on loan stock of debentures can be reduced by the tax benefit as the interest is deductible for tax purposes). This would not be so for preference shares that would have the same rate before and after tax.

The cost of issue of ordinary shares is more difficult to calculate:

$$\text{Gross dividend yield} = \frac{\text{current dividend per ordinary share}}{\text{market price per share}} \times 100\% \times \frac{100}{75}$$

The multiplier 100/75 is to allow for the tax credit that varies according to the tax rate. The dividend yield of any company can be compared with dividend yields in general and with those of other companies in the same equity group. The dividend yield prior to the 1960s tended to be higher than the yield obtained on unredeemable government stocks, because of the greater risk associated with equities. Since that time, the effects of inflation have caused a reverse yield gap in which the yield for equities has fallen below that of gilts, as prices are bidded higher. This is because equities have an ability to protect the owner against inflation; they tend to be inflation-proof rather than inflation-prone as gilts are. Redeemable debentures and loans issued by companies would tend to have a higher yield than government stock because they have a higher risk, but they are also inflation-prone as the returns are fixed. The dividend yield cannot be regarded as an adequate measure of the cost of equity capital as it does not take into account future change in the dividend stream and general changes in share price levels (Isaac and Steley 2000).

Two possible measures of the cost of equity capital are the earnings yield and the dividend yield plus a growth rate built in. The earnings yield is:

$$\frac{\text{earnings per ordinary share after tax}}{\text{market price per ordinary share}} \times 100\%$$

but it is more usual to express this as a price:earnings ratio (*P/E ratio*), that is:

$$\frac{\text{market price per ordinary share}}{\text{earnings per ordinary share after tax}}$$

The higher the P/E ratio (or, alternatively, the lower the earnings yield), the more the market thinks of the company and the cheaper the cost of equity capital. Earnings per share are calculated after the deduction of tax and preference dividends.

Dividend cover is also an important tool for analysis. Since the market is interested in future dividends, it prefers to see current dividends reasonably well covered by current earnings; this is a form of guarantee that the dividend will be maintained in the future. The *Financial Times* measure of dividend cover is:

$$\frac{\text{earnings per share on a maximum basis}}{\text{ordinary dividend per share}}$$

Earnings per share on a maximum basis assumes that a company distributes all its profits and is liable to pay advance corporation tax on them.

An alternative approach to the cost of equity capital is to add a growth rate to the dividend yield. If one considers that a company's dividends will grow at the rate of, say, 8 per cent, then this is added to the gross dividend yield to give the total cost of equity capital.

A further approach to calculating the cost of equity capital is that developed by portfolio theory. This cost is estimated as:

$$\overline{R} = R_F + \beta(\overline{R}_M - R_F)$$

where R_M is the expected return on the market, R is the expected return on the security, R_F is the risk-free rate (from a riskless security such as a Treasury Bill) and beta is the measure of risk (a measure of the security's sensitivity to movements in any underlying factors in the market). Portfolio theory was discussed in some detail in Chapter 2.

Application of the cost of capital to a project

If a project has a return of 20 per cent to equity capital, it can be refinanced at different levels of debt. The gearing effect is shown by increasing the level of debt, which increases the return to equity capital dramatically.

Example

Assume that the project return = 30 per cent and debt capital costs = 15 per cent. The project is financed by 50 per cent equity and 50 per cent debt. The returns on the project are distributed as returns to the debt holders or to the equity holders on the basis of their holdings:

$$R_p = (0.5)\, R_e + (0.5)\, R_d$$

where R_p, R_d and R_e are the returns to the project, debt and equity capital respectively. Thus:

$$30\% = (0.5)\, R_e + (0.5)\, 15\%$$

$$R_e = \frac{30\% - 7.5\%}{0.5} = 45\%$$

The value of a project will not alter merely by the way it is financed, but this will affect the way the proceeds are distributed and thus the gearing is affected. If the project is financed 20 per cent equity and 80 per cent debt, then:

$$30\% = (0.2)\, R_e + (0.8)\, 15\%$$

$$R_e = \frac{30\% - 12\%}{0.2} = 90\%$$

The advantage of using debt is that besides the gearing effects on the return to equity, the interest on debt is tax deductible and the analysis can be further advanced by using the weighted cost of capital by calculating the returns to equity and debt, and adjusting the debt return for tax relief. Thus, a project may provide a valuable tax shield (Isaac and Steley 2000).

10.5   Gearing

The capital structure of a property company is a key factor in how a company is viewed in terms of its attractiveness by an investor or lender. The sector is characterised by a high level of gearing due to the availability of fixed interest finance during the first postwar boom from 1954 to 1964. This availability led to many property companies being highly geared. The term gearing in this context is defined as the proportion of debt to total capital (equity plus debt).

High gearing is of benefit when property values are rising ahead of interest charges but can be dangerous if the real rate of interest is rising at a greater rate than property values. As real interest rates remain higher than growth at the present time, it would appear that property companies should stabilise by de-gearing. However, there are prejudices against such moves: in the 1970s, it was argued that the issue of share capital in a well-established company should be restricted only to the acquisition of additional entrepreneurial talent and from takeovers. In the 1960s, corporate funding was not popular and leaseback became a major source of funds. This situation was caused in part by the Capital Issues Committee of the Stock Exchange which for a period of years denied development companies access to the Stock Exchange debenture market. Later, the prejudice against corporate funds was reinforced by the introduction of corporation tax in 1965, which made the institutions less keen to receive their equity interest through shares in development companies, since the corporate structure reduced their gross income.

Thus, the lack of institutional funding in the 1980s led to new funds being raised by property companies through loans and debentures, as previously outlined, not by increased equity expansion. It is debenture and loan stock that is being issued rather than ordinary share capital. The risk of even higher gearing has been accepted because of the risks apparent in equity expansion. The use of property company equity for expansion is a difficult process. First, it is not easy for a predator to show shareholders immediate benefits of an acquisition as these are not likely to become apparent for a number of years, and second, there is a fundamental problem that property companies stand at a discount to net asset value and rights issues, convertible rights issues and vendor placings tend to dilute net asset value unless the acquisition is of assets which stand at a greater discount to their net worth.

Capital performance is the most important determinant of share price performance. The discount to net asset value is used in theory, in recognition of the inherent capital gains tax liability within an investment portfolio and other factors discussed in this chapter, but it also acts against the companies having rights issues.

Property companies need to consider the overall level of gearing both in respect of loans that are on the balance sheet and off-balance sheet loans. This overall level of gearing may depend on a number of factors, including the following:

1 Whether the company involved is an investment company or a trader (i.e., whether the property assets are intended to be held for long-term investment or sold);
2 The level of floating debt as against fixed rate debt. This is a measure of the control that the company has over its borrowing costs; the fixed rate interest rate can be calculated but floating rates will need to be forecast. This balance of debt has to be viewed in the context of the portfolio held by the company, the certainty of income arising and any risks involved. A portfolio held for trading will differ in terms of the risk profile from a portfolio developed and then held as an investment; this in turn will differ from the risk associated with a portfolio of investment property already let with different risks related to rent voids;
3 Whether the company's borrowing is secured or unsecured. If the company is borrowing unsecured, the maximum permitted level of borrowing will be set relative to the amount of the shareholders' funds. However, if the borrowing is secured, then the lender is unlikely to advance more than 70 per cent of the value of the property and thus an input of equity may be required. This input is a major constraint on development activity;
4 Any constraints on gearing levels. Some companies will have structures development vehicles that allow off-balance sheet funding, which will reduce the real gearing ratio. However, any lending on investigation of the accounts will calculate the loan and its price on the basis of the overall risks involved (Beveridge, 1988).

Box 10.3   An example of gearing

Assume a property asset with the following data (Freeman Publishing 2000):

Gross purchase price	£10 million
Initial yield	7.5%
Holding period	5 years
Exit price	£12.5 million
Interest on senior debt	7.75%
Interest on mezzanine debt	14%

Scenario	Equity input (£ million)	Sum of net rental income and sale proceeds (£ million)	Internal rate of return (IRR) (%)
100% equity	10	16.1	10.8
20% equity 80% senior debt	2	5.0	18.7
10% equity 10% mezzanine debt 80% senior debt	1	3.1	20.8

A study by Liow (1998) of the growth of property companies in Singapore between 1986 and 1995 concluded that the key determinants for sustainable growth were return on capital, earnings retention and debt-to-equity ratios. Many companies (around 50 per cent) tended to expand beyond their sustainable growth, and these higher growth companies introduced additional gearing through long-term debt to support this growth.

Thus, gearing enhances the investment returns, reduces the percentage of equity and increases the percentage of lower interest-bearing debt. If the overall investment return outstrips the debt return, there will be increased returns to equity. This is the gearing effect, which will increase as the proportion of debt to total financing increases. An example of gearing is set out in Box 10.3.

Debt finance will increase the volatility of an investment's returns and therefore its risk. By reducing the equity input, the investor's equity can be diversified between projects. As debt finance rises, so does the specific risk of the investment, but the release of equity will lead to a reduction in the overall portfolio risk. Debt can also increase liquidity: it can release part of the capital value to an investor whilst retaining some equity on which the investor can benefit in terms of future increases in capital value. The disadvantages of debt as indicated are that the increased volatility of increasing the debt will increase the specific risk and will lead to reduced control over the investment by the investor (Freeman Publishing 2000).

10.6   Property trading companies and property investment companies

A property dealing or trading company is a company primarily concerned with trading or dealing in property. The company buys or constructs with a view to sale and its stock of properties is included in the balance sheet as a current asset and is thus, under accounting conventions, shown in terms of value as the lower of cost and market value (see Chapter 13 for details on accounts).

A property investment company retains property and profits from the rental income and capital growth of its assets. A property company can be both an investment and a dealing/trading company.

Profits arising from capital transactions or growth in investment companies are taxed at the capital gains tax rate, whereas dealing/trading companies are taxed at corporation tax rates. The rates are now the same for companies but in the past there was a tax advantage if the profit was deemed to be a capital transaction. This was especially true before March 1983 when the corporation tax was at 52 per cent. All income to both investment and trading companies is taxed at corporation tax rates. If activities are mixed in a company, then all disposals are viewed as trading transactions by the revenue. There is a need to form separate companies for investment and trading. Revenue reserves are called retained earnings in most other industries but in property the distinction is mainly in investment companies between the capital and revenue reserves. Capital reserves arise in revaluation of assets, and for property investment companies their articles prevent distribution. If an investment company is being purchased or if it is borrowing funds, it will need to be valued. This can be done internally by a qualified employee. If investment properties form a significant part of the resources of an enterprise, such valuations should be made annually and supplemented by an independent valuation every 5 years. If the valuation exceeds the book value, this is termed a revaluation surplus and is subject to the rules of distribution outlined above.

The boundary between investment and trading companies was fairly clear until the tax year 1987/88. Before this, there were lower tax rates on capital gains than on income from profits, and therefore companies were careful to preserve the distinction between the two activities. Large groups have separate investment and trading companies. Investment companies still formed 85 per cent of the market capitalisation of the quoted property sector in 1988, while the remaining 15 per cent were trading companies or service companies including chartered surveying practices (Millman 1988). However, because of acquisitions and mergers, property investment companies are shrinking in number. Before the downturn in the market in 1990, trading companies had increased dramatically in numbers. Whereas the stock market values property investment companies and investment trusts on a discount to net asset value, other companies such as traders or service companies are valued on a multiple of their earnings. Hybrids do exist where development is combined with investment portfolios. Trafalgar House and Taylor Woodrow were examples where civil engineering and contracting were combined with a property portfolio. An example of a hybrid is Sterling Guarantee Trust (SGT). Sir Jeffrey Sterling, the founder, was a shrewd proponent of aligning cash flow businesses with a property portfolio. The development of SGT is shown in Figure 10.4.

Canary Wharf Group entered the FTSE 100 Index in 2000 and it uses net realisable value (NRV) as the Group's benchmark performance figure rather than the standard NAV. This is because of the size of its development programme. Conventional NAV figures underplay the value of undeveloped land. NRV is essentially an estimate of the value of the whole development when completed and let

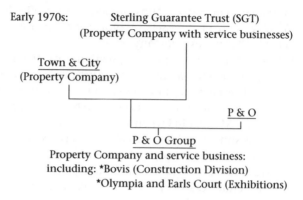

Figure 10.4   Sterling Guarantee Trust: development of hybrid business
Source: Millman (1988), p. 180.

after deducting all future costs (Whitmore 2001a). In March 2001, the group was trading at a discount of 17 per cent to NRV.

Recent analysis (2001) of the returns in the property sector have suggested that large quoted property companies are continuing to underperform in comparison to other companies in the sector, the wider stock market and often the direct property market. The analysis covering periods of 3, 5, 10, 15, 20 and 25 years prior to 2001 shows that no property company with a market capitalisation above £1 billion has ever provided top quartile total returns (Cooper 2001).

10.7   Takeovers

Introduction

Acquisitions of other companies are investment decisions and should be examined on the same criteria as other investments. However, there appear to be two main differences. In the first place, because takeovers are often contested, there may be little information beyond the published date on which the investment decision can be made. Second, many takeovers are for longer-term strategic reasons, which may be difficult to quantify now and may be even more difficult to quantify in the future when a company's 'goalposts' may have changed, along with those of competitors and those of the market. Many of the large takeovers of companies generally in the market in the 1980s failed because of the lack of information and lack of a clear strategy. Experience has shown that any problems arising will be accentuated if the size of company acquired is large, especially relative to the bidder. Risk analysis confirms that when acquisitions have highly uncertain outcomes, the larger they are, the more catastrophic the impact of any adverse outcomes (Pike and Neale 1993).

Motives for takeover

The motives for takeover often concern a feeling that the assets of the company to be acquired are valued at less than market value or there is some synergy in

Box 10.4 Motivation for takeovers

The motivation for takeovers include:
- the acquisition of skilled/technical management
- the obtaining of a supply of sites and projects
- the obtaining of potential benefits from the merging of property interests
- the ability to restructure funding facilities
- diversification (geographical or sectoral)
- if the acquired assets are at a discount to the share price, then they are cheap
- tax advantages
- access to cash or advantageous loan facilities

operating the organisations together. Thus, the motives concern the assets, which may be undervalued, or the marriage value in purchasing a management team, using your own or merging the skills. The choice between assets and management team in a takeover may also be linked to whether a bidder is looking to invest or trade in the property portfolio. In the latter case, management and entrepreneurial skills may be critical. Motivation for takeover is summarised in Box 10.4. A recent example is the case of Boots Company plc; it was realised here that, despite top management understanding of the potential of the sites, many of the company's real estate assets were underperforming. The senior management thus felt increasingly vulnerable to a takeover. The assets were revalued at the end of 1990 to a value of £769 million (Weatherhead 1997).

Discount to net asset value

The traditional discount on net asset value experience in the share price of an investment property company may lead to a discouragement of takeovers and rationalisation in the property investment sector. Takeover situations raise the share prices of the company being taken over and thus narrow the discount. Subsequently, the share price will tend to fall towards the previous discount level (the extent of the fall depending on the view the market takes). Thus, the takeover will generally mean a dilution of net asset value per share and a greater discount, unless the company being taken over is standing at a greater discount to the bidder (Isaac and Woodroffe 1987).

Takeovers: procedure

A takeover could proceed by an offer of shares in the predator company, a cash offer or offer of other securities (for instance, convertible loan stock issued by the predator). These offers would have to be at a higher level than the market price of the company being acquired to induce sale or swaps by the investors. Any tax liabilities in the portfolio of the company being acquired would need to be considered (Brett 1990b).

Hostile takeovers had their origins in the postwar property sector. There have been recent suggestions by stockbrokers that many of the quoted property companies could disappear over the next few years as a result of liquidation, receiverships or takeovers. In the past, takeovers were more prominent in the early stages of an upswing in the property cycle as predators sought to take advantage of discounted net asset value or exploit marriage values (Temple 1992).

The Takeover Code and statutory background

Takeovers are regulated as follows (Temple 1992):

1 *The Takeover Panel* – the rules are set out in the City Code on takeovers and mergers;
2 *The Office of Fair Trading* – which considers investigation of takeovers if competition, consumer choice or the public interest is threatened;
3 *The Companies Acts* – there has been a progressive reduction in the level at which substantial share investment must be disclosed and this is now at 3 per cent (as at 1992). The use of nominees to build up share ownership is now more difficult; a section 212 notice under the Companies Act 1983 can be served requiring disclosure of the bidder. Other aspects also serve to deter a potential bidder, for example:
   (a) if the bidder buys 10 per cent of the shares prior to an offer being made, the subsequent offer must include a cash alternative equivalent to the highest price paid for the shares;
   (b) if the bidder buys more than 30 per cent of the shares, an offer is usually mandatory at the highest price previously paid with a fully underwritten cash alternative.

Hostile takeovers are best avoided by ensuring a good track record, low overheads and enhancement of shareholder value. It is important as well that others know how well you are doing to discourage bidders and encourage a good press and investor/institutional loyalty.

Analysis for takeovers

The stock market can be an efficient medium for raising capital finance but it also enables control of existing companies to be effected. The ability to identify and evaluate suitable takeovers in the property sector will depend on the investigation of a number of factors including:

- the company's property assets, existing and potential income, value and trading potential
- the overall state of the company's financial position, its borrowings, liabilities and earnings
- The price and performance of the issued shares, dividend history and market capitalisation.

Techniques of analysis for takeover and other purposes include the following:

1 *Assessment of the price/earnings ratio,* which can be shown by:

$$\frac{\text{Market price per share}}{\text{Earnings per share}} = \frac{1}{\text{Earnings yield}}$$

A high P/E ratio indicates a strong expectation of growth and confidence in the share (comparable to a high year's purchase or YP in property valuation). Property companies tend to have higher P/E ratios but this income approach to valuation of the companies is used only for trading companies and not investment companies;

2 *Net asset value per share* – The property assets are shown in the accounts at valuation, cost or net realisable value, if different;

3 *Share price discount* – In the past there have been substantial discounts on the net asset value as expressed by the share price. This makes the undervalued assets vulnerable to predators;

4 *Share dividend* – The dividend provided over a period of time;

5 *Dividend cover* – The number of times current dividends are covered by the profits available for distribution: that is, earnings divided by dividends.

In Chapter 7, when talking about debt securitisation, it was mentioned that one of its benefits was that it was immune from 'event' risk, where an unforeseen event such as a merger or takeover can reduce the credit quality of a company. Thus, takeovers and buy-outs are prime causes of event risk and these have been dominant features of the UK property market in the period from 2000. These events will result in a change in the risk profile of the company. The change may not be large if the target company and the acquirer have similar capital structures and there is to be no substantial change in corporate strategy after the takeover. DTZ Research (2001) indicates that this may not be so in the takeovers and buy-outs seen in this period and suggests that new management often sought higher target rates of return and employed strategies and risk profiles necessary to realise these returns. In the case of the GE Capital and Hermes buy-out of MEPC, there was a dramatic change in strategy and capital structure, both of which had a substantial effect on the risk of holding MEPC's long-term unsecured bonds. The rating agencies Fitch and Standard & Poor cut the private company's rating of BBB+ to BB, which is a sub-investment grade. As a result, investors whose mandate prevents them from holding junk bonds have been forced to sell (DTZ Research 2001).

10.8 Summary

To summarise, the criteria for the successful financing of property companies can be considered as set out below:

1 The ability to raise equity if and when required.

2 The flexibility to use fixed or floating rate finance and to have access to a wide range of secured and unsecured finance.

3 The ability to achieve financing with long maturity money. This is especially important to property investment companies where the length of maturity of the loan is more important than interest margins. If interest can be fixed, then future income can be more confidently forecast.

4 The importance of flexibility in the financial structure, because each individual property company and project is unique and thus each company must be in the position to achieve the appropriate mix of financing required.

Above all a wide variety of financial sources and instruments should be available so that the directors of the company can make decisions as to the appropriate mix given the prevailing market conditions (Beveridge 1988).

In research reported in 1999, Looi found that asset structure, business orientation and level of investment in property development were key determinants of the debt policy of property companies (Looi 1999b). In the analysis of the UK property sector between 1985 and 1996, Looi found that:

- shareholders' equity was very sensitive to the underlying market conditions
- the level of indebtedness rose sharply through the study period
- despite rising debt, gearing ratios have improved because of strong property values and share capitalisation
- Debt raising capability is constrained by the inability to service loans rather than from a lack of collateral (Looi 1999a).

References and further reading

Barter, S. L. (1988) 'Introduction', in S. L. Barter (ed.), *Real Estate Finance*, Butterworths, London.

Barkham, R. (1995) 'The performance of the UK property company sector: a guide to investing in British property via the public stock market', *Real Estate Finance*, 12(1), 90–8.

Barkham, R. and Ward, C. W. R. (1999) 'Investor sentiment and noise traders: discount to net asset value in listed property companies in the UK', *Journal of Real Estate Research*, 18(2), 291–312.

Beveridge, J. (1988) 'The Needs of the Property Company', in S. L. Barter (ed.), *Real Estate Finance*, Butterworths, London.

Brett, M. (1990b) *Property and Money*, Estates Gazette, London.

Cooper, M. (2001) 'Top property firms still not delivering decent returns', *Estates Gazette*, 20 October, 53.

DTZ Research (2001) *Money into Property*, DTZ Research, London, edition 26, June.

Evans, P. H. (1993) 'Statistical Review', *Journal of Property Finance*, 1(4), 75–82.

Fraser, W. D. (1993) *Principles of Property Investment and Pricing*, Macmillan, London.

Freeman Publishing (2000) *Guide to the Property Industry*, Freeman Publishing, London, June.

Ghosh, C., Guttery, R. S. and Simons, C. F. (1994) 'The Olympia and York Crisis: Effects on the Financial Performance of US and Foreign Banks', *Journal of Property Finance*, 5(2), 5–46.

Hoesli, M. and MacGregor, B. D. (2000) *Property Investment: Principles and Practice of Portfolio Management*, Pearson Education, Harlow.

Isaac, D. (1986) 'Corporate finance and property development funding: An analysis of property companies' capital structures with special reference to the relationship between asset value and share price', Unpublished thesis, Faculty of the Built Environment, South Bank Polytechnic, London.

Isaac, D. and Steley, T. (2000) *Property Valuation Techniques*, Macmillan, London.

Isaac, D. and Woodroffe, N. (1987) 'Are property company assets undervalued', *Estates Gazette*, London, 5 September, 1,024–6.

Isaac, D. and Woodroffe, N. (1996) *Property Companies: Share Price and Net Asset Value*, Greenwich University Press, London.

Kynoch, R. (1993) 'Firms predict £2 bn spending surge', *Chartered Surveyor Weekly*, 26 August, 18–21.

Liow, K. H. (1998) 'An Empirical Investigation of Corporate Growth of Property Companies', *Journal of Financial Management of Property and Construction*, 3(3), 5–16.

Looi, J. T. L. (1999a) 'Financial structure of UK property companies: a research agenda', *Journal of Financial Management of Property and Construction*, 4(1), 5–30.

Looi, J. T. L. (1999b) 'The determinants of capital structure: evidence on UK property companies', *Journal of Property Investment and Finance*, 17(5), 464–80.

Mallinson, M. (1988) 'Equity Finance', in S. L. Barter (ed.), *Real Estate Finance*, Butterworths, London.

Millman, S. (1988) 'Property, Property Companies and Public Securities', in S. L. Barter (ed.), *Real Estate Finance*, Butterworths, London.

Paribas Capital Markets (1993b) *Monthly Property Share Statistics*, Banque Paribas, November.

Pike, R. and Neale, B. (1993) *Corporate Finance and Investment*, Prentice-Hall, London.

S. G. Warburg Research (1993) *U.K. Property: Monthly Review*, S. G. Warburg, London, November.

S. G. Warburg Securities (1993) *U.K. Property: Review of 1992 and Prospects for 1993*, S. G. Warburg, London.

Savills (1989) *Financing Property 1989*, Savills, London.

Savills (1993b) *Investment and Economic Outlook*, Savills, London, Issue 3, October.

Temple, P. (1992) 'How to Beat a Hostile Takeover', *Journal of Property Finance*, 2(4), 476–83.

The Times (2001) 'Property sector share prices', *The Times*, 5 July.

Weatherhead, M. (1997) *Real Estate in Corporate Strategy*, Macmillan, London.

Whitmore, J. (2001a) 'Canary Wharf value soars after hyperactive half year', *Property Week*, 16 March, 18.

Woodroffe, N. and Isaac, D. (1987) 'Corporate Finance and Property Development Funding', Working Paper of the School of Applied Economics and Social Studies, Faculty of the Built Environment, South Bank Polytechnic, London.

11
Joint Ventures

11.1 Introduction

There are a number of different types of joint venture arrangements but basically they involve the joining together of two or more parties to undertake a transaction. These parties may include institutions, banks, contractors, overseas investors, local authorities and public sector bodies.

The reasons for forming a joint venture may be numerous, but essentially they are about two activities: finance and expertise. A property company may not have sufficient finances to enable it to complete a transaction and find the development costs, and in such a case financial advisers may market the scheme to attract a third party investor. Developers may also form joint ventures and other forms of partnership with owners of land or a development where the latter do not have the expertise to develop. This may be the case where the landowner may be unused to the process of development and engaged essentially in non-property oriented activities. In recent years, other factors have influenced the formation of joint ventures and these basically relate to the reduction of debt in the arrangements for development and, related to this, the reduction in risk.

Thus, additional reasons for forming joint ventures could be listed as:

- the increased risk in property development
- the lack of equity in the property market and property companies unable to raise new funds by themselves in the market
- pressure to reduce debt in the property sector, by the Bank of England and lenders
- demands of overseas investors who have a preference for joint venture arrangements in their dealings.

DTZ Research (2001) has suggested that co-ownership through joint ventures is a popular route to acquiring property assets and expertise. It provides access to markets which may be denied to certain operators because of a lack of specialist expertise, inability to fund a project alone, or because of the distorting effect that a large asset may have on the risk profile of the portfolio of assets held. UK property companies such as British Land, Pillar, Chelsfield and Land Securities have been active in this area.

11.2   Criteria for choice of joint venture structure

The main types of joint venture structure are the partnership and the joint venture company (JVC) which are now explained. The decision to choose between the two will rest on a number of criteria, including:

- favourable tax treatment
- tax benefits
- limitations of liability
- control mechanisms
- the number of participants
- the timescale for the development, its disposal and whether this is a one-off or one of a number of schemes
- proposed methods of financing the development.

In the analysis, it is generally assumed that the joint venture has been formed for trading purposes: that is, to develop a property, let it and sell on the investment created to a third party. An example of the factors to be considered in negotiating a joint venture agreement to develop a business park is set out in Box 11.1.

11.3   Types of joint venture

The main types of joint venture structure considered here are the limited company and the partnership. As well as these common forms, a limited partnership and management agreement are also considered. Joint ventures will also differ on the funding arrangements. Examples of these types of partnership, including profit sharing and forward funding which relate to the division of profits, rather than the structure of the joint venture vehicle, will also be discussed. The material in this chapter will need to be updated for details of legislation, company law and accounting procedures that are constantly changing, so this is intended as a brief historical review only.

Box 11.1   Factors to be considered when negotiating a joint venture agreement to develop a business park

1 Level of funding to be provided
2 Infrastructure, amount and timing
3 Who is in control of the decision-making process?
4 How is the scheme to be phased and what types of building are going to be developed in terms of investment or owner-occupied property?
5 On completion of the first phase, how are subsequent phases going to be financed?
6 How is the profit to be divided following a substantial increase in the land value due to the success of the first phase?
7 How is the profit going to be distributed?
8 What are the dissolution provisions in the event of failure?
9 How are disputes to be settled?

11.4   Joint venture company (limited liability company)

Trading companies will often form a separate company for carrying out a particular project; it may be that the company will only have one site and finance is obtained on a project by project basis relating to each company formed. The advantage of the use of a limited company is that the structure is well known and can be utilised to provide a range of debt and equity interests which, as with any other corporate financial structure, can reflect the risk and rewards of the shareholders and creditors. The limited company is a separate legal entity and shareholders are limited, in terms of losses, to the extent of capital provided.

There are tax benefits and disbenefits: group relief will be available to the parent companies who have shareholdings but this advantage may be offset by the disadvantage that liabilities from subsiding companies will need to be consolidated in group accounts. Previously 50:50 joint companies were established to keep the borrowings of the JVC out of the consolidated accounts. Traditionally, the definition of a subsidiary company is one where the parent has a shareholding and controls the composition of the Board of Directors, or where it has more than 50 per cent of nominal equity capital. To avoid consolidation of accounts, a different type of company was established, termed a 'controlled non-subsidiary'. This in effect meant that although the subsidiary was controlled, its accounts were not consolidated into the group accounts of the parent. The Companies Act 1989 has changed this and the accounts of a joint venture will now have to be consolidated into one or more of the parent companies. A number of tests will determine whether consolidation of the accounts take place, including a revised definition of subsidiary based on the board of directors and voting control. The most significant test in the context of a 50:50 joint venture is whether a parent has the right to or can exercise a dominant influence (Albert and Watson 1990). Thus, a controlled non-subsidiary would be treated as a real subsidiary in the company accounts. A controlled non-subsidiary was regarded as a company, trust or other vehicle, directly or indirectly controlled and a source of benefits or risks that were, in substance, no different from those that would arise were the vehicle a subsidiary (Bramson 1988). The joint venture company is thus distinguished, if it is a subsidiary as defined above, from an associated company in which a parent has a significant stake but may not have technical control. In the case of an associated company, the debts may be regarded as off-balance sheet and not consolidated. This may thus give a false accounting picture because although profits may be apportioned from the associate company and consolidated in the accounts, interest charges may not. In all events, a company owned 50:50 with another party, where each party has the same number of directors and votes, will probably not constitute a subsidiary of either (Brett 1990b), but see the comments in Chapter 13.

Although the joint venture company, because of the Companies Acts, may provide a lack of flexibility and secrecy of operation, the corporate structure could be used as a vehicle that could be expanded in the future. This could be done by increasing the portfolio being developed and attracting more funds by the issue of new shares; the vehicle could then be floated on the Stock Exchange.

11.5 Partnerships

Partnerships are governed by the Partnership Act 1890. Partnership is a form of joint venture where each partner has a direct interest in the property and will (with its fellow-partners) be a co-owner of the whole of the property. If companies want to set up a joint venture, they could acquire the property jointly, but usually wholly-owned subsidiaries are used which may have been established particularly for this transaction. A co-ownership structure may be difficult for those dealing with the partnership property. The property itself may be held by a nominee company whose shares in turn are held by the partners. A partnership is easy to form and has a flexible structure. The disadvantage is that each partner has unlimited liability; however, this can be avoided by the use of limited liability companies. Minority interests are protected as they have the ability to dissolve the partnership at any time and ask for assets to be sold. Partnerships are taxed as if they are a company by assessing the trading profit, and once this has been done the profit or loss is allocated to the partners. The partners then pay tax on the allocated amount.

Limited partnerships may be feasible as another form of joint venture and the regulations for these are laid down under the Limited Partnership Act 1907. The limited partnership has two kinds of partner: general partners and limited partners. The obligations of a limited partner will be limited by the amount of capital originally invested provided the limited partner does not take part in the management of the partnership (Albert and Watson 1990). General partners have full liability and are thus liable for losses beyond the original capital subscribed. Limited liability partners are able to make some strategic decisions without losing their limited liability; these could include decisions to end the partnership. Also, it would be possible for the general partner to be a limited company, thus effectively limiting the liabilities of both parties (Bramson 1988).

The Limited Liability Partnerships Act 2000 has created the Limited Liability Partnership (LLP) which exists as a corporate body separately from its members in the same way as a limited company exists separately from its shareholders and officers. Like a company, an LLP can sue or be sued, grant fixed and floating charges over assets, own property, enter into contracts and can continue its existence even though its individual members may change. It can have a partnership agreement and is taxed as a partnership, and is therefore tax transparent for tax purposes (*Chartered Surveyor Monthly* 2001). By 2001, there were more than 120 limited partnerships with a combined value of more than £14 billion in real estate. Most of these limited partnerships had emerged in the previous five years; they accounted for around 12 per cent of the UK's direct institutional property market (Catalano 2001b). The popularity of LLPs is tax transparency, an investment that is a proxy for direct property, specialist management and access to specific stock. The problems are, however, as follows:

1 Liquidity – is there enough dealing for a secondary market?;
2 Valuation – an interest in an LLP is calculated as gross value of property held, divided by percentage of shares held.

There is no premium or discount, but with a secondary market there needs to be market pricing since a commingled vehicle (meaning 'of varied ownership') must be able to move to premium and discount.

11.6   Other types of joint venture

Management agreements are also possible where one party will hold on to the property on completion. These agreements could be on a project management basis with a developer assisting a landowner/investor for a project management fee or else sharing in the profits of the scheme. Possible arrangements for profit sharing in partnership arrangements are discussed later.

11.7   Partnership arrangements

These relate more to a method of funding a development rather than a true joint venture and are explored more fully elsewhere. These may include arrangements such as participation lending and forward funding. In participation lending, the lender will take a share of the proceeds of a scheme and this may occur where a lender is taking a higher risk, by lending more or at more advantageous rates of interest.

Forward funding is where the purchaser of a development assists the funding of the development, which provides the security for the purchaser of having some control as the development proceeds. It may be that the forward funder will fund the development at a lower rate of interest. The subsidy of the interest rate and the reduction of risk to the developer will thus lead to a reduced developer's profit payable and a higher yield on purchase of the completed development (because of reduced risk and reduced cost to the developer). Thus, the purchaser purchases at a reduced price.

The problem with joint ventures and more general partnership arrangements is that the interests held by the parties are going to be difficult to resell until the development is complete, so the partners involved have no security to offer to tenders. Property partnering, an adjunct to partnering in construction, can also be considered here.

In 1992, the UK government launched the Private Finance Initiative (PFI), which was intended to increase the involvement of the private sector in the provision of public sector services. The premise underlying the PFI is that enhanced value for money and cost effectiveness will result from the partnership, and thus the taxpayer will have greater value for money and the various risks involved with the projects will be placed with those parties best able to handle them. Subsequent studies have indicated that the initiative has been hindered by different views of the risk problem being taken by the various key participants (Gallimore, Williams and Woodward 1997).

In the Private Finance Initiative, a single point of contact takes responsibility for financing, physical procurement and ongoing management of capital project which replaced a lot of the traditional type of public sector funding and changed the way capital projects were procured. By December 1999, there were in existence over 250 agreements for PFI projects with an aggregate capital value of £16 billion. These agreements were signed by central and local government for the procurement of services across a wide range of sectors, including roads, railways, hospitals, prisons, office accommodation and information technology systems. Corporate PFI, however, which can be viewed as a corporate solution which outsources all non-core operations, had not really taken off (Freeman Publishing 2000).

Partnerships in a variety of forms can be used for encouraging urban regeneration; the usual forms in the UK are public–private partnerships (PPPs), limited partnerships and companies limited by guarantee. PPP is an extension of the Private Finance Initiative discussed previously. PFI is a means in this sense of funding public sector capital projects from future revenue streams. The minimum value for PFI schemes launched by central government is usually £8–10 million but projects as small as £2 million have also been started. The ability to access cheaper sources of finance via the capital markets should help develop the market for private sector PFI-style deals. Securitisation techniques may be seen to be the way to boost PFI-style deals in the corporate sector, but regard must be had to credit risk (Rodney and Clark 2000).

11.8   The formal agreement

The participants in a joint venture need to ensure there is proper documentation between them. The nature of the agreement needs to look at the overall control of the projects, the day-to-day operation and the exit of the parties. In detail, the agreement governing the activities of a joint company will be embodied in its Articles of Association. In the joint venture arrangement, it is important to distinguish between the overall control and day-to-day management. The important point is to avoid destructive deadlocks.

The formal agreement should clearly indicate elements such as:

- the level of funding proposed
- the development period
- the control mechanism for decision-making
- provision for dissolution
- arrangements for settlement of disputes.

If things go wrong in a joint venture, then dissolution of the joint venture may be the only option. This could be done by one party buying out the other parties at an agreed valuation. The formula for the valuation could be previously agreed, and it might well be that the triggering of such dissolution might be at an inappropriate time for one or other of the joint venture partners, especially in respect of the valuation of any work in progress. One approach suggested is that if there is a deadlock, either party may offer to purchase the other's interest within a given timescale and at a figure quoted by the offeror. The offeree then has the option of either accepting the offer or buying the offeror's interest at the same price.

If interests are not equal then this will need to be done on a pro rata basis. This approach is known as the 'Texas Option', amongst other things (Bramson 1988).

11.9   Example of a joint venture

Rosehaugh Stanhope Developments (Peat 1988)

In 1987, Rosehaugh and Stanhope Properties set up a joint venture, Rosehaugh Stanhope Developments (Holdings) PLC (RSD). RSD developed the Broadgate Complex in the City of London. The accounts of the joint venture partners were prepared prior to the changes that tightened up on off-balance sheet finance for joint venture companies. The separate accounts for Rosehaugh and Stanhope were prepared separately to 30 June 1987. These disclosed RSD's affairs. Rosehaugh's debt relating to RSD included in the consolidated balance sheet was £71 million and Stanhope's was £8.5 million. The debt of RSD was £183 million; thus, the borrowing included in the consolidated balance sheets of Rosehaugh and Stanhope understated the true level of the group's indebtedness. However, both partners followed existing accounting conventions and made detailed disclaimers; the issue here is whether the conventions allow the balance sheet to show the proper financial position.

Box 11.2   Summary of joint ventures

Forms of joint venture
Limited liability companies
Partnership
Partnership arrangements for profit division

Purposes of joint venture
One off, or for a number of projects
Tax advantages
Attract financial investment
Attract development expertise
Reduce debt/risk
Buy into an existing development programme

Joint venture agreements
Should contain details of:
   funding level
   development period
   control
   profit distribution
   dissolution
   disputes

Potential joint venturers
Landowners without development expertise or finance
Developers without finance or land
Owner-occupiers with land banks
Banks and other lending institutions

11.10   Summary

A summary of the points discussed previously in this chapter is shown in Box 11.2. If a property development is undertaken through a joint venture it has the advantage of bringing together the resources and expertise of the parties. It also spreads the risk of the project between the parties. Before the 1989 Companies Act, the borrowings of neither a joint venture company nor its related property interests needed to appear in the balance sheets of the parent companies. Because joint venturers tend to set up a separate joint venture company for each project, finance can be applied to the project as a non-recourse or limited recourse loan. The changes in the Companies Acts suggest that the accounts of a company should reflect the commercial effect of a transaction rather than the form. The practice of not showing the borrowings of 'off-balance sheet' companies may continue in the case of genuine 50:50 joint ventures even though the definitions of what constitutes a subsidiary company are being tightened (see Chapter 13).

References and further reading

Albert, D. and Watson, J. (1990) 'An Approach to Property Joint Ventures', *Journal of Property Finance*, 1(2), 189–95.

Bramson, D. (1988) 'The Mechanics of Joint Ventures', in S. L. Barter (ed.), *Real Estate Finance*, Butterworths, London.

Brett, M. (1990b) *Property and Money*, Estates Gazette, London.

Catalano, A. (2001b) 'Limit to LP's attractions', *Estates Gazette*, 3 November, 61.

Chartered Surveyor Monthly (CSM) (2001) 'Limited Liability Partnerships Act 2000', *CSM*, November and December, 8.

Chesterton Financial, Internal uncirculated reports, Chesterton Financial, London.

DTZ Research (2001) *Money into Property*, DTZ Research, London, edition 26, June.

Freeman Publishing (2000) *Guide to the Property Industry*, Freeman Publishing, London, June.

Gallimore, P., Williams, W. and Woodward, D. (1997) 'Perceptions of Risk in the Private Finance Initiative', *Journal of Property Finance*, 8(2), 164–76.

Peat, M. (1988) 'The Accounting Issues', in S. L. Barter (ed.), *Real Estate Finance*, Butterworths, London.

Rodney, W. and Clark, P. (2000) 'Financing Urban Regeneration', *Real Estate Finance and Investment Research Paper*, No. 2000.04, City University Business School, December.

12
Securitisation and Unitisation

12.1 Definitions

Securitisation is the creating of tradable securities from a property asset. *Unitisation* is also the creation of a tradable security but the aim in this case is to parallel a return comparable to direct ownership.

This distinction may sound confusing but it is based on an analysis relating to debt and equity investments. To begin with, one must consider a single property rather than a portfolio. For a single property, if we divide the interest into a number of holdings, then we divide the equity and this is unitisation. If we divide the interest and add debt securities, in the way a company may have shares and loan stock, this is securitisation. In fact, securitisation is rather like imposing a corporate finance structure on a property (i.e., a single asset property company), but this approach simplifies matters because it is important to understand the objectives of securitisation and unitisation which will differ from the operation of a property company. From the above, securitisation thus includes unitisation and can be used as a general term incorporating unitisation, and this will be done here except when discussing securitisation historically or when the securitisation of the equity alone is considered. The distinction between securitisation and unitisation is shown in Figure 12.1.

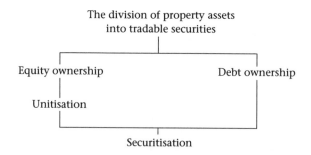

Figure 12.1   Securitisation and unitisation

Securitisation

	Equity	Debt
One property asset	Unitisation Securitisation	Securitisation
Portfolio of assets	Unit trusts Shares in a property company	Mortgage backed securities Loan stock/debentures in a property company

Figure 12.2   Securitisation matrix

Table 12.1   Unitisation and securitisation vehicles

Vehicle	Ownership		Securitisation of equity (unitisation)	Securitisation of debt (total securitisation)
SPOTs	Direct	⎫	'Unitised Property	Yes	No
SAPCO	Direct	⎬ Market'	Yes	Yes
PINCs	Income owned	⎭	Yes	Possible (Initially unitised but debt securities could be added.)

The distinction of a single property is important to this analysis. If a portfolio of properties is considered, then unitisation is basically akin to property units as in an authorised property unit trust whilst securitisation of a portfolio would be equivalent to a property company's shares and loan stock/debentures. A matrix of options will clarify this, as shown in Figure 12.2.

A further analysis was used in the past by the Barkshire Committee (Barkshire 1986) related to the distinction between the unitised property market (in which the investor gets a percentage interest in the ownership of the property investment) and property income certificates (where an investor gets a percentage income that the investment produces). This distinction of structure is not very useful and confuses the elements of debt and equity. Nevertheless, as another structure for clarification, the framework is outlined in Table 12.1.

The vehicles originally conceived for unitisation and/or securitisation were:

- Single Property Ownership Trusts (SPOTs)
- Single Asset Property Companies (SAPCOs)
- Property Income Certificates (PINCs).

From Table 12.1, it can be seen that SPOTs, because they only deal with equity, are vehicles for unitisation whereas SAPCOs and PINCs can be securitised. To summarise, securitisation in general is the conversion of an asset into tradable securities (these are certificates of ownership or rights to income). In the property context used here, securitisation is the conversion of a single property and the tradable securities may be debt- or equity-based. Unitisation is included in securitisation but specifically refers to the securitisation of the equity interest. In its simplest form, this unitisation will provide a share of the rental and capital growth with no obligation of management. This approach contrasts to property share ownership in the sense that, with unitisation, the investor selects specific property assets in which ownership is held rather than having to accept an existing managed portfolio. In this respect Barter, writing in 1988, suggested the income yield which could arise from unitisation (which, because of its tax transparency will be the equivalent of investing directly in property) might be twice the dividend yield from property company shares (Barter 1988).

12.2   History

The pattern of investment in commercial property has changed substantially over the postwar period. There has been a collectivisation of savings and the property investment market has become dominated by the major institutions, the insurance companies and the larger pension funds. This has been less true in recent years where property investment and development have been funded by banks and by raising equity in property companies. Problems with the ownership of property investments have arisen because of the lack of liquidity in the market. There are difficulties in transferability; extended negotiations are necessary to achieve matched deals. Other investment media, such as quoted shares, have a centralised market and do not experience these problems. Further problems with illiquidity have been experienced in terms of the increasing size of investments available. A number of recent property developments are too large to fit neatly within the portfolio of existing institutions. Institutions would not commit a large proportion of their available funds to a single property investment where this may be contrary to existing policy or where overcommitment to one project may increase risk within the portfolio related to the balance of the investments. The number of potential purchasers for a larger investment (say, more than £20 million) is thus limited and this will affect the price of the asset. The problem of illiquidity will affect the demand, supply and value of large projects because of the way the asset is traded.

Other problems with large investments may relate to situations where a partial disposal is required or where developers may wish to retain the investment but recoup some of the project cost. There is also a lack of opportunity to spread investment portfolios by incorporating larger buildings which, because of location and prestige, may be attractive assets. Finally, there will be problems associated with the valuation of such properties by traditional methods where comparable evidence is lacking. Also, a bulk discount relating to size or a discount reflecting the lack of ease of transferability, especially important in the event of a forced sale, will need to be incorporated.

For a long period, indirect investment in property shares and unit trusts has been readily available to investors and to some extent has addressed the problems of illiquidity. For a long period until recently, property unit trusts (PUTs), where they were unauthorised, had not been able to invest in real property. Exempt unauthorised unit trusts could not under previous law (the Prevention of Fraud (Investment) Act 1958) be openly offered for sale to the public. The result is that only the main institutions had been involved in this form of investment. Property bonds existed but also suffered from illiquidity problems, and some contained provisions that delayed repayment of investments for up to 6 months. Property share investment has been popular since the Second World War and the growth of property investment companies over this period has been a major factor in the property market. Property company share ownership suffers from three major difficulties. First, there is a tax problem relating to double taxation of income (the shares are not tax transparent). Second, there is no purity of investment in that the portfolios of properties can be large, varied and changing, and it is therefore difficult to identify the asset ownership related to the share ownership. Finally, the net asset values are discounted on the stock market in respect of property investment companies whilst property trading companies are valued on the assessment of future profitability, which may not readily relate to existing asset values.

As indicated earlier, three major vehicles had originally been suggested to deal with the problems. For simplicity, these structures have been considered as single asset property companies, single property ownership trusts and property income certificates. In the first two cases, the single property vehicles are divided up on the basis of ownership of the asset. In the case of SPOTs, the interest is divided up into equity units which are identical; in the case of SAPCOs, the division is by securitisation, the layering of negotiable interests in the investment on a risk/reward basis and including debt as well as equity interests. Different interests are thus created in relation to the assets in much the same way as companies are financed through a variety of corporate funding techniques. Finally, PINCs differ from the previous two vehicles in that they provide ownership rights to the income arising from the investment rather than direct investment in the asset. Other vehicles that have been considered are property unit trusts (PUTs) and mortgage backed securities (MBSs) which are common in the USA.

Mortgage backed securities had originally developed in the residential market; they enabled a building society or specialist mortgage lender to raise funds using a pool of mortgages as collateral, the strength of which meant that the issue received a high credit rating. MBS allows issuers to repackage their mortgage assets for sale in capital markets, freeing up capital for additional loans. Subsequent to the Building Societies Act 1986 the building societies have been committing funds to the commercial property sector, although there have been some bad experiences in their investments. Despite this, the presence of building societies in the market may accelerate the take up of MBS issues (Savills 1989).

Objectives of securitisation: a summary

Securitisation does all of the following:

1 Provides for liquidity in the market and, associated with this, the need to keep values up by increasing the size of the market and speeding up the time taken for transactions;
2 Assists in the diversification of risk. Securitisation provides a range of opportunities to have a mixed portfolio and to invest in different development proposals more precisely. Securitisation offers the ability also to invest in debt and equity security, in themselves having different risk profiles;
3 Provides the opportunity to avoid the management of property that occurs with direct ownership and to leave the task to the more skilled and experienced;
4 Provides tax transparency and avoids the double taxation which exists with property company shares;
5 Provides a more flexible financial structure to encourage debt instruments, and thus gearing situations, making the funding market more flexible for the sale of the developer's interest or part interest, and provides a better opportunity for refinancing development funds with long-term investment.

12.3   Problems in the development of securitisation

A number of statutory and legal constraints have stalled the development of equity securitisation in the property field. These basically relate to legal ownership, financial disclosure, tax and share listings.

Legal ownership

The Law of Property Act 1925 basically reduces the number of legal owners to four, and where there are more than four, then separation must be made between legal owners and those receiving the beneficial interests. If those joining together form a trust for sale or a partnership, then both of these structures have important limitations and, in respect of the latter, the risk of unlimited liability. Really, only a company or a unit trust, where the asset is held by trustees on trust for members holding units, are suitable vehicles for securitisation of a single property (Royal Institute of Chartered Surveyors 1985, Appendix II).

Financial disclosure

Before 1986, the Prevention of Fraud (Investments) Act 1958 prevented dealings of the public in unauthorised unit trusts. The Department of Trade and Industry would not authorise trusts made up of property assets because of the perceived illiquidity and lack of diversification of interests. The Financial Services Act 1986 introduced 'collective investment schemes' for property, and authorised property unit trusts (APUTs) have now been established. Single property schemes could now be promoted under this legislation.

Taxation

Tax transparency is defined as the ability through securitisation to achieve the same level of net after-tax return as would be achieved through direct ownership. The primary objective of securitisation was to avoid the double taxation that shareholders in property companies suffer. This relates to both capital gains tax and income tax, and has been discussed in Chapter 3.

Share listing

The Stock Exchange would not permit the listing of single property vehicles and thus there was no ready market for the shares. In May 1987, the International Stock Exchange permitted listing of single property schemes.

12.4   The vehicles

Single Property Ownership Trusts

This is envisaged as vehicle rather like an existing property unit trust, but which will involve investment in a single property asset. The trust would be authorised and would enable multiple direct ownership in a property on financial terms no less favourable than those available for single direct ownership in property (Royal Institute of Chartered Surveyors 1985). SPOTs involve a trustee holding the legal title to the property with the trust deed providing details of the operating framework for the scheme. Income accruing to the trust as a result of rents received passes straight to the investor (unit holder). Rental income is secured by the covenant of the tenant and by the form of lease agreement. Thus, the vehicle is a trust that could be floated on the Stock Exchange, management is through trustees who retain the ownership, and there are no debt interests. SPOTs require the law to be changed to achieve tax transparency; the Inland Revenue classed them as unauthorised unit trusts and thus liable to corporation tax (Savills 1989). In 1988, the Treasury confirmed it would not grant SPOTs tax transparency and thus the vehicle is in abeyance (Barter 1988).

Single Asset Property Companies

A SAPCO is a company structure rather like a property company, only in this case the company holds a single property rather than a portfolio. SAPCOs can be listed on the Stock Exchange but suffer from the same problems as a property company in that they are not tax transparent. SAPCOs are the best examples of complete securitisation and an example is given later. SAPCOs fulfil the opportunities of securitisation by providing various financial instruments such as debt, preferred equity and equity secured on a single asset in order to access the widest possible pool of investment capital and thereby enhance liquidity through tradability. Layers of securities of different characteristics are created to appeal to different classes of investor who will be looking for different returns and notes (Gibbs 1987).

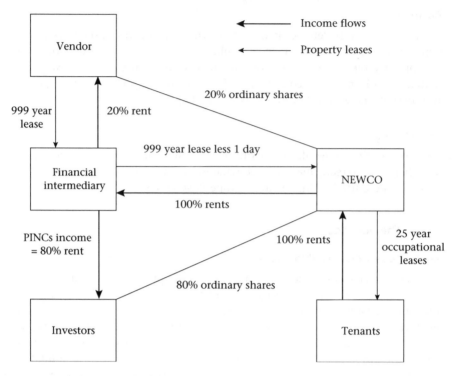

Figure 12.3   PINCs structure
Source: Orchard-Lisle (1987).

Property Income Certificates

A PINC is a tradable share. The share represents a right to the income arising from rent and capital appreciation of the single property asset. It has the benefit of tax transparency and the ability to be listed. Debt instruments can be issued to create gearing. A PINC is a composite security encompassing two elements:

- the right to receive a share of the property's income
- an ordinary share in a company that exercises control and management.

A PINC is a limited liability equity share in a tax transparent single asset property company. The structure for an 80 per cent flotation, where the developer or vendor retains 20 per cent, is shown in Figure 12.3.

12.5   Issues in securitisation

Problems of valuation of the units

The units may change hands at a discount to the asset value as perceived by the valuer and will thus mirror the market movement of shares in property invest-ment companies. The possibility of discount runs counter to the views of the organisers of the market who suggest that there should be a premium on the price of units because of liquidity. By taking the whole and dividing it into smaller units, the increased liquidity should avoid any bulk discount on the whole and thus trade at a premium to the value. The initial value may vary; the issue price will reflect the market conditions. There will be problems of revaluation in the sense of when these should take place and by whom. The significance is that, like company accounts, there needs to be an adjustment of market value. The valuation here will be the assessment of profit and net asset value (NAV) through the company accounts. Periods for revaluation could be 1 year or 5 years. There may be problems for the valuation profession in the sense that there may be less need for valuations of properties generally, but still the need for these revaluations. The basis of valuation may be different here to reflect the discount and the increased liquidity.

Problems of management of the units

The managers of the units will need to make decisions relating to the sale of the asset, refurbishment and financial management. For instance:

- they will need to provide maintenance and sinking funds
- they will need to decide on any programme for refurbishment
- they will have to provide guarantees to perform and to protect the investor's interests.

Problems of marketability

The problems of marketability will depend on demand, premiums and discount trading, the size of the market and alternative investments including property shares.

Size and membership of the market

There needs to be a critical mass for the market to operate properly. The net worth of the members of the market will need to be decided both for market makers and others. The initial fee and subsequent membership fee will need to be decided. There needs to be a diversity of investors, otherwise one party can manipulate the market. The property consultant will have a role here in the provision of financial services. The initial number of properties will have to be agreed. There is a debate as to whether freehold or long leasehold properties should be unitised.

Conflicts of interest and insider trading

There may be rent review considerations of tenants' versus the landlord's surveyors, as the unit holders may be tenants as well of the buildings that are securitised or of comparable buildings. 'Chinese walls' (which establish clear divisions of information so that inside information obtained in one area of the firm cannot be used elsewhere) will need to be established within firms. This will prevent transactions on the basis of insider information, although what constitutes insider information may be difficult, given the nature of the property market. Disclosure of property information (including structural defects and dangerous materials) will be necessary.

Box 12.1   Securitisation: an example

Case study: Billingsgate, Lower Thames Street, EC2
Joint developers: London & Edinburgh Trust
                        S. & W. Berisford

$£20$ million raised internally (30 per cent construction cost)
$£44$ million raised on market (70 per cent construction cost)

The money raised on the market was non-recourse borrowing from a syndicate of banks. Finance for the construction and letting was to be repaid on resale or refinancing.

Valuation: Let to Samuel Montagu on a 35-year lease with 5-year upward only reviews.

Rental	£5,000,000
Yield	6.2 per cent
Capital Value	£79,000,000

London & Edinburgh Trust sold out interest to S. & W. Berisford who in turn did not wish to hold a £79 million investment.

Securitisation solution:
3 layers of security:

(a) *Debt security*
$£52.5$ million of $6\frac{5}{8}$ per cent deep-discounted first mortgage bonds expiring 2006 offered at 32.5 per cent discount. (This represents a gross redemption yield of 10.6 per cent which was 1.15 per cent over the yield provided by Treasury 13.5 per cent 2004–8, the equivalent gilt.) This raised £35.5 million.

(b) *Preferred equity security*
$£25.8$ million cumulative preferred equity shares of 1p each at a price of 100p per share. Shareholders were guaranteed 30.2 per cent of the rental income to be paid as dividends (on basis that the current rent showed a 5.9 per cent return). The gross dividend rises to 20 per cent p.a. by year 2000 from the initial 5.9 per cent.

(c) *Ordinary equity security*
The rest was kept as ordinary shares. These are highly geared. There was no dividend entitlement until the next review. The shareholders get a 69.56 per cent increase in rental and capital growth. The value of the shares is £79 million, less debt and preferred equity = £17 million.

There was little investor interest in the shares despite the booming market at the time in City offices and the massive leap in rents expected at the next rent review. In September 1988, Berisford made a bid for the outstanding preference shares and now controls more than 50 per cent. The Billingsgate experience may have damaged prospects for further SAPCOs (Savills 1989).

12.6   Example of securitisation

An example of securitisation, taken from Gibbs (1987) is given in Box 12.1.

12.7   Liquidity and securitisation

The vehicles discussed above have floundered for a number of reasons, including the inability to be listed and problems of developing in a market that is rapidly changing. Securitisation does offer an approach to counter the illiquidity of the property market. Securitisation and liquidity will provide certainty about market prices but will mean that investors will no longer have direct control.

The Royal Institute of Chartered Surveyors (RICS) in their research have provided the following advantages for holding a property in multiple ownership (Maxted 1988):

- to stimulate investment in large urban renewal projects
- to enable small investors to enter the market
- to create a vehicle which would supplement the involvement of the major institutions in the market
- to introduce liquidity to the benefit of all classes of investor
- to open a wider range of property investment opportunities and enable an investor to spread risk through a tax neutral vehicle.

A survey by Rydin, Rodney and Orr (1990) asked a number of financial institutions about the prospects for a unitised property market. The respondents considered unitised property as a substitute for direct property holding and not as a substitute for equities or gilts; thus, for these respondents securitisation would not increase the size of the property market, but merely substitute for existing property investment. The need for an active market was stressed by respondents before they would become involved. The main criteria stated for the emergence of an active unitised market were:

- the choice of quality properties
- the installation of active management to ensure capital growth.

In the analysis, 43 per cent considered the opportunities for gearing unimportant; thus, they were satisfied with a unitised rather than a completely securitised market. The response of those surveyed as to what they believed unitisation acted as a substitute for, in term of alternative investments, is shown in Figure 12.4.

Christopher Jonas has suggested that: 'Illiquidity is one of the major drawbacks inherent in property investment. At a time when the pensions and life regulatory regime is increasing valuation and solvency requirements, property does not sit

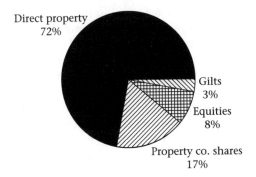

Figure 12.4 Unitisation: substitution for other types of investments (%)
Source: Rydin, Rodney and Orr (1990).

comparably in many portfolios' (Jonas 1995, p. 52). Jonas's view is that a paper security should be provided to enable institutional investors to be exposed to the market without the associated cost of direct ownership, and he suggests the principal criteria to judge the success of any new security would be:

- one which gives the owner, as nearly as possible, a share in the whole of the rental income and the whole of the capital value of a building
- one which can be issued within existing tax and regulatory rules
- one which would quickly attract a following among market makers so that a fully liquid market was available to investors daily, through third party market makers.

Liquidity has been defined as the tradability of an asset, which on disposal does not lead to a discount on the net asset value.

At the end of 1995, it was estimated that there were over 400 commercial properties in the UK, each of which had a capital value above £40 million, making a combined value of around £30 billion or one-seventh of the total value of UK commercial property. Investors cannot generally afford to buy these investments and those who can are worried about aspects of liquidity when alternative asset classes offer better opportunities. Regulations under the Pensions Act 1995 may provide a further disincentive to fund investment in property. A minimum funding requirement under the Act will mean that funds must match assets and liabilities closely. The proposed basis for valuing the liabilities is by reference to the yields on UK equities and gilts, depending on the maturity of the pension scheme. Property does not appear to figure highly in the arrangements for these regulations (Goodwin 1995). The need for liquidity has become even more apparent and a number of approaches have been suggested which involve new types of Stock Exchange-quoted property investments and derivative financial products which base their returns on indices of property market performance. Commercial property investment trusts have also been considered, with tax breaks in which investors buy-in pools of property assets rather than single buildings. Unlike property companies, investment trusts are exempt from tax on capital gains, so tax-exempt investors such as pension funds can swap buildings for shares without a tax penalty. The model for the initiative is based on the US Real Estate Investment Trust market, which was valued at £38 billion in 1996, and is used as a way for pension funds in the USA to gain access to the property market. A similar market in the UK is restricted because the Treasury would not historically extend investment trust benefits to commercial property (London 1996). Attempts to recreate US investment trusts by other means have been tried, such as PUTs (which can be quoted on the Stock Exchange and benefit from tax advantages). These vehicles, however, are not ideal for commercial property investment because, unlike companies and investments trusts, the unit trust is open-ended so the capital available to the fund expands and contracts depending on the demand for units. If investors want to sell units when property values fall, then it can be difficult to sell buildings to raise the cash needed for redemptions.

In 1995, the Investment Property Forum produced a report on property securitisation, and in it they argued for the establishment of a securitised property market. By comparison with successful securitised markets in the USA, Australia and Belgium, they showed the relative failure of securitisation exercises in the UK. In a serious lobbying of the government they, the RICS and other members of the property profession were insistent that, in order to create a successful market, an instrument was required which was tax neutral, tradable and available to a wide market. In the USA, the market in Real Estate Investment Trusts (REITs), which commenced in the early 1960s, was now a sizeable one, as was the market in Australia for Australian Listed Property Trusts (ALPTs: Investment Property Forum 1995). The report suggested that securitisation would address the constraints of the direct property market in terms of liquidity, divisibility, problems of management and costs, price signalling (meaning a traded securities market place with real-time price information providing immediate indications of value and performance), risk control, information transparency, investment timing, diversification and breadth of investment opportunity. The recommendations of the report were as set out below:

1 An approach should be made to HM Treasury to seek government agreement to accepting income and capital gains tax neutrality for a Stock Exchange tradable pooled property vehicle. Such an approach needs to have the widespread support of the property industry through its representative bodies and institutions.
2 The approach to HM Treasury will need to be accompanied by an assessment of the likely tax revenue implications of the introduction of securitised property vehicles. A study undertaken by the RICS in 1993 in relation to single properties concluded that the introduction of tax transparency for SPOTs would be revenue-positive in overall terms.
3 The existing DTI (Department of Trade and Industry) regulations that apply to single properties will need amendment to encompass pooled property vehicles.
4 An approach should be made to the London Stock Exchange to permit the existing rules relating to the listing of single properties to be extended to pooled securitised property vehicles.
5 The precise vehicle/vehicles which might be most suitable and which must address the needs for tax neutrality, Stock Exchange promotion, trading and regulation should be left open at this stage for discussion with HM Treasury. Such vehicles could involve:
   (a) the extension of the OEIC (open-ended investment company) regime to include tax neutral and listable direct property trusts;
   (b) the extension of the criteria that govern investment trusts to include direct property.

The definitions of securitisation used in the report are summarised in Box 12.2.

In 1996, the government changed the rules to allow both Authorised Property Unit Trusts (APUTs) and Housing Investment Trusts (HITs) to trade on the stock market. The RICS has written subsequently to the Treasury to set out its concern that other countries, particularly Belgium and the Republic of Ireland, have securitised vehicles and that, in the absence of appropriate vehicles in the UK, a securitised market in UK property could be run from Brussels, Dublin or elsewhere (*Chartered Surveyor Monthly* 1996).

Box 12.2   Definitions of securitisation

Property equity securitisation – The conversion of property assets into tradable paper securities. Property Unitisation refers to vehicles based on a unit structure (e.g. property unit trusts) rather than securities.

Property debt securitisation – The conversion of property assets into tradable paper debt securities – now commonly applied to property debentures (a long established instrument), zero coupon and deep discount bonds, residential property mortgages and, more recently, the refinancing of portfolios of commercial property mortgages into rated tradable paper and the securitisation of income-producing portfolios through a financial instrument.

Debt/equity instruments – Tradable paper debt securities that provide investors with an option at a future date either to redeem their debt securities for a pre-determined cash sum or to convert them into new equity shares in the company owning the underlying property assets.

Synthetics and derivative instruments – A *synthetic* is a tradable instrument which is designed to track the performance characteristics of a benchmark index on a one-to-one basis.

A *derivative* is a tradable instrument that comprises either a futures contract or an option agreement to buy or sell a given commodity at a pre-specified date in the future at a predetermined exercise price.

A *futures* contract is a legally binding contract where the parties to the transaction are bound to give and take delivery of the commodity (or a cash settlement when an index or synthetic is involved) at the expiry date. Usually these contracts are tradable during the life of the contract.

An *option* contract is similar to a futures contract, but differs in that the purchaser of the option to buy (or sell) has the option and not the legal obligation to buy (or sell).

Source: Investment Property Forum (1995).

Robinson (1996) has argued that portfolios are undiversified in property because the investment vehicles which would allow agents cheaply, quickly and conveniently to modify their exposure to property (and thus allow an efficient transfer of risk from those who want less exposure, such as households, companies and banks, to those who want more such as institutional investors) do not exist. He argues that current investment vehicles offer only a limited exposure to the property market and says that Real Estate Investment Trusts in the USA have limited use because:

- certain classes of property (e.g., residential) may not be held by investment companies
- prices of REITs are correlated with the stock market rather than the property market, thus rendering them ineffective as hedging instruments.

As an alternative to REITs, Robinson suggested the establishment of a market in property derivatives (futures, forwards, options, etc.) directly linked to property price indices, thus assisting in portfolio construction because of property's performance which has an inverse correlation with bonds and low correlation with equities. Investors could lay-off risks in many ways using derivatives, and property companies could hedge their exposure. Property companies are often trapped between high gearing, rising interest rates and falling asset prices in an illiquid market;

property derivatives could be used to hedge these exposures and thereby reduce the equity capital required to support any project. Institutional investors could modify their exposure to property without the costs and uncertainties of transacting in the 'cash' market. The inclusion of commercial property results in a better risk/return trade-off. The advantages of derivatives are summarised below:

1 Transaction costs would be lower.
2 The time of execution of transactions with derivatives could be chosen with more precision by the investor. Even those investors who prefer strategic holdings of physical property would find derivatives useful, as they would allow the investor to maintain exposure to property until transactions in the physical market could be effected.
3 Because they derive from broad-based property indices, derivative securities would offer property investment in a diversified form, even for a limited outlay.
4 They remove the need for property management.

Other detailed analysis of REIT performance investigated the key characteristics of REIT performance and found that the financial ratios (gross cash flows, leverage or gearing, asset size), regional location of properties and types of real estate investment determine the risk-adjusted performance (Redman and Manakyan 1995). This study suggested that, specifically, investment in securitised mortgages provides a positive effect on the risk-adjusted return.

In 1994, BZW (part of Barclays Bank) launched its Property Income Certificates (PICs1), a simple instrument which pays a return pegged to the income and returns registered by Investment Property Databank's (IPD's) index. The first issue of £150 million attracted 43 investors composed of UK pension funds, insurance companies and property companies, as well as some overseas buyers. The second version of PICs (PICs2) was launched in July 1995 and dealt with two of the drawbacks of the first launch. PICs1 could not be bought and sold on the open market, although Barclays did undertake to arrange trades on a matched bargain basis. PICs2 was only being sold to professional investors such as financial institutions but could be subsequently traded by a listing on the London Stock Exchange as a Barclay debt security. The second problem with PICs1 was that it carried a 12 per cent discount on the income return and investment managers, worried about the performance relative to the IPD index, considered this to be too large a discount to the index. PICs2 pays the full return registered by IPD, less an annual charge of 0.15 per cent of the capital value for expenses (Catalano 1995). BZW has now launched a forward contract based on the Investment Property Databank's annual capital growth index called PIFs; these are over-the-counter (OTC) forward contracts, where one party agrees to buy and another agrees to sell an asset (the IPD Annual Capital Growth Index) at a certain time in the future for a certain price. The contract is settled at the expiry date, one or two years on, by a cash payment made between the two counter-parties according to the percentage rise or fall in the IPD index. Barclays Bank will initially act as a counter-party to all PIF transactions and BZW market makers will quote bid/offer prices on Reuters. A futures contract is simply an exchange-traded forward contract (Catalano 1996b).

This requirement for liquidity in the investment market was shown in a recent survey by solicitors Cameron Markby Hewitt (1996), 'The Future of Investment Property'. Liquidity was a major concern of respondents to the survey who suggested (in order) the following to deal with the lack of liquidity:

- having a central property register
- up-to-date 'logbooks' to be maintained by vendors
- shorter and less complex occupational leases
- sellers to provide detailed warranties and a full certificate of title.

Logbooks should include not only management information such as tenancy schedules, payment records, arrears, service charge accounts, progress of rent reviews and turnover rent computations, but also copies of summaries of the title and occupancy documentation (Bourne 1995).

The respondents to the Cameron Markby Hewitt survey suggested new products for the property market, and these were, in order of priority:

(a) securitisation or unitisation of property with full tax transparency;
(b) tax-effective products that enable the property investor to generate funds in other areas without disposing of the property (e.g., a forward sale of rental flow or capital allowances);
(c) property investment companies that pursue full benchmarking relative to competitors;
(d) property futures based on a recognised property index.

The need for securitisation is international because of the global nature of finance and investment. In Australia, there are already securitised instruments but, in a study of investors' attitudes, Newall and Fife (1995) found that the underlying assumptions and expectations of investors in Australia concerning the need for liquidity matched those in the UK. Investors in the survey provided the following conclusions:

1 The principal benefit of property securitisation was seen as the ability to access physical property assets that would otherwise be beyond prudent investment levels;
2 The desire for investment liquidity and the use of securitised property as an effective portfolio management tool to obtain geographic and property type diversification and allocation benefit;
3 Unit trusts were the preferred method of securitised property investment with listed property trusts being the preferred trust format.

Some derivative products have been discussed by McAllister and Mansfield (1998b), and these include:

- London FOX Property Futures
- BZW's Property Index Certificates (PICs), Property Index Forwards (PIFs) and Property Index Notes (PINs)

- Property basket warrants issued by Goldman Sachs and SBC Warburg
- The real estate index market (REIM).

The first two groups of products have been covered elsewhere but, to recap, the property futures launched by London FOX in 1991 came to an abrupt end the same year when the market was suspended because of an illegal practice of boosting sales volumes. *Property basket warrants* gave exposure to indirect property equity, in this case for four quoted property companies (Land Securities, MEPC, British Land and Slough Estates), when the warrant was issued in 1994. A warrant is the right to buy shares at a given price at a fixed date in the future (see Chapter 6); the investor pays a premium for this right (11.5 per cent) and usually exercises the right if the value of the warrant increases. If the right is not exercised, then the premium is lost. The *real estate index market* (REIM) was a product developed to allow investors to take positions in the institutional property market without the need to acquire or dispose of property. Problems with legislation and taxation, and thus the product's liquidity, prevented it being launched; we have seen these problems associated with other initiatives in this chapter.

By 2001, no great progress had been made in the securitisation of equity. Catalano (2001a) suggested that it was clear that no UK government of any political hue was going to concede the tax breaks necessary to commercial property vehicles to make securitisation work. This was despite the fact that in the USA (in the form of REITs) and in many European countries – including Germany, Italy, Portugal, Spain, Belgium and Turkey – such vehicles are available. Catalano's view was that the way forward was to give up on trying to get tax transparency from the government and to develop separately a transparent, benchmarked and public market for property investment in tax-efficient formats that exist. The simplest vehicle could be a variant of PIFs and PICs (already discussed earlier in the chapter): that is, a tracker fund that follows the IPD index in the same way that tracker funds for equities let you buy into the FTSE index (the stock market index).

Forward and futures markets

In summary, one of the most significant innovations in corporate finance has been that associated with markets in currency and financial futures leading on to the development of options markets. The value of such markets is that traders on the market can lock into future interest rates or currency values. The nature of this commitment and the critical distinction between forward and futures markets and that of option markets varies between a binding contractual agreement to deal at that price within a stated period and the purchase of a discretion to exercise such a right only when it is beneficial to do so.

The differences between forward markets and futures contracts are explained below:

1 Forward markets are about advance pricing which provides for forward contracts stipulating the exchange of commodities and money at a future date and a stated price.

2 Futures contracts are standardised forward contracts that are traded in an open market, usually with a central location. Unlike forward contracts, futures contracts are not bilateral transactions between traders because, on completion of the contract, the exchange itself assumes the role of the clearing house for every transaction. Further, whilst most forward contracts involve delivery of the commodity between two parties at a future date, the standardisation of futures contracts means that physical delivery of the commodity is unlikely on maturity of the contract. Most futures contracts are closed out by offsetting transactions with sale contracts offset or closed out by purchase contracts.

In financial futures, the holder of a cash position in a financial security can lock into a specified interest return by the use of a financial future. By contrast, an option contract holder has the right, but not the obligation, to buy or sell a specified amount of the asset at a specified rate on or before a specified date (Davis and Pointon 1994).

Summary

As at 2001, it would appear that the necessary prerequisites for a securitised equity market are not in place. It is unlikely that the UK government will allow legislation to enable the launch of a tax-transparent or tax-neutral vehicle. Without this vehicle there is no point in trying to establish an appropriate market through, say, listing on the Stock Exchange. In contrast, debt securitisation has developed and there have been a number of successful examples. Usually the arrangement costs for debt securitisation are high, so such flotations are limited to transactions between £50 and £100 million. Examples included £555 million of debt raised by Canary Wharf in 1998 and £1.54 billion raised by British Land on its Broadgate scheme in the City of London. The British Land issue was the largest property securitisation transaction in Europe at that time. It is essentially a bond issue based on the securitisation of the rental income stream from 12 of the properties in the Broadgate development. The £1.54 billion issue was split into four tranches, each with a different credit rating from AAA to BBB (the basis of credit rating is discussed in Chapter 7). The credit rating of the rental stream determines the interest rate of the bond because the credit rating determines the perceived element of risk attached to the income stream, and therefore the risk premium or spread that is required by investors above the gilt rate. For instance, an AAA rated bond is likely to incur an interest rate equal to the gilt rate plus a spread of 100–125 basis points (1 basis point = 0.01 per cent). A BBB spread would be 150–200 basis points. The attraction of securitisation as a method of raising debt finance is that, because the debt is based on gilt rates, not swap rates (as is typical for bank debt), it is cheaper. Also the spreads required by the bond investors are smaller than those required by a bank on the senior debt finance of a comparable income stream. The disadvantages of securitisation are that arrangement fees may be more than 2 per cent, compared to 0.3–0.5 per cent for bank debt. It also takes longer to complete the transaction, say 3–4 months, compared to bank finance which takes half this time (Freeman Publishing 2000).

There are also additional problems related to the introduction of a securitised market beyond those of secondary markets and tax transparency, and these relate to a lack of enthusiasm for securitisation amongst the professional practices dealing in property investment. This lack of enthusiasm arises from two concerns.

1 *Valuation* – in a secondary securitised market, the investment will be bought and sold at market prices, and thus the valuation service provided by property professionals will no longer be required.
2 *Loss of best product* – if securitisation uses the best properties, the remainder of the investment market will be left with a poorer product which will be difficult to shift and may lead to less interest in direct investment and thus less activity amongst property investment advisers in direct markets.

Pressure for securitisation will also involve the reform of legislation that governs UK-registered limited partnerships. With reform, the UK will have a chance to establish a legal structure relevant to a property industry operating within a globalised market (Rodrigues 2001).

References and further reading

Ball, M., Lizieri, C. and MacGregor, B. D. (1998) *The Economics of Commercial Property Markets*, Routledge, London.
Barkshire, R. (1986) *The Unitised Property Market*, Working Party of the Unitised Property Market, London, February.
Barter, S. L. (1988) 'Introduction', in S. L. Barter (ed.), *Real Estate Finance*, Butterworths, London.
Barter, S. and Sinclair, N. (1988) 'Securitisation', in S. L. Barter (ed.), *Real Estate Finance*, Butterworths, London.
Bourne, T. (1995) 'Accelerating towards best returns', *Estates Gazette*, 10 June, 44–5.
Cameron Markby Hewitt (1996) 'The Future of Investment Property', *Property Update*, Cameron Markby Hewitt, Summer.
Catalano, A. (1995) 'Property paper chase', *Estates Gazette*, 1 July, 52.
Catalano, A. (1996a) 'An industry hungry for change', *Estates Gazette*, 18 May, 44.
Catalano, A. (1996b) 'MEPC taps US market with $225 million bond issue', *Estates Gazette*, 18 May, 43.
Catalano, A. (2001a) 'No safe haven for small punters', *Estates Gazette*, 27 October, 54.
Chartered Surveyor Monthly (CSM) (1996) 'RICS presses Treasury on securitisation', *CSM*, October, 7.
Davis, E. W. and Pointon, J. (1994) *Finance and the Firm*, Oxford University Press, Oxford.
Freeman Publishing (2000) *Guide to the Property Industry*, Freeman Publishing, London, June.
Gibbs, R. (1987) 'Raising Finance for New Development', *Journal of Valuation*, 5(4), 343–53.
Goodwin, M. (1995) 'A recipe for liquifying property', *Chartered Surveyor Monthly*, November/December, 28–9.
Investment Property Forum (1995) *Property Securitisation*, IPF, London.
Jonas, C. (1995) 'Liquidity and property', *Estates Gazette*, 3 June, 52.
Lennox, K. (1996) 'Future perfect', *Estates Gazette*, 24 August, 30.
London, S. (1996) 'Lure of the property magnet', *Financial Times*, 23 September, 19.
Maxted, B. (1988) *Unitisation of Property*, College of Estate Management, Reading.
McAllister, P. and Mansfield, J. R. (1998b) 'Investment property portfolio management and financial derivatives: Paper 2', *Property Management*, 16(4), 208–13.
Newall, G. and Fife, A. (1995) 'Major property investors' attitudes to property securitisation', *Journal of Property Finance*, 6(1), 55–63.

Orchard-Lisle, P. (1987) 'Financing Property Development', *Journal of Valuation*, 5(4), 343–53.

Redman, A. L. and Manakyan, H. (1995) 'A Multivariate Analysis of REIT Performance by Financial and Real Asset Portfolio Characteristics', *Journal of Real Estate Finance and Economics*, 10(2), 169–75.

Robinson, G. (1996) 'Derivatives: filling a gap in the market', *Estates Gazette*, 2 November, 179–81.

Rodrigues, M. (2001) 'Get the REIT response', *Estates Gazette*, 1 December, 125.

Royal Institution of Chartered Surveyors (1985) *The Unitisation of Real Property*, RICS, London.

Rydin, Y., Rodney, W. and Orr, C. (1990) 'Why Do Institutions Invest in Property?', *Journal of Property Finance*, 1(2), 250–8.

Savills (1989) *Financing Property 1989*, Savills, London.

Whitmore, J. (1993) 'Debt securitisation to aid the market', *CSW – The Property Week*, 28 January, 15.

13
Financial Accounts

13.1 Property accounts

As a preliminary note, views on the use of accounts, legislation and standards applying are constantly changing. This chapter will provide only an historic overview and readers should update the material through reading and review of journals and by taking appropriate professional advice where necessary.

Company financial statements

A company's financial statements are contained in the reports sent to their shareholders. The reports provide details of the operations of the company. It contains a Chairman's review that looks at the preceding year and prospects for the future. There is also a Director's Report which comments on such matters as profits, dividends, fixed assets and finance, and includes the report of the auditors and a summary of the accounting policies of the company which can be useful in the analysis of the position of the firm. Accounting policies are important in the property sector in respect of asset valuation and there will be different bases according to whether a property company is an investment or a trading company. Attached to the report are the financial statements, including:

- the profit and loss account
- the consolidated statement of total recognised gains and losses (discussed later in the chapter)
- the balance sheet
- the cash flow statement
- note of historical costs, profits and losses
- notes to the accounts
- report of the auditors.

The balance sheet and the profit and loss account are the main statements of the financial situation of the company. The balance sheet would be for an individual or group of companies but, if there were a parent company, then this may be included in addition. The main accounts would be in accordance with historic cost conventions but current cost accounts would attempt to take into account inflation

Box 13.1   The users of published accounts

Who are the users of published accounts?

The equity investor group including existing and potential shareholders and holders of convertible securities, options or warrants.

The loan creditor group including existing and potential holders of debentures and loan stock, and providers of short-term secured and unsecured loans and finance.

The employee group including existing, potential and past employees.

The analyst-adviser group including financial analysts and journalists, economists, statisticians, researchers, trade unions, stockbrokers and other providers of advisory services such as credit rating agencies.

The business contact group including customers, trade creditors and suppliers and, in a different sense, competitors, business rivals, and those interested in mergers, amalgamations and takeovers.

The government including tax authorities, departments and agencies concerned with the supervision of commerce and industry, and local authorities.

The public including taxpayers, ratepayers, consumers, and other community and special interest groups such as political parties, consumer and environmental protection societies and regional pressure groups (Westwick 1980).

---

of asset values. It is useful to remind ourselves at this stage of those particular groups who need to use published accounts, because it is their needs for information which will have to be satisfied. These are set out in Box 13.1. The accountancy profession is debating accountancy practice at the present time; the approach used is normally a 'modified historic cost accounting' approach with the revaluation of some assets, usually real estate (Weatherhead 1997); see also section 13.6 on 'Recent changes'.

The balance sheet

The balance sheet lists the balances of assets and liabilities as at the accounting date. As a result of the European Union's fourth directive on company accounts, balance sheets are now in a standardised form. Balance sheets are built up from three categories of entry: assets, liabilities and shareholders' funds. Thus, total assets are equal to the sum of shareholders' funds plus liabilities if one looks at the balance sheet from the point of view of the company. Alternatively, from a shareholder's view, one can see that the difference between assets and liabilities is the shareholders' funds, and thus:

Business view: assets = shareholders' funds + liabilities
Shareholders' view: assets − liabilities = shareholders' funds

Also, we can see that: fixed assets + net current assets (current assets less current liabilities) = capital employed (shareholders' funds + long-term liabilities). This is a modification of the business view, taking current liabilities to the asset side of the equation.

The balance sheet model of the firm, first introduced in Chapter 1, is set out in Figure 13.1 to clarify these concepts.

Profit and loss account

Whilst the balance sheet is for a particular moment, a profit and loss account is for a year ending on the accounting date; it is the result of the year's activities.

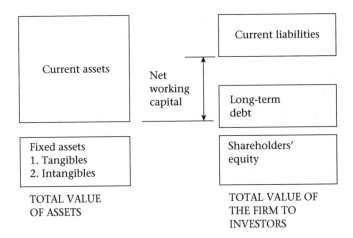

Figure 13.1   Balance sheet model of the firm
Source: Ross, Westerfield and Jaffe (1993), p. 5.

The profit is shown before and after tax; profit attributable to minority interests arises from investment in other companies amounting to 50 per cent or less of ownership, and these profits are now allowed to be consolidated in the sheet. The accounts also show the proportion of profit distributed and retained. To grow, a company will need to increase its assets. The balance sheet shows that assets = liabilities plus shareholders' funds, so that the ways to grow would be to increase liabilities (borrow more) or increase shareholders' funds. There are two ways of increasing the shareholders' funds: by issuing more shares or ploughing back profits. Ploughing back profits is not necessarily the cheapest source of long-term funds for the company, and it also restricts the payment of dividends.

Consolidated statement of total recognised gains and losses

This is an important additional statement as individual components in the accounts are often more significant than total figures, which can mask the fact that gains and losses may cancel out. Gains and losses included are ones that have been recognised during the accountancy period. So, if balance sheet assets are revalued, it is probable that the change in value has been building up or declining over a number of years but the result is shown as a lump sum in the year of revaluation (Weatherhead 1997).

Cash flow statement

The cash flow statement (or source and application of funds statement) shows the expenditure on fixed assets and the funds raised from their sale. Some companies break this down to show real estate items separately. It will show whether the company is funding its operation from the sale of real estate, whether it is selling real estate to prop up a weak trading position or whether it is using real estate to fund expansion (Weatherhead 1997). See Box 13.2.

Box 13.2   Examples of a balance sheet and a profit and loss account

Balance sheet as at 31 March		
	£000	£000
Fixed assets		
(Investment properties for property companies)		3,000
Land and buildings for occupation		400
Plant and machinery		200
Fixtures and fittings		200
		3,800
Current assets		
Stocks (Trading properties for property companies)	3,000	
Debtors	100	
Cash	100	
	3200	
Current liabilities		
Bank overdraft	400	
Trade creditors	600	
	1,000	
Net current assets		2,200
Total assets less current liabilities		6,000
Capital and reserves		
Issued share capital		2,000
Revenue reserves		1,000
Capital reserves		1,000
Shareholders' interest		4,000
Long-term liabilities (over one year)		
Loans		2,000
Total long-term capital		6,000
(Adapted from Asch and Kaye 1989)		

Notes to balance sheet:

In the notes to these accounts, set out in the following paragraphs, references are for an ordinary trading company; notes relating to the peculiarities of property companies are in brackets.

Fixed assets

Assets were originally valued at historic cost for an ordinary company. Land and buildings were shown at original cost less depreciation in normal accounts but, because this does not reflect worth, companies now revalue to market value. Depreciation is an annual allowance for wear and tear and reduces the balance sheet valuation; it is deducted from profit as a cost. (For a property company, the valuation should be market value for an investment property or the lower of cost and realisable value for a property in the course of development, but intended as an investment property: i.e., intended as a fixed asset.) Fixed assets are intended to be permanent features of the company's assets; current assets are turned into cash, usually within one year. Plant and machinery and fixtures and fittings are shown at cost less depreciation.

Current assets

Stocks are valued at cost. For a property company, properties to be traded are stocks and are valued at the lower of realisable value or cost. Cost includes the expenses paid out on a property since purchase and interest.

Current liabilities

These are the amounts due to creditors within 1 year. The balance of current assets less current liabilities is called the net working capital.

Capital and reserves

Issued share capital is the amount paid in by the shareholders when they originally bought the shares in the company. Reserves arise because profits are not distributed to shareholders but ploughed back into the company; these are called revenue reserves. Revenue reserves have to be distinguished from capital reserves which arise on the revaluation of assets and which may then give rise to a capital surplus. (Capital reserves are especially important in property companies when they arise from revaluation of the property assets rather than profits from rents or trading.)

Long-term liabilities

These are amounts owed by the company at a future date, longer than one year.

Profit and loss account for the year ended 31 March

		£000	£000
Turnover			10,000
less cost of sales (direct costs)			6,500
Gross profit			3,500
less (indirect costs)	Administration expenses	1,000	
	Selling and distribution costs	200	
	Interest on loans	150	
			1,350
Net profit before tax			2,150
Corporation tax			750
Profit on ordinary activities after tax		1,400	—
Extraordinary item after taxation			200
Profit for the year		1,200	—
Dividends			600
Transfer to reserves			600

(Asch and Kaye 1989)

Notes to profit and loss account:

Whereas the balance sheet reveals the state of affairs of the company at one point in time, the profit and loss account shows how much net cash has been generated by activities over the accounting period by matching the expenditure of the year against the revenues. The cost of sales is the cost of raw materials, production or direct labour, power and other factory costs. An extraordinary item is an unusual one in terms of its size or frequency; they are infrequent and thus need to be omitted when considering profit trends over a period of years. For instance, a large profit may have been made from disposal of part of the business, an event that is unlikely to occur again and which distorts the profit figure for that year.

Basic accounting concepts

The financial statements are produced and based on accounting concepts. Four rules or concepts are observed in all published accounts unless it is otherwise stated. These rules are:

- the going concern concept
- the accruals concept

- the consistency concept
- the prudence concept.

The going concern concept assumes that the business will be continuing its activities for the foreseeable future on a similar scale. Thus, the values attaching to assets and liabilities in the balance sheet reflect going concern values. This concept is important in property asset valuation for accounts purposes. The accruals concept says that it is vital, for an accurate assessment of profit and loss for the accounting period, to compare costs and benefits accurately. It is important to assign costs and financial returns to the period incurred which may not be the same time period when money costs are incurred or financial returns received. For instance, if a sale has legally taken place, whether or not cash has been received from the customer for the goods delivered, the transaction will be taken as a sale and included as part of the sales revenue appearing in the profit and loss account. The consistency concept is necessary so that approaches to the formulation of the accounts remain the same, and so valid comparisons and analysis can be made against previous results and with other companies. The prudence concept covers the attitudes of dealing with costs and revenues; it is the cautious way an accountant approaches the problem unless it is certain. Based on the above concepts, the Companies Acts make it a legal requirement that a company's balance sheet should show a true and fair view.

Techniques for analysis

The analysis of company accounts involve the initial consideration of three problems:

1 Is the company making a satisfactory profit?
2 Is the company short of cash or cash rich?
3 What should be the source of long-term funds?

These problems relate to profitability, liquidity and capital structure, and are as applicable to individual property projects as they as are to property companies or any firm. The techniques applied are based on relationships between the elements in the financial statements (financial ratios) and rates of return (yields). The area of capital structure is of major interest to financing arrangements and also has parallels in the financial structure of property projects.

Profitability measures

The key ratios used to analyse the profitability of an enterprise are shown below:

1 Trading profit as a percentage of turnover
2 Profit before interest and tax as a percentage of average capital employed
3 Earnings per share, either basic (based on issued share capital) or fully diluted (based on authorised share capital, which is the total share capital that can be issued)
4 Dividend per share
5 Number of times covered; that is the number of times a dividend is covered by earnings. This is also a measure used by property managers to assess the security

of a tenant by testing the number of times the rent is covered by the net profit of the tenant company

6 Assets per share; the asset backing of shares based on the value of the net assets divided by the number of shares. There has been much discussion of this in relation to the share price of property investment companies, as one would expect the asset value per share to relate to the market price of the share. However, historically, the stock market has discounted the net asset values of property investment companies by an average of approximately 20 per cent. The discount is measured by:

$$\frac{\text{Share price} - \text{Net asset value per share}}{\text{Net asset value per share}} \times 100\%$$

(Isaac and Woodroffe 1987)

Return on investment

This is defined as

$$\frac{\text{Profit}}{\text{Assets}} \times 100\%$$

Thus, profit is looked at as a percentage of capital, and this is further influenced by two further ratios comprising the profit margin (profit as a percentage of sales) and the rate of asset turnover (sales dividend by assets).

$$\frac{\text{Profit}}{\text{Assets}} = \frac{\text{Profit}}{\text{Sales}} \times \frac{\text{Sales}}{\text{Assets}}$$

or:

Return on capital = Profit margin × Turnover

The return on capital may vary from one industry to another but wider variations may be found in the profit margin and rates of turnover. For instance, a return of 20 per cent could be achieved by a high profit margin and a low turnover (the corner shop) or low profit margin and high turnover (the supermarket piling the goods high and selling cheaply).

A sector comparison should show that capital intensive industries with long production cycles would have a low rate of turnover but a high profit margin. From the key ratios above, a number of subsidiary ratios relating costs or assets to sales can be formulated. Depending on the use to which the ratio is put, the definition of profit and assets will differ. Generally, a wider view of company performance is taken:

$$\text{Return on capital} = \frac{\text{Profit before tax, interest and dividends}}{\text{Total capital employed}}$$

The comparison of profitability ratios enables firms within a business sector to be compared against one another and for differing sectors to be compared.

Liquidity and cash flows

As well as being profitable, it is also important that a company should be liquid. A profitable and fast expanding company may find that it has tied up its profits in fixed assets, stocks and debtors and that it has difficulty paying its debts as they fall due. Two main ratios examine the liquidity of a company: the liquidity ratio and the current ratio.

The liquidity ratio is also called the acid-test ratio because it is a most important test. It is the ratio of liquid assets to current liabilities and a 1:1 ratio means that a company has sufficient cash to pay its immediate debts. Liquid assets are defined as current assets excluding stocks of goods (that cannot be quickly turned into cash). In effect, liquid assets are debtors, cash and any short-term investments such as bank deposits or government securities. A company can survive with a liquid ratio of less than 1:1 if it has an unused bank overdraft facility.

The other test of a company's liquidity is the current ratio; that includes stock and work in progress on the grounds that stock eventually turns into debtors and then into cash itself. It is calculated by relating all current assets to current liabilities. A norm of 2:1 is generally regarded as being satisfactory, but this will depend on the benchmark for a particular industry.

Thus:

Liquidity ratio = Liquid assets : Current liabilities
Current ratio = Current assets : Current liabilities

Gearing ratio and interest cover

Two important measures of financial analysis are the gearing ratio and interest cover.

The gearing (or leverage) ratio is the ratio of debt to shareholders' funds. This could be expressed as the ratio of debt to net operating assets and this is the approach used in most economic texts, but often in the market it is stated as:

$$\text{Gearing ratio} = \frac{\text{Debt (borrowings)}}{\text{Shareholders' funds}}$$

also known as the debt to equity ratio.

Interest cover is the profit available to pay interest charges.

$$\text{Interest cover} = \frac{\text{Profit before interest and tax}}{\text{Net interest}}$$

An example of an interest cover calculation is given in Box 13.3.

The gearing ratio is used to compare levels of debt between companies. Interest cover indicates the safety margin before profits become inadequate to cover the interest charge. Gearing and interest cover are used by lenders to determine whether a company's borrowings are at a reasonable level and whether it is prudent to lend more. Also, investors are concerned with the company's capacity to absorb a downturn in profit without having to sell assets in possibly unfavourable market conditions. Gearing is also a measure of the potential to finance expansion

Box 13.3 An example of an interest cover calculation

	Co. A	Co. B
Balance Sheet	£ million	£ million
Net Operating Assets	100	100
Financed by: Debt	20	80
Shareholders	80	20
	100	100
Profit and Loss Account		
Operating Profit	15.0	15.0
Less interest payable @10 per cent	(2.0)	(8.0)
Profit before tax	13.0	7.0
Tax @ 35 per cent	(4.55)	(2.5)
Net Profit	8.45	4.5
Gearing Ratio	$\dfrac{20}{80} = 25\%$	$\dfrac{80}{20} = 400\%$
Interest cover	$\dfrac{15}{2} = 7.5$ times	$\dfrac{15}{8} = 1.88$ times

without recourse to shareholders that would depress the share price. If a company requires additional debt to fund a new project, the resultant gearing effect may depress the share price and restrict flexibility to respond to future opportunities. There is thus pressure to record the project, the asset and debt off-balance sheet.

Financial gearing and operational gearing

Many organisations have some control over production methods: that is, they can use either a highly automated process with its associated high fixed costs, but low variable costs, or alternatively, a less-automated process with lower fixed costs, but higher variable costs. If the enterprise chooses to use a high level of automation, its break-even point is at a relatively high sales level, and changes in the level of sales will have an exaggerated effect on profits. In other words, the degree of operating gearing is high. This is the same effect as that produced with financial gearing in that the higher the gearing factor, the higher the break-even sales volume and the greater the impact on profits.

The degree of operating gearing can be defined as the percentage change in operating profits associated with a given percentage change in sales volume. Operating gearing can be calculated using the following formula:

Degree of operating gearing $= (S - VC)/(S - VC - FC)$,

where S represents the level of sales (quantity $\times$ value), VC is total variable cost, and FC is total fixed cost (Asch and Kaye, 1989).

For example, let us suppose that a firm has a level of sales of £100,000 total variable costs of £50,000 and total fixed costs of £20,000. Its degree of operating gearing would be:

$$\frac{(100,000 - 50,000)}{(100,000 - 50,000 - 20,000)} = 1.67 \text{ or } 167\%$$

Therefore, if sales increase by 100 per cent, profit increases by 167 per cent. Operating gearing affects earnings before interest and taxes (EBIT), whereas financial gearing affects earnings after interest and taxes (i.e., the amount available to equity holders in the company). Financial gearing will intensify the effects on earnings available to equity after the effect of operating gearing has been taken into account.

The degree of financial gearing can be defined here as: the percentage change in earnings available to equity that is associated with a given percentage change in earnings before interest and taxes (EBIT); that is, the change in equity return relative to overall return before tax. An equation has been developed for calculating the degree of financial gearing:

Degree of financial gearing = $EBIT/(EBIT - I)$

where EBIT is earnings before interest and taxation and I is interest paid (which is the return to debt capital so $EBIT - I$ is the return to equity capital).

Thus, in the earlier example, we can now compute the degree of financial gearing. If we now assume that further debt is required involving interest payments (I) of £5,000, the degree of financial gearing would be:

30,000/(30,000 − 5,000) = 1.2 or 120%

If EBIT were to increase by 100 per cent, this would result in an increase of 120 per cent in the amount available to equity. We can combine operating and financial gearing to reveal the overall effect of a given change in sales on earnings available to the owners as follows (which, in effect, reflects the addition to the interest cost relative to fixed costs):

Combined gearing effect = $(S - VC)/(S - VC - FC - I)$

which for our example would be:

(100,000 − 50,000)/(100,000 − 50,000 − 20,000 − 5,000) = 2 or 200%

Therefore, if sales change by 100 per cent, this would cause the earnings available to equity investors to change by 200 per cent. In this example, the combined gearing effect of 2 was obtained from a degree of operating gearing of 1.67 and financial gearing of 1.2, but clearly other combinations would have produced the same effect. It is possible to make trade-offs between financial and operating gearing. The concept of the degree of gearing allows an organisation to predict the effect of changes in sales on the earnings available to ordinary shareholders, in addition to revealing the interrelationship between financial and operating gearing. The concept can be used to predict, for example, that a decision to finance new plant and equipment with debt may result in a situation where a small change in sales volume will produce a large variation in earnings, whereas a different operating and financial gearing combination may reduce the effect on earnings (Asch and Kaye 1989).

Analysing a property company: a summary

In order to analyse a property company, its accounts and finances, the following criteria will be important (from Brett 1990b):

1 *Net asset value per share*
   If the net assets are £10 million and the issued share capital is 5 million shares at £1, then the net asset value per share is £10 million/5 million (i.e., £2 or 200p per share).
2 *Gearing*
   If the shareholders' funds are £5 million and the debt capital is £3 m, then the gearing is £3 million/£5 million, (i.e., 0.66 or 66 per cent).
3 *Composition of interest rates in the debt*
   What is the percentage of variable rate loans to total loans? A company with a lot of debt with floating rates may find its share price suffering, especially in a period of volatile interest rates.
4 *Valuation of assets*
   When were they last valued? Property companies are meant to value their properties internally annually and have an external independent valuation every five years.
5 *Comparison of the amount of properties shown at cost* (development properties in the process of being developed) *with the amount shown at value* (investment property)
   This analysis gives an indication of the level of development activity.
6 *The legal interests in properties held*
   The breakdown of properties into freeholds, long leaseholds and short leaseholds can give an indication of the type and amount of income arising and the nature of rent reviews.
7 *Comparison of profit*
   A year-on-year comparison excluding extraordinary items is a valuable analysis.
8 *Capital*
   How is it financed and what capital commitments are there?
9 *Contingent liabilities*
   Has the company guaranteed the borrowing of associate companies, which increases its liabilities? Are there any off-balance sheet transactions?

13.2   Property accounts: issues

Capitalisation of interest for property companies

One aspect of financial reporting attracts more adverse comment than others; this is the process of capitalising interest into the cost of property developments rather than treating it as an expense. Thus, the cost increases the asset value in the balance sheet rather than reducing the profit in the profit and loss account. The difference between capitalising and expensing interest can have a high impact on the reported results and net assets of business during the development period. It is somewhat surprising that generally accepted accounting practice in the UK permits both policies (Smee 1992). The capitalisation of borrowing costs into most types of property development appears a logical and appropriate policy. Interest is a development cost and is no different from construction and land costs in this respect. The policy of capitalising interest is mandatory in the USA and looks set to become so elsewhere in the world.

The arguments against capitalisation are set out in Exposure Draft (ED) 51 (1990) and are, briefly:

(a) it is illogical to treat finance costs as a period expense normally and then treat them as a cost during the period of construction and revert to treating them as a period expense once the asset is complete, as finance costs are probably continuing to be incurred;
(b) borrowing costs are often for the whole enterprise and allocation of cost to a particular fixed asset will be arbitrary;
(c) capitalisation of borrowing costs results in similar fixed assets carrying different levels of interest (a highly geared company will carry its fixed assets at a higher amount than one that is not).

Smee (1992) suggests that capitalisation results in a proper matching of income and capital return with the development expenditure and best reflects, from an accounting view, the management's judgement of a project's viability rather than being creative accounting.

The treatment of interest on debt instruments is dealt with in section 13.5.

Goodwill

When a company acquires a business, it often seeks to write off the goodwill against capital reserves to avoid having to amortise the goodwill in its profit and loss account. The company can thus increase net profit and earnings per share. On resale of the business, the company can record a greater gain, as the original price will not reflect the additional sum paid for goodwill. After 23 January 1992, the profit and loss account on the date of disposal should be determined by reference to the attributable amount of purchase goodwill where this has not previously been charged to the profit and loss account. This ruling was made by the Urgent Issues Task Force set up by the Accounting Standards Committee and the Accounting Standards Board (see Ryland 1992).

Structure of financial statements: reporting in financial statements

The Accounting Standards Board (ASB) has issued an exposure draft on financial statements; this requires additional matters to be included in the statements to make it more difficult for companies to inflate net profits and earnings per share. The ASB requires each company to prepare a cash flow statement as part of their financial statements for accounting periods ending after 23 March 1992 (Ryland 1992).

Valuation of assets

Through time, the value of investment property will increase and the upward revaluation will create a surplus, being the difference between the open market value and its historic cost. This gain (loss) can be dealt with in three ways:

1　It can be passed through the profit and loss account as an ordinary, exceptional or extraordinary item.
2　If the company's articles prevent option (1), then the gain can be transferred to the capital reserve.
3　It can be shown in a separate capital profit and loss account. This is best practice, to place gains or losses in a proper reserve and show it in the accounts as a capital profit and loss account which thus makes a distinction between realised and unrealised surpluses (Purdy 1992).

Information in property company accounts

In May 1990, chartered accountants Stoy Hayward and researchers from the University of Reading set up a panel of experts to look at the provision of information in property company accounts and the main areas of problems relating to loans and interest, the nature of the assets and joint ventures. The recommendations of the panel are listed below (Purdy 1992):

1　Property company accounts should be placed in context, in terms of what has happened over the year; how the company has been performing over the last five years; a view of the future; and what accounting policies are used.
2　More details should be included about loan arrangements, the payment of interest and the capitalisation of interest.
3　An analysis of properties should be included showing their use as trading stock, investment properties or development properties.
4　A list of properties with a worth greater than 5 per cent of the total property portfolio should be included.
5　An external revaluation on an open-market basis should be carried out in accordance with the guidelines of the Royal Institution of Chartered Surveyors.
6　All revaluation gains or losses should be passed into a property revaluation reserve, shown in the accounts as a capital profit and loss account which distinguishes between realised and unrealised amounts.
7　Details of costs and revenues from all developments relating to, and details of, all joint ventures should be included.

Off-balance sheet and off-profit and loss account finance is covered later in this chapter.

13.3　The regulation of accounts

There are several sources of regulation with which statutory accounts have to comply:

1　The Companies Acts, which describe the principles that should be followed in preparing statutory accounts. They indicate that accounts should show a true and fair view. The Companies Acts also set out the detailed disclosure requirements.

2 The accounting profession publishes SSAPs (Statements of Standard Accounting Practice) and these cover accounting and disclosure.
3 If the company is listed, the Stock Exchange specifies mandatory disclosure requirements.

The company accounts are independently examined by auditors who have to report to the shareholders that the accounts show a true and fair view and are properly prepared in accordance with the Companies Act. Auditors are under a professional obligation to ensure the accounts comply with SSAPs. If the accounts do not accord with the regulations, the auditors must state this in their report unless, in exceptional circumstances, they concur with a departure from an SSAP; this seldom happens. If the auditors are going to qualify the accounts they will discuss this with the directors and often the directors will amend the accounts to avoid qualification. The auditors will also advise of any failure to observe the relevant requirements of the Stock Exchange.

13.4   Off-balance sheet funding

Section 13.6 on 'Recent changes' has greatly affected this section; this section thus provides an overview of procedures which have been adopted in the past but which may no longer be allowable. Off-balance sheet funding has become common in the last few years because there is less equity and more debt in balance sheets, since small developers have limited equity resources and banks have become more competitive, flexible and innovative in their lending. In the 1980s, banks contrived with the lenders to encourage off-balance sheet funding to increase their market share, thus adding to the problem (Peat 1988). Also, in the UK, SSAPs have never been intended to be applied mechanistically but rather to set out the broad principles which are to be applied in drawing up accounts; there is thus a tendency for the broad approach of the SSAPs to be ignored and for some property lenders to pursue accounting treatments which, while consistent with the letter of accounting standards, may be at variance with their spirit.

Examples of previous off-balance financing structures were provided by Peat (1988) and these are set out and discussed in the following paragraphs.

(a)   Controlled non-subsidiary

If a developer sets up a debt-financed subsidiary to undertake a project, the consolidated balance sheet of the parent company would have to show the debt of the subsidiary. An alternative is to form a company that is not technically a subsidiary within section 736 of the Companies Act 1985. A company is a subsidiary of another if the latter is a member of the company and controls the board. If the parent company has only the right to appoint half the board but its directors each have two votes whilst the others have one, it will not control the composition of the board although it will effect almost total control. Similarly, a company is a subsidiary of another if the latter holds more than half its equity share capital in terms of nominal value. The technique in this respect is for a company to own shares which represent no more than half of the nominal value of the share capital but give a right to, say, 99 per cent of the company's profits. The company would not technically be a subsidiary, even though its 'parent' enjoyed 99 per cent of its profits, as referred to previously, and effectively controlled the Board. This kind of structure is called a 'diamond structure'.

Example of a 'Diamond structure'

The definition of a subsidiary set out in section 736 of the Companies Act 1985 provides that a company is a subsidiary of a parent company only if:

(a) the parent is a member of the board and controls the board of directors of the subsidiary;
(b) the parent company holds more than half the nominal value of the equity share capital of the subsidiary;
(c) the subsidiary will be regarded as a subsidiary of the parent, if it is itself a subsidiary of a subsidiary of the parent.

The diamond structure set out in Figure 13.2 avoids the definition of subsidiaries indicated in the previous paragraphs.

A and B shares have the same number of votes except on a vote to appoint directors. The holders of the A shares have the right to appoint three directors without reference to the holders of the B shares; similarly the B shareholders have the right to appoint three directors without reference to the holders of the A shares. However, at Board meetings of the off-balance sheet vehicle (the quorum for which requires an A director), the A directors each have six votes while the B directors have one each. Rights to dividends and returning capital on a winding-up may be split so that the A shareholders received 99 per cent and the B share-holders 1 per cent.

Although the parent receives nearly all the profit and can control decisions because the membership of the Board is 50:50, it was not considered under the Companies Act 1983 to be a subsidiary; the fact that the directors appointed by the parent carry a majority of the votes which may be cast at board meetings is not addressed in this legislation.

This diamond structure also means that the parent does not hold more than half of the nominal value of the equity share capital. A and B shares are equity share capital within the meaning of the Act. Equity share capital is defined as the issued

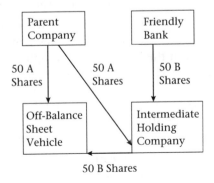

50 B Shares

Figure 13.2   Off-balance sheet funding: diamond structure

share capital excluding capital that carries rights to participate beyond a specified amount in the distribution. In this example there is no specified amount as a ceiling. Although the dividend right of the A shares is far greater than that of the B shares, the definition of a subsidiary requires that the measure of the relative weight of the shares is to be their nominal value.

A similar result to above could be arranged by having the B shares of the off-balance sheet vehicle held by the bank, but the structure above exists for tax reasons. For example, it may be necessary to ensure that the off-balance sheet vehicle and its parent would be treated as falling within the same group for group relief purposes or for corporation tax on capital gains, or it may be necessary to minimise the stamp duty payable on transfers of property between the parent and the off-balance sheet vehicle.

Prior to the publication of the draft SSAP on Accounting for Special Purpose Transactions (Exposure Draft 42), most accountants held that it was not permissible to consolidate a company which was not a legal subsidiary; thus, a note to the accounts would disclose these interests. This approach is not appropriate if the notes present a view contradictory to the main accounts rather than supplementing them.

Other examples of off-balance sheet funding were:

- sale and leaseback
- sale and repurchase
- options
- lease and finance leaseback
- joint ventures
- non-recourse debt.

(b)   Sale and leaseback

If the sale and leaseback are at fair market values, the accounting transaction is that summarised as follows:

- the property is taken off-balance sheet
- the net sale proceeds are included as cash or debtors in the balance sheet
- the profit or loss is recognised (difference between net sale proceeds and value in accounts)
- the rent payable is charged to profit over the term of the lease.

Variations in this may include put and call options where the seller has a right to buy back the property at a pre-determined price (preserving an interest in the capital growth of the asset) and the lender has a put option to require the seller to repurchase at the same price (protecting the lender from capital losses). Accounting for leases is dealt with in SSAP 21. This distinguishes between a finance lease and a standard lease. A finance lease is defined as 'a lease that transfers substantially all the risks and rewards of ownership of an asset to the lessee'. Any other lease is an operating lease. In property, a lease is likely to be an operating lease where:

(a) there are regular rent reviews to a market rent;
(b) there is a reversion of the asset to the landlord on the expiry of the lease, and thus the landlord takes the risk/rewards of the rental income and the capital appreciation.

The categorisation of the leaseback as a finance or operating lease determines whether the asset and the related financing can be taken off-balance sheet. This can only really be done if the lease is an operational lease; the presumption with other leases is that they are finance leases on the basis that the lessee has uninterrupted use of the property. If the lease is a finance lease, then under the provisions of SSAP 21 it will need to be capitalised by the lessee, the property asset is included in the balance sheet at its fair value and the obligation to pay rentals included as a liability of a similar amount; alternatively, the sale proceeds can be included on the balance sheet as a liability.

(c) Sale and repurchase

This comprises two agreements, one for sale and one for the repurchase, entered into simultaneously. The price payable to repurchase will be the sale price plus interest. The intended effect is that the seller's balance sheet after sale and before repurchase includes the sales proceeds but neither the property nor the obligation to repay (the debt is taken off-balance sheet). It is not likely that the auditors would accept that the property and obligation to repay should be off-balance sheet because the seller (repurchaser) retains substantially all the beneficial interest in the property. A more sophisticated approach has been used by house builders to finance show houses and can take the finance off-balance sheet:

Example of sale and repurchase

(a) a builder sells the completed show houses to the financier;
(b) the financier grants the builder a right to use houses for a fee that equals the interest on funds advanced by the financier;
(c) the builder undertakes to sell the show houses as an agent for the financier;
(d) the builder retains from sale proceeds an agency fee equal to the excess sale proceeds over the amount due to the financier.

The critical difference here is that the sold houses are unlikely to revert to the house-builder, and the builder will probably not have to make good any shortfall in sale proceeds. The builder will guarantee that the houses will be sold in a certain period of time and the builder will make good the shortfall but the time period and the values included in the agreement would be such that he would be unlikely to have to do so. The builder may also report a profit in the period he enters into the sale agreement rather than waiting for the actual sale.

(d) Options

Property transactions frequently involve the grant of options to purchase a property. The accounting profession has no prescribed rules for options. Options are often used as an alternative to secured borrowings and to create off-balance sheet structures, as with buy-back options in sale and finance leaseback.

Example of an option arrangement

The direct purchase of a property may look like:

Equity	£1 m
Debt	£9 m
Value	£10 m

These elements could be shown on a balance sheet. As an alternative, a bank could purchase the property on the investor's behalf for £10 million and the investor could pay £1 million for an option to purchase the property at some future time for a predetermined price. The predetermined price equals the purchase price plus the bank's interest and other costs less rent received. The bank will have a put option, if the value declines, to force the investor to acquire the property for the same amount as the purchase price. The idea is to take the asset and debt off the balance sheet because here it appears that the beneficial ownership has been acquired by the financier. However, as before, because the investor has the cost/benefits of the option, the option will be shown in the accounts with disclosure of the contingent obligation under the put option. More strictly, it would be viewed that the effect of the option, because of the likelihood of repurchase, is to purchase the property.

(e)   Lease and finance leaseback

This is a variant of the sale and leaseback and is a useful means of structuring the finance of a property that is going to be developed by a developer.

For instance, if a manufacturer acquires a site on which to build a building for its own use, the finance agreement with the bank might be as follows:

1   The manufacturer grants the bank a lease for 25 years with no premium and a peppercorn rent;
2   The bank enters into a contract with a builder to build the warehouse;
3   The bank leases back the building to the manufacturer for 25 years. No premium is paid; the rents reimburse the bank for development costs and interest.

This approach is a finance one rather than an attempt to obtain an accounting advantage. Thus, the property and the obligation to pay would be on the balance sheet. This approach is motivated by tax considerations, and the desire for the bank to obtain the benefit of capital allowances. This benefit (reducing the bank's tax) will be shared with the manufacturer, as it will be reflected in the lower rentals payable under the leaseback.

(f)   Joint ventures

Joint ventures were covered in Chapter 11. Joint ventures are reflected in the accounts of the parent companies (the joint venturers) as an investment asset, at the cost of the investment plus investor's share of profits; the borrowings of the joint venture company, however, may not appear.

(g)   Non-recourse debt

Lenders' rights are restricted to a charge over a particular asset that is pledged as security. Some suggestions, especially by bankers, are that non-recourse debt in the balance sheet be netted against the asset it is financing. These suggestions reflect the bankers' and lenders' primary interest in the balance sheet, which in their case is used to determine whether there are sufficient assets available to repay future and existing debt. Netting-off non-recourse debt is not generally an acceptable approach as accounts extend beyond just credit and liquidity assessment.

Moves to account for off-balance sheet transactions

Exposure draft (ED) 42 says that transactions should be accounted for in accordance with their economic substance, having regard to their effect on the enterprise's assets and liabilities. ED 42, as incorporated in the Companies Act 1989, affects the off-balance sheet vehicles described above dramatically. For instance:

Controlled non-subsidiary	should be accounted for as a subsidiary.
Sale and leaseback	would be treated as a borrowing transaction and the terms of arrangement need to be reworded.
Sale and repurchase	need clearly to account for transaction as borrowing.
Options	transaction or arrangement should be accounted for on the basis of the likelihood that the option would be exercised, if it is probable that it would be exercised. This would be the case where two options, one to sell and one to buy, exist.
Lease and finance leaseback	unaffected.
Joint ventures	if a joint venture is a genuine sharing of risk and reward, a participant who has an interest of 50% or less will not need to disclose separate joint venture asset and borrowing on the parent companies' balance sheets.
Non-recourse debt	it is not appropriate to offset the asset against its liability. If the accounts are used solely for lending decisions, there may be a basis for netting-off. Assets and liability should be separate categories in the balance sheet (Peat 1988).

Implementation of the EU Directive on Company Law

This deals with group accounts, and with voting rights and problems discussed with the diamond structure. There is a new definition of a subsidiary. It is a subsidiary if the parent holds a participating interest in the subsidiary and either:

(a) exercises a clear influence over the subsidiary; or
(b) the subsidiary and parent are managed on a unified basis.

Overall, there is still the requirement that the accounts present a true and fair view.

13.5   Off-profit and loss account funding

Note that section 13.6, 'Recent changes', has greatly affected this section. This approach basically charges operating costs directly to shareholders rather than in the profit and loss account. Share options remuneration, for instance, where directors and employees receive share options rather than income, is a dilution of share capital and not charged to the profit and loss account. Another example is convertible loan stock that has a lower interest rate but which gives the holder rights to convert to equity at a fixed price (Peat 1988). Other structures that provide off-profit and loss account financing are discussed below.

Deep-discount debentures

These bonds are issued at a lower rate of interest, which may remain at this level or be stepped up. The accruals concept of accounting (see earlier in the chapter) should mean that revenues and expenses should be matched for the appropriate time period. The real rate of interest should be thus accounted for over the life of the bond, which reflects the use of the loan over the period, and this should be taken out of profit.

Share premium accounts

There is a need to credit the share premium account when the proceeds of an issue of shares exceeds the nominal value. At the same time, one is able to write off costs of the issue of shares and debentures (including commission and discounts) against the account. It is possible therefore to write off the deep discount of a bond against the share premium account. The appropriate method should be to amortise the discount through the profit and loss account (as notional interest) then transfer (by way of a movement of reserves) an amount from the share premium account to retained profits.

Redeemable convertibles

These are redeemable, convertible loan stock. The interest coupon is lower than on the conventional convertible and this is compensated for by the inclusion of a redemption option. If the share price does not increase sufficiently to make conversion worthwhile, the holder may opt for redemption at a premium over issue price, and this has an appropriate return to compensate. The issue is, should the potential redemption premium be accrued and charged to the profit and loss account as interest to the date when it may be exercised? The approach should be that the potential premium should be accrued and charged to the profit and loss account rather than held as a contingency for a possible claim.

Convertible preference shares

This has the same problems and issues as redeemable loan stock. Convertible issues are usually bonds, but convertible preference shares with a redemption premium option have been issued. The preference shares thus convert to ordinary shares under this procedure but, if the price is low, they can be redeemed with a premium to make up for the low yield. Systematic accrual should be made through the profit and loss account for the potential redemption premium, however remote its potential redemption appears to be.

Debt with equity warrants

This is an issue of debt with equity warrants, which are rights to subscribe for shares at a fixed price. These warrants are redeemable; that is, the amount paid for the warrant is repayable if the warrant is not exercised. The debt instruments and the warrants are traded separately. The objective is (as for convertible debt) to secure lower interest rates for the debt issued. Thus, to account properly for this, the proceeds from the issue should be allocated between debt and the warrants and accounted for separately. If the warrant is redeemable, accrual should be made through the profit and loss account for potential redemption.

13.6 Recent changes

The Accounting Standards Board has now made it more difficult to keep debts 'off-balance sheet'. The problem in accounts has been to differentiate profits and cash; profits can be increased by receivable sums which are anticipated but which have not been paid for in cash actually received. The profit and loss account can be misleading as to the cashflow of a company; for instance, interest receivable from related companies could be included in the income. The requirement now, as noted at the beginning of the chapter, is for companies to publish a cashflow statement to show the precise cash position. Financial Reporting Standards (FRS) in FRS3 have now indicated quite clearly what is to be included in the profit and loss account to increase clarity in the accounts; for instance, it was possible previously in the accounts to exclude items which were regarded as extraordinary items. These items were not included in the pre-tax profits but were written off from the profit after tax. New financial reporting standards make it more difficult to develop financial structures that have off-balance sheet advantages (Ryland 1994).

A new financial statement, the 'Statement of total recognised gains and losses', is now also to be published in addition to the profit and loss account. This will also help in clarifying the accounts, and key information from the statement will need to be included in the profit and loss account (Brett 1999). In the past, the profit included gains from trading and also net surpluses or deficits thrown up by property revaluations that were incorporated into the accounts. The new statement highlights the gains and losses from revenue. FRS4 now regulates the way companies treat financial instruments in accounts so that the accounts give a true reflection of the cost of finance.

Another Financial Reporting Standard (FRS5) has clarified accounting treatment. The standard looks at what is behind the transaction, not merely its legal form. It will outlaw many of the ways in which property companies have, in the past, tried to keep the full extent of their debts from appearing in the group accounts. The exception will only be when money is borrowed by a genuine joint venture company that is not owned or controlled by the company in question.

Two further aspects of accounts are under review:

1 *The use of valuations in accounts*. Non-specialist properties in accounts have to be revalued on a regular basis, as do fixed assets generally; this revaluation is being extended to trading stock as well. Commercial companies may be required to have their operational premises revalued regularly and provide for depreciation of the buildings.
2 *Accounting for leases*. The different treatment of financial and operating leases might be ended (Brett 1997).

A further development is to include a second income statement in property companies' annual accounts. This is a suggestion from the European Public Real Estate Association (EPRA) which would allow companies reporting under national guidelines to also present figures following the International Accounting Standards (IAS) guidelines. This would bridge any reporting problems for property companies as the IAS guide comes into force at the end of 2005, and it would also provide clarity and consistency for investors when comparing companies across the sector (*Estates Gazette* 2001). These moves also arise from the fact that the European Commission has proposed that all listed companies in the European Union comply with International Accounting Standards by 2005, and the UK Accounting Standards Board is committed to this development.

References and further reading

Accounting Standards Committee (1990) *Exposure Draft 51: Accounting for Fixed Assets and Revaluations*, ASC, May.

Asch, D. and Kaye, G. R. (1989) *Financial Planning: Modelling Methods and Techniques*, Kogan Paul, London.

Asch, D. and Kaye, G. R. (1996) *Financial Planning: Profit Improvement through Modelling*, Kogan Paul, London.

Barkham, R. J. and Purdy, D. E. (1992) 'Financial company reporting: Potential weaknesses', *Journal of Property Valuation and Investment*, 11(2), 133–44.

Brett, M. (1990a) *How to Read the Financial Pages*, Hutchinson, London.

Brett, M. (1990b) *Property and Money*, Estates Gazette, London.

Brett, M. (1997) *Property and Money*, Estates Gazette, London.

Brett, M. (1999) 'Accounting changes will give a clear view', *Estates Gazette*, London, 7 August, 32.

Cairns, D. (2001) 'Value of land in the balance', *Estates Gazette*, 27 October, 178–9.

Calachi, R. and Rosenburg, S. (eds) (1992) *Property Finance: An International Perspective*, Euromoney Books, London.

Dunckley, J. (2000) 'Financial reporting standards: is market value for the existing use now obsolete?', *Journal of Property Investment and Finance*, 18(2), 212–24.

Estates Gazette (2001b) 'Accountancy board calls for greater consistency in sector', *Estates Gazette*, 6 October, 51.

Evans, M., French, N. and O'Roarty, B. (2001) 'Accountancy and corporate property management – a briefing on current and proposed provisions relating to corporate real estate', *Journal of Property Investment and Finance*, 19(2), 211–23.

Isaac, D. and Woodroffe N. (1987) 'Are property company assets undervalued', *Estates Gazette*, London, 5 September, 1024–6.

Peat, M. (1988) 'The Accounting Issues', in S. L. Barter (ed.), *Real Estate Finance*, Butterworths, London.

Pike, R. and Neale, B. (1993) *Corporate Finance and Investment*, Prentice-Hall, London.

Purdy, D. E. (1992) 'Provoking awareness through the provision of relevant information in Property Company Accounts', *Journal of Property Finance*, 3(3), 337–46.

Ross, S. A., Westerfield, R. W. and Jaffe, J. F. (1999) *Property Finance*, McGraw-Hill, London.

Ryland, D. S. (1992) 'Changes in Accounting Rules', *Journal of Property Finance*, 3(1), 28–37.

Ryland, D. S. (1994) 'Financial Reporting Standard 5', *Journal of Property Finance*, 5(1), 7–8.

Smee, R. (1992) 'Capitalisation of Interest for Property Companies', *Journal of Property Finance*, 3(1), 13–22.

Weatherhead, M. (1997) *Real Estate in Corporate Strategy*, Macmillan, London.

Westwick, C. A. (1980) *Property Valuation and Accounts*, Institute of Chartered Accountants in England and Wales, London.

14
Financial Services

14.1 Introduction

The central task of a financial intermediary is to deploy capital from those who have it to those who need it, ensuring the rights of the former are preserved over time. Gumerlock (1999) suggests three fundamental paradigms for managing the risk of intermediates. These are shown in Figure 14.1, and offer a conceptual framework for developing this more applied and practical chapter.

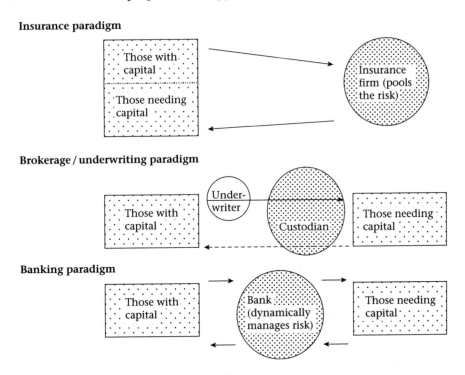

Figure 14.1 Managing the risks of intermediation

Source: Adapted from Gumerlock (1999).

The provision of financial services by property consultants will obviously vary according to the expertise of the firm, its clients and any niche market in which the firm is operating. This section initially relied heavily on the study of the operation of Chesterton Financial, the financial services company of Chesterton International, international property consultants in the early 1990s. Chesterton Financial dealt mainly with:

- debt finance
- joint ventures
- equity participation
- professional advice
- tax-based leasing.

Most activity is in the area of debt finance.

The role of financial services is to make contact with a number of funders; these will include banks, building societies, insurance companies and finance houses operating in the UK market. Chesterton Financial in 1992 was in contact with 170 such lenders. The role of financial services is to be an intermediary and to know the lending criteria of the various institutions, their likes, dislikes and procedures, and also to know the staff and personnel who may be doing the lending. When a client approaches a financial services company, the company will ascertain the requirement and then refine it to convert the enquiry into an application to a lender. In addition, the terms are agreed on which the financial services company will act for the client. Typical fees for acting are set out in the following section. In the early stages of discussion with the client, a general idea of the terms of the loan can be guessed but it is necessary to research the market, and to telephone lenders who may be interested, outline the deal to them and ask if they wish to look at it in more detail.

The research should provide three or more options for the transaction. An information memorandum is then prepared for those lenders who have expressed an interest in the deal that, in most instances, covers the following basic headings:

1 Introduction to the transaction
2 Background to the transaction
3 Description and history of the borrower
4 Amount and purpose of the loan
5 Description and location of the property for which the loan is sought
6 Costs and valuations related to the property
7 Financial analysis of cash flows and analysis of return
8 The equity investment proposed and the proposals for securing the loan
9 The terms of the loan and its proposed interest rate margin
10 The security being provided for the loan, the status of the borrower
11 A summary of the proposal with recommendations
12 Appendices which may include detailed and financial analysis, structural surveys, formal valuations and legal report on the property, planning permissions, and so on. Also, accounts and site plans/maps. Whilst most of the material will

be readily available from the client, detailed cash flows are usually prepared by the financial services company.

The proposal is then sent to the lender who may reject the application outright once the full proposal is known, or else put the application to the Credit Committee. Usually, however, the lender will ask for more information. This process will continue with one or more lenders until an acceptable deal is structured.

The financial services company will follow the process, giving legal and commercial advice through to the drawdown of the loan. This process may mean providing relevant information to the solicitors involved and ensuring all the information needed is available. Any fresh valuations will need to be provided and any conditions set by the lender will need to be fulfilled.

14.2 Providers of financial services

Besides the special departments and companies working with surveying firms and property consultants, there are financial services ranging from the large insurance groups to small specialist property finance intermediaries. Lenders thus have thousands of sources of potential new business.

Lenders will tend to differentiate between the intermediaries on two counts:

- quality clients (borrowers)
- quality transactions (quality of security, property transaction, cash flow, etc.).

Chartered surveyors who have some activity in the financial services area include the major property consultants. Savills (1989) carried out research on the average size of debt issued in 1989 and on the types of financial structure used; this information is given respectively in Figures 14.2 and 14.3. More recent analysis of the types of financial instrument used in 1991 shows a much more restricted range based on term loans, revolving credit and bonds with a very small rights issue

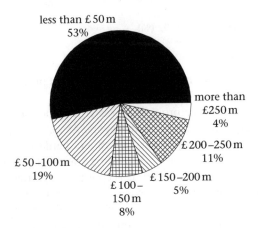

Figure 14.2 Average size of debt issued, 1989 (%)
Source: Savills (1989).

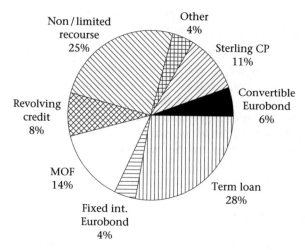

Figure 14.3 Types of debt issued, 1989 (%)
Source: Savills (1989).

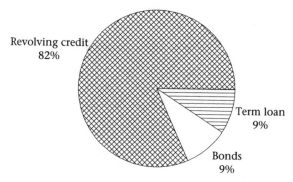

Figure 14.4 Types of debt issued, 1992 (%)
Source: Savills (1993).

usage (see Figure 14.4). This may reflect the problems of property in the post-boom market.

New forms of finance have brought increased competition in the markets for property professionals, the chartered surveyors. As debt finance and the capital markets have become more important, investment banks have attempted to compete more openly with surveyors in providing specialist property financing services. Competition has also come from accountants, particularly in the area of project management and corporate advice. The key argument for property professionals is whether to act as principal or adviser, in certain corporate transactions it is necessary to take a principal role, but historically professional partnerships have given advice. For the more financial services-orientated firms, there is a need to have capital so they are able to take principal positions: for instance, the ability to underwrite a debt financing facility or an equity placing for a development or property company. In the context of securitisation, there is the need to underwrite a flotation or make markets (Barter 1988). The ability to structure or arrange deals may not be sufficient to ensure the appropriate instructions. Clients may want to see the arranger of the finance taking the lead with its own funds, whilst accepting that the majority of the funding will be syndicated elsewhere.

The training for people in financial services is very important; it is a key opportunity for developing property professionals in the finance field. The weak players in this market at the moment are the medium-sized firms; they do not have the niche markets of the small firms and lack the international perspective, specialised departments and research backing of the larger diversified practices.

The funding of property

The decision as to which funding strategy to pursue depends on the financial policy of the client. Major perspectives may include the following:

Private versus public client

Clients in the private sector may have firm views on the use of public sector money, especially where management control or equity share may be dissipated. Funding may be available from the public sector in terms of grants or loan facilities from European, national and local government bodies. Public sector clients, because of preference policy or legislation, may be limited in their use of different sources of funds.

Debt versus equity alternatives

The extent to which a developer is willing to share the risks and rewards of a project will determine the more likely source of funds and the terms that might apply.

Tax considerations

Fiscal measures impinge on the process of property development and are crucial in assessing the viability of a given project and in deciding the best way of organising a programme of acquisition, construction and disposal.

Current arrangements

Many client developers will have access to existing sources of finance; large organisations will often have multiple funding arrangements with funds and banks. A general funding facility could be provided giving wider flexibility to project finance.

14.3 Fees for providing financial services

The fees charged by Financial Services Companies may be options of the following:

1 An abortive fee plus a success related fee on the facility. This could be, say, a £10,000 fee (payable even if project is abortive) plus a success-related fee of, say, 0.5 per cent of the facility;

2 A speculative fee (say, 1 per cent of the facility). This is the traditional approach;
3 A partnership approach: perhaps 1 per cent if the agent brings in the funding partner, 0.66 per cent if the client brings in a partner (if they have contacts).

If the fees are based exclusively on transaction costs, fees for acting will be greater, perhaps on the following scale:

Transaction Size	Fee
£250,000 plus	2%
£500,000 plus	1.5%
£1 million plus	1%

14.4   The debt finance market

In the 1990s, the debt market was tough going. The banks were highly exposed in property, the highest since the collapse of 1973/4. If the problems of the banks had been confined to property, then the debt finance market would not have been too badly affected, but bank lending problems were not confined to property and there were problems in other sectors including retailing, housing construction and manufacturing. Banks themselves also had operational problems. Bad debt problems thus made banks reluctant to lend unless an improvement in the economic situation could be seen. This made the work of financial services and the placing of the loans more difficult.

The financial services intermediaries did have two positive aspects to look to, though.

1 Banks need to lend money to make money. They need to lend it more so now. A bank that loses £1,000 may need to lend £50,000 for a year to make up that loss. The clearing banks wrote off billions of pounds in the last property slump and this must act as an incentive to lend.
2 As finance becomes more difficult to obtain, so intermediaries with wider contacts become more important, as do their skills in negotiating and presenting the deals. Thus, the paradox is of greater importance for financial services in a more discerning lending market.

14.5   Presentation of loan proposals

Proper presentation of loan proposals is essential, especially for those developers and investors whose credibility and track record is unknown. Leading institutions put great store by the proper presentation of material backed up by appropriate research, comparable evidence, valuations and cash flow projections. Obviously, in a situation such as this, it is also important for the lender to be aware of the business strategy of the borrowers, their background and experience. The CVs of the key people involved in the project will be required. For small developers this is especially important. Research by Isaac and O'Grady (1993) indicates that there are four main reasons why lenders turn down applications for funding from small developers. These are given below, in order.

1 Lenders are not convinced of the overall viability of the development;
2 Lack of adequate equity provided by the developers;
3 Poor presentation of the documents applying for finance;
4 Unfavourable results arising from investigations into the developer's past record.

This presentation approach is best seen through an example of how an agreed facility is presented, as shown in Box 14.1.

Box 14.1 Example of a presentation of an offer of a facility

Consists of:

(a) Principal terms and conditions
(b) Description of premises
(c) Details of the group of companies

Enclosures:

(d) Property particulars
(e) Valuation report
(f) Certificate of title
(g) General brochures of borrowing company
(h) Annual company report of borrower
(i) Financial accounts of borrower

Principal Terms and conditions:

Description:	e.g., Medium term loan facility
Borrower:	
Guarantor:	
Underwriters:	
Lender:	
Arranger:	lead manager and agent
Amount:	
Purpose:	say, to assist the finance of the purchase
Term:	e.g., 5 years from the signing of the facility document
Drawdown:	e.g., in one amount
Repayment:	Minimum instalment amounts

e.g.,	Months from signing	Instalment amounts (£ m)
	12	7
	24	4
	36	4
	48	2.5

Interest:

e.g.,   The aggregate of:
– Margin of 7/8 per cent (year 1) or if later till all monies guarantee is released of 3/4 per cent
– LIBOR (1, 3 or 6 months, borrower's option, or 12 months subject to availability to bank)
– Associated costs rounded up to the nearest 1/16 per cent

14.6　Criteria of acceptance

Both sides are looking at basic investment criteria of risk and return:

Lender looks at:

- risk of borrower defaulting
- risk of property not achieving a sale price to cover debt
- return on capital relative to cost of capital

Borrower looks at:

- risk of falling values
- risk of higher interest rates
- risk of unemployment or inability to pay
- return on equity in property.

A simple comparison of what is required in terms of information by a lender can be made in an area with which we are all generally familiar: the mortgage application to purchase a house. The principal area of interest to the lender and the fundamental criteria are the same (see Box 14.2). Wyles (1990) suggests a number

Box 14.2　Information required for loan proposal

An example of information required when applying for a mortgage on a domestic house for owner occupation.

1　Information required by lender

  (a)　Details of borrower:
    Status
    Date of birth
    Nature of employment
    Length of service
    Financial commitments
    Evidence of bankruptcy
  (b)　Details of property to be mortgaged
    Age
    Location
    Type
    Use, may need to be wholly residential
  (c)　Details of occupants
  (d)　Details of previous applications
  (e)　Details of loan requirements
    – payment details

2　Information required by borrower

  (a)　Maximum loan:
    – multiplier of income
    – per cent property value
  (b)　interest rate and repayment period
  (c)　fixed/variable rate
  (d)　arrangement costs/redemption costs.

of criteria that would be used in underwriting commercial mortgage indemnities (CMIs: see Chapter 4 for a discussion of these). These criteria are useful as lending criteria on which a proper presentation of a loan proposal should be based. These criteria are presented as two lists, one for investment property and one for speculative development:

Investment Property	*Speculative Development*
Financier – nature of/requirements	(see also comments in left column)
Borrower – details/requirement	
Asset – details, value	Financier
Cash flow – projections, assumptions	Development – proposals
Estimated rental value (ERV) – comparables	Site appraisal
Site – details/constraints	Basis of feasibility
Loan duration	Voids – repercussions
Structure of finance	Profit on cost
Costs and values	Cost overrun risk
Loan to value ratio	Completion risk

14.7 Comparison of finance terms

There are four main areas to be considered prior to entering into a facility to ensure that a suitable structure can be arranged. These are cost, flexibility, risk and accounting presentation:

Cost	Best rates are available for the best quality covenants. Where the lending institution takes more risk, a higher return is required. For non-recourse transactions an interest rate between 1 and 2 per cent over LIBOR is currently required.
Flexibility	The greater the level of security and recourse, the less likely is there will be any restrictions on management control. Flexibility depends on the interest rate structure.
Risk	The greater the lender's risk, the greater the cost to the borrower.
Accounting	A number of creative packages are available which can remove debt from the balance sheet.

14.8 Financial regulations

The rules on financial advisers have changed radically over the last five years or so. There is now a clear line between independent advice and straight salesmanship. All independent advisers are regulated by the Financial Intermediaries, Managers and Brokers Regulatory Association (FIMBRA). The idea of the regulation was to encourage protection for the investor; however, the amount of paperwork and accounting procedure has made the process difficult for the individual operator and thus many FIMBRA members have now linked themselves to a single insurance company.

The Financial Services Act has introduced new administrative and disclosure obligations. Authorisation to advise under the Act may include other departments or practices including investment agents and property management. The Act has brought new regulations and issues of compliance and conflicts of interest. Whilst there will have to be formal compliance requirements within the authorised part of a surveyor's business, the inevitable consequence of the more diversified firm may be a need for compliance policy and a compliance officer for the whole firm. The compliance officer would have knowledge of all transactions being undertaken within the firm as a whole and would have the power to enforce disclosure of conflicts of interest, establish 'Chinese walls' and discipline staff (Barter 1988).

Financial Services Act 1986

The Financial Services Act 1986 is an act to regulate investment business. The main principle of the Act is the requirement that a person be authorised or exempted in order to carry out an investment business. Sections 3 and 4 of the Act provide that it is a criminal offence to carry on an investment business without authorisation. Section 5 provides that contracts entered into by an unauthorised person, are unenforceable against the client dealing with that unauthorised person.

Part 1 of the Act regulates investment business and investment protection has been delegated to the Securities and Investments Board (SIB). It is financed by a levy on self-regulating organisations (SROs) and recognised professional bodies. The SROs are listed in Box 14.3. The rulebooks used by these regulators encompass principles of fairness, skill and diligence, and stipulate the minimum required financial resources required to operate a business.

To be within the scope of the Act, the business activity must be concerned with an investment. Business is defined as dealing in investments, arranging deals in investments, managing investments, giving investment advice and establishing

Box 14.3 Self-regulating organisations and recognised professional bodies under the Financial Services Act

---

Self-regulating organisations (SROs) are:

SFA (the Securities and Futures Authority) which is made up of members of the Stock Exchange, market makers, brokers and those working in the futures and options markets;
IMRO (the Investment Managers' Regulatory Organisation) which is made up of managers of large investment portfolios;
LAUTRO (the Life Assurance and Unit Trust Regulatory Organisation) which is concerned with the marketing of life assurance and unit trusts;
FIMBRA (the Financial Intermediaries, Managers and Brokers Regulatory Association) which concerns itself with the selling of investment services.

Recognised Professional Bodies (RPBs) are:

The Institutes of Chartered Accountants of England and Wales, Scotland and Ireland;
The Association of Certified Accountants;
The Law Society;
The Institute of Actuaries;
The Insurance Brokers Registration Council.

collective investment schemes. Investments are defined in the following way (*Estates Gazette* 1991):

- stocks and shares
- debentures, loan stock, bonds and certificates
- loan stock, bonds and other documents of indebtedness to government or to local authorities or to public authorities
- warrants or other instruments entitling the holder to subscribe for any of the above
- certificates respecting any of the above
- unit trusts
- options to acquire (among other things) investments, currency, gold or silver
- futures
- contracts for differences
- long-term insurance contracts
- rights and interests in investments.

Financial services and investment

Financial services organisations are involved in property fund management and it is appropriate to consider their investment strategies and performance here. Freeman Publishing (2000) suggests that financial services organisations in investment management will have three specific objectives: to try to increase market share, to match the performance of competitors and also to match the business risk. The suggestion is that they will try to stay 'close to the pack' and operate to a benchmark of competitors' risk profiles and returns. A more absolute benchmark for the return would be to look at the Investment Property Databank Index (IPD) to see if the fund being managed is outperforming the index. Multi-asset managers are encouraged to invest in property as an asset class so as to avoid the risk of performing differently from competitors with a given property weighting. Departure from the standard weighting leading to a loss of performance relative to competitors can lead to withdrawal of investment. Risk is important as the deviation from the index or benchmark figure (called the tracking error) rather than absolute risk.

References

Barter, S. L. (1988) 'Introduction', in S. L. Barter (ed.), *Real Estate Finance*, Butterworths, London.

Estates Gazette (1991) 'Mainly for Students: The law of financial services', *Estates Gazette*, London, 16 November, 193–4.

Freeman Publishing (2000) *Guide to the Property Industry*, Freeman Publishing, London, June.

Gumerlock, R. (1999) 'The future of risk', *Euromoney*, London, June, 362, 112–14.

Isaac, D. and O' Grady, M. (1993) 'Thorough Approach the Key to Development Funding', *Property Valuer*, Dublin, Winter.

Savills (1989) *Financing Property 1989*, Savills, London.

Savills (1993a) *Financing Property 1993*, Savills, London.

Wyles, M. (1990) 'Mortgage Indemnity – A Risk/Reward Arbitrage', *Journal of Property Finance*, 1(3), 378–86.

Bibliography

Accounting Standards Committee (1990) *Exposure Draft 51: Accounting for Fixed Assets and Revaluations*, ASC, May.

Albert, D. and Watson, J. (1990) 'An approach to Property Joint Ventures', *Journal of Property Finance*, 1(2), 189–95.

Armon-Jones, C. H. (1992) 'Underwriting Property Sales', *Journal of Property Finance*, 2(4), 497–500.

Asch, D. and Kaye, G. R. (1989) *Financial Planning: Modelling Methods and Techniques*, Kogan Paul, London.

Asch, D. and Kaye, G. R. (1996) *Financial Planning: Profit Improvement through Modelling*, Kogan Paul, London.

Ashurst, R., Blundell, G., Booth, P., Cumberworth, M., Griffiths, G. and Morrell, G. (1998) 'Property investment for UK pension funds post MFR', *Journal of Property Investment and Finance*, 16(1), 7–20.

Balchin, P. N., Isaac, D. and Chen, J. (2000) *Urban Economics: A Global Perspective*, Palgrave, Basingstoke/New York.

Balchin, P., Isaac, D. and Rhoden, M. (1998) 'Housing policy and finance', in P. Balchin and M. Rhoden (eds), *Housing: The Essential Foundations*, Routledge, London.

Ball, M., Lizieri, C. and MacGregor, B. D. (1998) *The Economics of Commercial Property Markets*, Routledge, London.

Bank of England (1990) *Quarterly Bulletin*, 30(2), May.

Bank of England (1991) *Quarterly Bulletin*, 31(2), May.

Bank of England (1992) *Quarterly Bulletin*, 32(2), May.

Bank of England (1993) *Quarterly Bulletin*, 33(3), August.

Bank of England (1994a) *Quarterly Bulletin*, 34(3), August.

Bank of England (1994b) *Quarterly Bulletin*, 34(4), November.

Bank of England (1995) *Quarterly Bulletin*, 35(3), August.

Baring, Houston & Saunders (1991) *Property Report*, Baring, Houston & Saunders, London, November.

Barkham, R. (1995) 'The performance of the UK property company sector: a guide to investing in British property via the public stock market', *Real Estate Finance*, 12(1), 90–8.

Barkham, R. J. and Purdy, D. E. (1992) 'Financial company reporting: Potential weaknesses', *Journal of Property Valuation and Investment*, 11(2), 133–44.

Barkham, R. and Ward, C. W. R. (1999) 'Investor sentiment and noise traders: discount to net asset value in listed property companies in the UK', *Journal of Real Estate Research*, 18(2), 291–312.

Barkshire, R. (1986) *The Unitised Property Market*, Working Party of the Unitised Property Market, London, February.

Barter, S. L. (1988) 'Introduction', in S. L. Barter (ed.), *Real Estate Finance*, Butterworths, London.

Barter, S. and Sinclair, N. (1988) 'Securitisation', in S. L. Barter (ed.), *Real Estate Finance*, Butterworths, London.

Baum, A. E. and Schofield, A. (1991) 'Property as a Global Asset', in P. Venmore-Rowland, P. Brandon and T. Mole (eds), *Investment, Procurement and Performance in Construction*, RICS, London.

Berkley, R. (1991) 'Raising Commercial Property Finance in a Difficult Market', *Journal of Property Finance*, 1(4), 523–9.

Beveridge, J. (1988) 'The Needs of the Property Company', in S. L. Barter (ed.), *Real Estate Finance*, Butterworths, London.

Beveridge, J. A. (1991) 'New Methods of Financing', in P. Venmore-Rowland, P. Brandon and T. Mole (eds), *Investment, Procurement and Performance in Construction*, RICS, London.

Booth, P. and Rodney, B. (2000) 'The Repayment of Mortgages by Endowment Assurances in a Low Interest Rate Environment', *Real Estate Finance and Investment Research Paper*, no. 2000.01, City University Business School, November.

Booth, P. and Walsh, D. (2000) 'Cash Flow Models for Pricing Mortgages', *Real Estate Finance and Investment Research Paper*, no. 2000.02, City University Business School, November.

Bourne, T. (1995) 'Accelerating towards best returns', *Estates Gazette*, 10 June, 44–5.

Bramson, D. (1988) 'The Mechanics of Joint Ventures', in S. L. Barter (ed.), *Real Estate Finance*, Butterworths, London.

Brett, M. (1983a) 'Growth of financial institutions', in C. Darlow (ed.), *Valuation and Investment Appraisal, Estates Gazette*, London.

Brett, M. (1983b) 'Indirect Investment in Property', in C. Darlow (ed.), *Valuation and Investment Appraisal, Estates Gazette*, London.

Brett, M. (1990a) *How to Read the Financial Pages*, Hutchinson, London.

Brett, M. (1990b) *Property and Money, Estates Gazette*, London.

Brett, M. (1991a) 'How property futures work', *Estates Gazette*, 18 May, 71.

Brett, M. (1991b), 'Property and Money: Mortgages which convert into property', *Estates Gazette*, 17 August.

Brett, M. (1997) *Property and Money, Estates Gazette*, London.

Brett, M. (1999) 'Accounting changes will give a clear view', *Estates Gazette*, London, 7 August, 32.

Briscoe, G. (1988) *The Economics of the Construction Industry*, Mitchell, London.

Brooks, C., Tsolacos, S. and Lee, S. (2000) 'The cyclical relations between traded property stock prices and aggregate time-series', *Journal of Property Investment and Finance*, 18(6), 540–64.

Brown, G. R. (1991) *Property Investment and the Capital Markets*, E. & F. Spon, London.

Brown, G. R. and Matysiak, G. A. (2000) *Real Estate Investment: A Capital Market Approach*, Pearson Education, Harlow.

Cadman, D. and Catalano, A. (1983) *Property Development in the UK – Evolution and Change*, College of Estate Management, Reading.

Cairns, D. (2001) 'Value of land in the balance', *Estates Gazette*, 27 October, 178–9.

Calachi, R. and Rosenburg, S. (eds) (1992) *Property Finance, An International Perspective*, Euromoney Books, London.

Cameron Markby Hewitt (1996) 'The Future of Investment Property', *Property Update*, Cameron Markby Hewitt, Summer.

Catalano, A. (1993) 'Paribas trusts in the upturn', *Estates Gazette*, 23 October, 52.

Catalano, A. (1995) 'Property paper chase', *Estates Gazette*, 1 July, 52.

Catalano, A. (1996a) 'An industry hungry for change', *Estates Gazette*, 18 May, 44.

Catalano, A. (1996b) 'MEPC taps US market with $225 million bond issue', *Estates Gazette*, 18 May, 43.

Catalano, A. (2000) 'Extra cash at a premium', *Estates Gazette*, 29 January, 58–9.

Catalano, A. (2001a) 'No safe haven for small punters', *Estates Gazette*, 27 October, 54.

Catalano, A. (2001b) 'Limit to LP's attractions', *Estates Gazette*, 3 November, 61.

Central Statistical Office (1992) *Financial Statistics: Explanatory Handbook*, CSO, London, December.

Central Statistical Office (1993a) *Financial Statistics*, CSO, London, September.

Central Statistical Office (1993b) *Housing and Construction Statistics*, CSO, London, September.

Central Statistical Office (1994a) *Financial Statistics*, CSO, London, November.

Central Statistical Office (1994b) *Economic Trends*, CSO, London.

Central Statistical Office (1995a) *UK Economic Accounts*, no. 8, CSO, London, January.

Central Statistical Office (1995b) *Economic Trends*, CSO, London, July.

Central Statistical Office (1995c) *Economic Trends: Annual Supplement*, CSO, London.

Central Statistical Office (1996) *Financial Statistics*, CSO, London, November.

Central Statistical Office (1999) *Financial Statistics*, CSO, London, no. 452, December.

Chartered Surveyor Monthly (CSM) (1996) 'RICS presses Treasury on securitisation', *CSM*, October, 7.

Chartered Surveyor Monthly (CSM) (2001) 'Limited Liability Partnerships Act 2000', *CSM*, November and December, 8.

Chartered Surveyor Weekly (1991) 'Editorial: Crisis at London FOX leaves futures uncertain', *Chartered Surveyor Weekly*, 10 October, 5.

Chartered Surveyor Weekly (1991) 'Editorial: UPS offers new option to property strugglers', *Chartered Surveyor Weekly*, 17 October.

Chesterton Financial (1991) *Property Lending Survey*, Chesterton Financial, London, February.

Chesterton Financial (1992) *Property Lending Survey*, Chesterton Financial, London, February.

Chesterton Financial (1993) *Property Lending Survey*, Chesterton Financial, London, February.

Chesterton Financial/*CSW* (1993) *Property Confidence Barometer*, bi-annual survey 1991–1993, Chesterton Financial, London.

Chesterton Financial, Internal uncirculated reports, Chesterton Financial, London.

Clarke, R. J. (1990) 'Refinancing', *Journal of Property Finance*, 1(3), 435–9.

Cohen, P. (1992) 'Non-recourse Property Funding', *Journal of Property Finance*, 3(3), 319–24.

Cooper, M. (2001) 'Top property firms still not delivering decent returns', *Estates Gazette*, 20 October, 53.

Copeland, T. E. and Weston, J. F. (1988) *Financial Theory and Corporate Policy*, Addison-Wesley, Wokingham.

Cornes, D. and Isaac, D. (1998) 'Counting the cranes on the skyline', *Chartered Banker*, May, 39.

Danaher, T. (2001) 'The year of leverage', *Property Week*, 16 March, 12–13.

Darlow, C. (ed.) (1983) *Valuation and Investment Appraisal*, Estates Gazette, London.

Darlow, C. (1988) 'Direct Project Funding', in C. Darlow (ed.), *Valuation and Development Appraisal*, Estates Gazette, London.

Davis, E. W. and Pointon, J. (1994) *Finance and the Firm*, Oxford University Press, Oxford.

Debenham, Tewson & Chinnocks (1984) *Property Investment in Britain*, Debenham, Tewson & Chinnocks, London.

Dent, P. and Weeks, C. (1993) 'Is there LIFFE after FOX?', *Estates Gazette*, 9 October, 132–6.

Dianchun Jiang, Chen, J. and Isaac, D. (1999) 'Real Estate and Foreign Investment in China', *Journal of Financial Management of Property and Construction*, 4(1), 75–87.

DTZ Debenham Thorpe (1993) *Money into Property*, DTZ Debenham Thorpe, London, August.

DTZ Debenham Thorpe (1996) *Property Lending Survey*, DTZ Debenham Thorpe, London, September.

DTZ Debenham Thorpe (1999) *Money into Property*, DTZ Debenham Thorpe, London, May.

DTZ Research (2001) *Money into Property*, DTZ Research, London, edition 26, June.

Dubben, N. and Sayce, S. (1991) *Property Portfolio Management*, Routledge, London.

Dunckley, J. (2000) 'Financial reporting standards: is market value for the existing use now obsolete?', *Journal of Property Investment and Finance*, 18(2), 212–24.

Enever, N. and Isaac, D. (2001) *The Valuation of Property Investments*, Estates Gazette, London.

Estates Times (1993) 'Swaps not cash', *Estates Times*, 19 November, 24.

Estates Gazette (1991) 'Mainly for Students: The law of financial services', *Estates Gazette*, London, 16 November, 193–4.

Estates Gazette (2000) 'How to fuel the modern enterprise', *Estates Gazette*, London, 18 November, 188–91.

Estates Gazette (2001a) 'Market Indicators', *Estates Gazette*, 22 September, 64.

Estates Gazette (2001b) 'Accountancy board calls for greater consistency in sector', *Estates Gazette*, 6 October, 51.

Estates Gazette (2001c) 'Profiting from property', *Estates Gazette*, 17 November, 168–90.

Estates Gazette (2002) 'Property companies' bank borrowing tops £100 bn', *Estates Gazette*, 16 February, 47.

Euromoney (1999) 'The world's biggest banks', *Euromoney*, no. 362 (June), 209.

Evans, M., French, N. and O'Roarty, B. (2001) 'Accountancy and corporate property management – a briefing on current and proposed provisions relating to corporate real estate', *Journal of Property Investment and Finance*, 19(2), 211–23.

Evans, P. H. (1992) 'Statistical Review', *Journal of Property Finance*, 3(1), 115–20.

Evans, P. H. (1993) 'Statistical Review', *Journal of Property Finance*, 4(2), 75–82.

Fielding, M. and Besser, A. (1991) 'Syndicated loans – *caveat* borrower', *Estates Gazette*, 15 June, 78 and 103.

Fox, J. W. W. (1993) 'Sale and Leasebacks: A Case Study', *Journal of Property Finance*, 4(1), 9–12.

Fraser, W. D. (1993) *Principles of Property Investment and Pricing*, Macmillan, London.

Freed, N. (1992) 'Bridging Finance', *Journal of Property Finance*, 3(2), 187–90.

Freeman, D. J. (2001a) 'Property joint ventures', *Property Review*, D. J. Freeman, London, no. 37 (October), 1–2.

Freeman. D. J. (2001b) 'Security structures, the Insolvency Act 2000 and further proposal for reform', *Property Review*, D. J. Freeman, London, no. 37 (October), 4.

Freeman Publishing (2000) *Guide to the Property Industry*, Freeman Publishing, London, June.

Gallimore, P., Williams, W. and Woodward, D. (1997) 'Perceptions of Risk in the Private Finance Initiative', *Journal of Property Finance*, 8(2), 164–76.

Gallinger, G. W. and Healey, P. B. (1991) *Liquidity Analysis and Management*, Addison-Wesley, Wokingham.

Gemill, G. (1990) 'Futures trading and finance in housing market', *Journal of Property Finance*, 1(2), 196–207.

Ghosh, C., Guttery, R. S. and Simons, C. F. (1994) 'The Olympia and York Crisis: Effects on the Financial Performance of US and Foreign Banks', *Journal of Property Finance*, 5(2), 5–46.

Gibbs, R. (1987) 'Raising Finance for New Development', *Journal of Valuation*, 5(4), 343–53.

Goldsmith, G. C. (1992) 'Sterling Interest Swaptions', *Journal of Property Finance*, 3(3), 315–18.

Goodman, T. (1991) 'Property futures idea is still alive – just', *Chartered Surveyor Weekly*, 10 October, 11.

Goodwin, M. (1995) 'A recipe for liquifying property', *Chartered Surveyor Monthly*, November/December, 28–9.

Graham, J. (1995) 'New sources of finance for the property industry', *Estates Gazette*, 6 July.

Gumerlock, R. (1999) 'The future of risk', *Euromoney*, London, June, 362, 112–14.

Hargitay, S. E. and Sui-Ming, Y. (1993) *Property Investment Decisions*, E. & F. Spon, London.

Harvard, T. (2001) *Valuation Behaviour and Valuer Reliability*, Royal Institute of Chartered Surveyors Foundation, London (web address: http://www.rics-foundation.org).

Hoesli, M. and MacGregor, B. D. (2000) *Property Investment: Principles and Practice of Portfolio Management*, Pearson Education, Harlow.

Investment Property Databank (1993) *Annual Review 1993*, IPD, London, December.

Investment Property Databank (1995) *Annual Review 1995*, IPD, London.

Investment Property Forum (1995) *Property Securitisation*, IPF, London.

Isaac, D. (1986) 'Corporate finance and property development funding: An analysis of property companies' capital structures with special reference to the relationship between asset value and share price', Unpublished thesis, Faculty of the Built Environment, South Bank Polytechnic, London.

Isaac, D. (1994) *Property Finance*, Macmillan, London.

Isaac, D. (1996) *Property Development; Appraisal and Finance*, Macmillan, London.

Isaac, D. (1996) *Commercial Property Lending*, Inaugural Lecture Series, Greenwich University Press, London.

Isaac, D. (1996) 'The Property Lending Survey five years on', *Chartered Surveyor Monthly*, October, 40.

Isaac, D. (1998) *Property Investment*, Macmillan, London.

Isaac, D. (1998) 'Property Lending Survey 1998', *Journal of Property Valuation and Investment*, 16(5), 493–7.

Isaac, D. (1998) 'Property lending survey 1998', *Journal of Financial Management of Property and Construction*, 3(3), 87–91.

Isaac, D. (2002) *Property Valuation Principles*, Palgrave, Basingstoke/New York.

Isaac, D. and O'Grady, M. (1993) 'Thorough Approach the Key to Development Funding', *Property Valuer*, Dublin, Winter.

Isaac, D. and Steley, T. (1991) *Property Valuation Techniques*, Macmillan, London.

Isaac, D. and Steley, T. (2000) *Property Valuation Techniques*, Macmillan, London.

Isaac, D. and Woodroffe, N. (1987) 'Are property company assets undervalued', *Estates Gazette*, London, 5 September, 1,024–6.

Isaac, D. and Woodroffe, N. (1996) *Property Companies: Share Price and Net Asset Value*, Greenwich University Press, London.

Jennings, R. B. (1993) 'The Resurgence of Real Estate Investment Trusts (REITs)', *Journal of Property Finance*, 4(1), 13–19.

Jonas, C. (1995) 'Liquidity and property', *Estates Gazette*, 3 June, 52.

Jones, T. and Isaac, D. (1996) 'Finance for the Smaller Building Contractor', in D. Isaac (ed.), *Construction Management: Issues and Perspectives*, Greenwich University Press, London.

Jones Lang Wootton (1989) *The Glossary of Property Terms*, Estates Gazette, London.

Journal of Valuation (1989) 'Market Data', *Journal of Valuation*, 8(1), 87–9.

Keers, H. (2001) 'Property lending cools despite £15 bn increase', *Property Week*, 10 August, 68.

Kynoch, R. (1993) 'Firms predict £2 bn spending surge', *Chartered Surveyor Weekly*, 26 August, 18–21.

Lee, C. F. (1985) *Financial Analysis and Planning: Theory and Application*, Addison-Wesley, Wokingham.

Lennox, K. (1996) 'Future perfect', *Estates Gazette*, 24 August, 30.

Levy, H. and Sarnat, M. (1994) *Capital Investment and Financial Decisions*, Prentice-Hall, Englewood Cliffs, NJ.

Liow, K. H. (1998) 'An Empirical Investigation of Corporate Growth of Property Companies', *Journal of Financial Management of Property and Construction*, 3(3), 5–16.

London, S. (1996) 'Lure of the property magnet', *Financial Times*, 23 September, 19.

Looi, J. T. L. (1999a) 'Financial structure of UK property companies: a research agenda', *Journal of Financial Management of Property and Construction*, 4(1), 5–30.

Looi, J. T. L. (1999b) 'The determinants of capital structure: evidence on UK property companies', *Journal of Property Investment and Finance*, 17(5), 464–80.

Lucius, D. I. (2001) 'Real options in real estate development', *Journal of Property Investment and Finance*, 19(1), 73–8.

Maguire, D. and Axcell, A. (1994) 'Real Estate Finance: France, Germany and the UK', *Journal of Property Finance*, 5(1), 29–40.

Mallinson, M. (1988) 'Equity Finance', in S. L. Barter (ed.), *Real Estate Finance*, Butterworths, London.

Marriott, O. (1962) *The Property Boom*, Hamish Hamilton, London.

Marshall, P. and Kennedy, C. (1992) 'Development valuation techniques', *Journal of Property Valuation and Investment*, 11(1), 57–66.

Maxted, B. (1988) *Unitisation of Property*, College of Estate Management, Reading.

McAllister, P. and Mansfield, J. R. (1998a) 'Investment property portfolio management and financial derivatives: Paper 1', *Property Management*, 16(3), 116–19.

McAllister, P. and Mansfield, J. R. (1998b) 'Investment property portfolio management and financial derivatives: Paper 2', *Property Management*, 16(4), 208–13.

McIntosh, A. and Sykes, S. (1985) *A Guide to Institutional Property Investment*, Macmillan, London.

Millman, S. (1988) 'Property, Property Companies and Public Securities', in S. L. Barter (ed.), *Real Estate Finance*, Butterworths, London.

Mitchell, C. and Peake, J. H. (1991) 'The Management of Interest Rate Exposure', *Journal of Property Finance*, 1(4), 530–8.

Naylor, T. (1994) 'Aspects of senior debt used by and available to property development companies', *Journal of Property Finance*, 5(1), 23–8.

Neave, E. H. (1998) *Capital Investment and Financial Decisions*, Prentice-Hall, Englewood Cliffs, NJ.

Newall, G. and Fife, A. (1995) 'Major property investors' attitudes to property securitisation', *Journal of Property Finance*, 6(1), 55–63.

Nicolle, C. and Llewelyn, H. (2002) 'Shape up or ship out', *Estates Gazette*, 5 January, 30–1.

Ong, S. E. and Brown, G. R. (2001) 'Editorial: what are real options', *Journal of Property Investment and Finance*, 19(1), 6–8.

Ooi, J. (2000) 'Corporate reliance on bank loans: and empirical analysis of UK property companies', *Journal of Property Investment and Finance*, 18(1), 103–20.

Orchard-Lisle, P. (1987) 'Financing Property Development', *Journal of Valuation*, 5(4), 343–53.

Paribas Capital Markets (1993a) *European Equity Research: Rodamco*, Banque Paribas Nederland NV, October.

Paribas Capital Markets (1993b) *Monthly Property Share Statistics*, Banque Paribas, November.

Parker, R. H. (1983) *Understanding Company Financial Statements*, Penguin, London.

Peat, M. (1988) 'The Accounting Issues', in S. L. Barter (ed.), *Real Estate Finance*, Butterworths, London.

Pike, R. and Neale, B. (1993) *Corporate Finance and Investment*, Prentice-Hall, London.

Pike, R. and Neale, B. (1998) *Corporate Finance and Investment: Decisions and Strategies*, Prentice-Hall, London.

Plender, J. (2002) 'The slow demise of the cult of the equity', *Estates Gazette*, 12 January, 38.

Property Week (2001a) 'New model for reviews', *Property Week*, 19 October, 7.

Property Week (2001b) 'Property lending hits £67.5 bn', *Property Week*, 16 November, 17.

Property Week (2001c) 'Pillar and HBV go down new lending route', *Property Week*, 16 November, 19.

Pugh, C. (1991) 'The Globalisation of Finance Capital and the Changing Relationships between Property and Finance', *Journal of Property Finance*, 2(2) and (3).

Purdy, D. E. (1992) 'Provoking awareness through the provision of relevant information in Property Company Accounts', *Journal of Property Finance*, 3(3), 337–46.

Ratcliffe, J. (1978) *An Introduction to Urban Land Administration*, Estates Gazette, London.

Ratcliffe, J. (1984) 'Development Financing: drawing up the Agreement', *Architects Journal*, 22 and 29 August, 63.

Redman, A. L. and Manakyan, H. (1995) 'A Multivariate Analysis of REIT Performance by Financial and Real Asset Portfolio Characteristics', *Journal of Real Estate Finance and Economics*, 10(2), 169–75.

Richard Ellis (1986) 'Development Finance', *Property Investment Quarterly Bulletin*, Richard Ellis, London, April.

Richard Ellis (1991) 'A look at Commercial Property Futures', *Investment Research Review no. 2*, Richard Ellis, London.

Riley, M. and Isaac, D. (1991) 'Property Lending Survey 1991', *Journal of Property Finance*, 2(1), 74–7.

Riley, M. and Isaac, D. (1992) 'Property Lending Survey 1992', *Journal of Property Finance*, 2(4), 38–41.

Riley, M. and Isaac, D. (1993a) 'Property Lending Survey 1993', *Journal of Property Finance*, 4(1), 43–8.

Riley, M. and Isaac, D. (1993b) 'Commercial Property Lending: Confidence Survey', *Journal of Property Finance*, 4(3/4), 45–51.

Riley, M. and Isaac, D. (1994) 'Property Lending Survey 1994', *Journal of Property Finance*, 5(1), 45–51.

Riley, M. and Isaac, D. (1995) 'Property Lending Survey 1995', *Journal of Property Finance*, 6(1), 67–72.

Riley, M. and Isaac, D. (1997) 'Property Lending Survey 1996', *Journal of Property Finance*, 8(1), 85–91

Robinson, G. (1996) 'Derivatives: filling a gap in the market', *Estates Gazette*, 2 November, 179–81.

Rodney, W. and Clark, P. (2000) 'Financing Urban Regeneration', *Real Estate Finance and Investment Research Paper*, no. 2000.04, City University Business School, December.

Rodrigues, M. (2001) 'Get the REIT response', *Estates Gazette*, 1 December, 125.

Ross, S. A., Westerfield, R. W. and Jaffe, J. F. (1993) *Corporate Finance*, Irwin, Boston, MA.

Ross, S. A., Westerfield, R. W. and Jaffe, J. F. (1999) *Corporate Finance*, McGraw-Hill, London.

Royal Institution of Chartered Surveyors (RICS) (1985) *The Unitisation of Real Property*, RICS, London.

Rydin, Y., Rodney, W. and Orr, C. (1990) 'Why Do Institutions Invest in Property?', *Journal of Property Finance*, 1(2), 250–8.

Ryland, D. (1991) 'Authorised Property Unit Trusts', *Estates Gazette*, London, 9 November, 163–4.

Ryland, D. S. (1992) 'Changes in Accounting Rules', *Journal of Property Finance*, 3(1), 28–37.

Ryland, D. S. (1994) 'Financial Reporting Standard 5', *Journal of Property Finance*, 5(1), 7–8.

S. G. Warburg Research (1993) *U.K. Property: Monthly Review*, S. G. Warburg, London, November.

S. G. Warburg Securities (1993) *U.K. Property: Review of 1992 and Prospects for 1993*, S. G. Warburg, London.

Samuel, J. M., Wilkes, F. M. and Brayshaw, R. E. (1995) *Management of Company Finance*, Chapman Hall, London.

Savills (1989) *Financing Property 1989*, Savills, London.

Savills (1991) *Financing Property 1991*, Savills, London.

Savills (1993a) *Financing Property 1993*, Savills, London.

Savills (1993b) *Investment and Economic Outlook*, Savills, London, Issue 3, October.

Scott, I. P. (1992) 'Debt, Liquidity and Secondary Trading in Property Debt', *Journal of Property Finance*, 3(3), 347–55.

Scrimgeor Vickers & Co. (1986) *United Kingdom Research, Annual Property Report*, Scrimgeor Vickers & Co., London.

Sexton, P. and Laxton, C. (1992) 'Authorised Property Unit Trusts', *Journal of Property Finance*, 2(4), 468–75.

Shayle, A. (1991) 'The Use of Deep Discount and Zero Coupon Bonds in the UK Property Market', *Journal of Property Finance*, 2(1), 11–17.

Sharpe, W. F., Alexander, G. J. and Bailey, J. V. (1995) *Investments*, Prentice-Hall, Englewood Cliffs, NJ.

Sieracki, K. (1993) 'U.K. Institutional Requirements for European Property', *Estates Gazette*, 17 July, 116.

Smee, R. (1992) 'Capitalisation of Interest for Property Companies', *Journal of Property Finance*, 3(1), 13–22.

Temple, P. (1992) 'How to beat a hostile takeover', *Journal of Property Finance*, 2(4), 476–83.

The Times (2001) 'Property sector share prices', *The Times*, 5 July.

UBS Global Research (1993) *UK Equities: Property Perspective*, UBS Ltd, London, no. 3, April.

UBS Phillips & Drew (1993) *Global Research Group: UK Property Service*, UBS Ltd, London.

Van Horne, J. C. (1998) *Financial Management and Policy*, Prentice-Hall, London.

Venmore-Rowland, P. (1991) 'Vehicles for Property Investment', in P. Venmore-Rowland, P. Brandon and T. Mole (eds), *Investment, Procurement and Performance in Construction*, RICS, London.

Venmore-Rowland, P. (1998) 'Taking on corporate finance techniques', *Property Week*, 12 June, 44.

Wang J., Chen, J. and Isaac, D. (1996) 'Financing real estate in China: the development of a real estate investment bond market in Tianjin', *Journal of Financial Management of Property and Construction*, 1(3), 5–22.

Weatherhead, M. (1997) *Real Estate in Corporate Strategy*, Macmillan, London.

Westwick, C. A. (1980) *Property Valuation and Accounts*, Institute of Chartered Accountants in England and Wales, London.

Whitmore, J. (1993) 'Debt securitisation to aid the market', *CSW – The Property Week*, 28 January, 15.

Whitmore, J. (1997) 'Lending on the hoof', *Property Week*, 30 May, 31–8.

Whitmore, J. (1998) 'The REIT stuff', *Property Week*, 12 June, 36–9.

Whitmore, J. (2001a) 'Canary Wharf value soars after hyperactive half year', *Property Week*, 16 March, 18.

Whitmore, J. (2001b) 'Healthiest lending market for six years', *Property Week*, 16 November, 19.

Wolfe, R. (1988) 'Debt Finance', in S. L. Barter (ed.), *Real Estate Finance*, Butterworths, London.

Woodroffe, N. and Isaac, D. (1987) 'Corporate Finance and Property Development funding', Working Paper of the School of Applied Economics and Social Studies, Faculty of the Built Environment, South Bank Polytechnic, London.

Worzala, E. M., Johnson, R. D. and Lizieri, C. M. (1997) 'Currency swaps as a hedging technique for international real estate investment', *Journal of Property Finance*, 8(2), 134–51.

Wyles, M. (1990) 'Mortgage Indemnity – A Risk/Reward Arbitrage', *Journal of Property Finance*, 1(3), 378–86.

Index